THE HOMES OF THE PILGRIM FATHERS IN ENGLAND AND AMERICA
(1620–1685)

By the same Author

✭

IN THE HEEL OF ITALY
1910

BAROQUE ARCHITECTURE
1913

THROUGH EGYPT IN WAR-TIME
1918

MUHAMMADAN ARCHITECTURE IN EGYPT
AND PALESTINE. *1924*

A SHORT HISTORY OF THE BUILDING CRAFTS
1925

RUSTICUS : OR THE FUTURE OF THE
COUNTRYSIDE. *1927*

THE ARCHITECT IN HISTORY
1927

ENGLISH ARCHITECTURE : AN OUTLINE
1928

1. THE MASTER-WEAVER'S HOUSE, DEDHAM, ESSEX

THE HOMES OF THE PILGRIM FATHERS IN ENGLAND AND AMERICA

(1620-1685)

Martin S. Briggs, F.R.I.B.A.

HERITAGE BOOKS
2011

HERITAGE BOOKS
AN IMPRINT OF HERITAGE BOOKS, INC.

Books, CDs, and more—Worldwide

For our listing of thousands of titles see our website
at
www.HeritageBooks.com

A Facsimile Reprint
Published 2011 by
HERITAGE BOOKS, INC.
Publishing Division
100 Railroad Ave. #104
Westminster, Maryland 21157

Originally published
Oxford University Press
London and New York
1932

— Publisher's Notice —
In reprints such as this, it is often not possible to remove blemishes from the original. We feel the contents of this book warrant its reissue despite these blemishes and hope you will agree and read it with pleasure.

International Standard Book Numbers
Paperbound: 978-0-7884-1511-1
Clothbound: 978-0-7884-8906-8

TO THE MEMORY OF
PERCIVAL HALL LOMBARD
ONE OF THE
'MAYFLOWER DESCENDANTS'
(Died 22 January 1932)

PREFACE

NEW ENGLAND contains a number of charming wooden houses erected during the seventeenth century by the early colonists. Many of these buildings have perished, but now the survivors are more jealously guarded; and the Society for the Preservation of New England Antiquities, founded in 1910, is leading a movement which is likely to save most of those remaining. Many books have been published, illustrating and describing these humble dwellings, so that it is now common knowledge that they form a precious relic of the beginnings of American colonial history.

But hitherto no attempt seems to have been made to link these picturesque timber-framed houses with their predecessors, contemporaries, and counterparts in the districts of England from which the colonists came; to consider whether Holland, the refuge of the exiles before they became Pilgrims to the New World, had any share in dictating the form and construction of this rustic architecture; or to picture the conditions under which it came to be created by a miscellaneous company of political refugees united only by their common faith.

This is the theme of the present little book, and its genesis was almost accidental. Three years ago I was invited to assist Mr. P. H. Lombard, then President of the Historical Society of Bourne, Mass., by research into building methods in vogue in England during the early seventeenth century, especially in the district round Scrooby and Gainsborough from which the Pilgrim Fathers are supposed to have come. His immediate object was to reconstruct, on its original stone foundations, the little wooden trading-post built at Aptucxet near Bourne in 1627, picturesquely described in his Society's manifesto 'as the zero Milestone in America's commercial progress'. With patient care he uncovered, measured, and drew a plan of the foundations; but all the superstructure had gone, and its design had to be hypothetical. From England I sent him all the material I could find, in the form of notes, sketches and photographs, taken from contemporary and similar buildings 'on this side', because the few old documents describing the ancient original gave us little help. At last, on 3 September 1930, the reconstruction was finished and the Replica of the Trading Post was opened at a congress of the General Society of Mayflower Descendants. In the presence of more than 200 delegates from all over the States, one of the descendants of an old Pilgrim family lit the fire on the ancient hearth which had been cold for three centuries. For it was in the year 1627 that the early colonists of New Plymouth first began to trade with their Dutch rivals at New York, and it was perhaps this fact especially which gave significance to so unassuming a building.

But my own studies in this connexion revealed to me for the first time the extraordinary close kinship between the seventeenth-century timber houses of New England and certain parts of Old England, and thus induced me to offer to the public my

PREFACE xi

views on the English origins of the Pilgrim architecture of America. It appears that the south-eastern counties of England, and Essex in particular, were the main source not only of this architecture, but of the whole religious movement which led to the original *Mayflower* expedition and to subsequent migration on a larger scale. Names familiar in New England as the sites of some of the best surviving seventeenth-century houses (such as Dedham, Wethersfield, and Topsfield) have their counterpart in obscure Essex villages. And all these villages, as well as more familiar names such as Colchester, Chelmsford, Braintree, and Billericay—found in New England as in Old—were 'hot-beds of Dissent' in the sixteenth and seventeenth centuries.

It was not until I had laboriously traced these points of contact and completed my manuscript that I came across a recent book, *New Light on the Pilgrim Story* (by the Rev. T. W. Mason and the Rev. Dr. B. Nightingale), which confirms my theory of the prominent part played by Essex in the beginnings of New England history, though the question of architecture is not treated therein.

Throughout the preparation of this work I received valuable help, kindness, and advice from the late Mr. P. H. Lombard, of Brookline, Mass. The news of his untimely death reached me on the very day when my book was completed for press. He allowed me to reproduce three of his photographs (Figs. 65, 66, and 91), and obtained permission for me to use many other photographs by his own friends from the copyright collections of American learned societies (Figs. 67, 80, 81, 84, 89, 90, 92). Fig. 68 is reproduced by the courtesy of the *Monograph Series* from a photograph by the late Kenneth Clark, Figs. 86, 93, and 94 by the courtesy of the Topsfield Historical Society, and Fig. 83 by the courtesy of the Metropolitan Museum of New York. Mr. J. F. Kelly and the Yale University Press, author and publishers respectively of the fine book *Early Domestic Architecture of Connecticut*, have kindly allowed me to reproduce seven

PREFACE

photographs (Figs. 69, 70, 75, 76, 78, 79, 87) and six line drawings (Figs. 73, 74, 77, 82, 85, 88), also to redraw Figs. 71 and 72 from illustrations to that volume. Except Figs. 11, 30, and 31, the whole of the remaining photographs, sketches, diagrams and maps are my own work.

In conclusion I acknowledge my gratitude to a number of architect friends who have helped me with their views on local English building practice in the seventeenth century, and to several Congregational ministers, who have provided me with local information.

M. S. B.

MILL HILL,
29 February, 1932.

Post-Mill at Torksey, near Gainsborough (England).

CONTENTS

PREFACE	*page* ix
I. THE ORIGINS OF THE PILGRIM MOVEMENT (*c. 1570–1608*)	1
II. PILGRIM HOMES IN SCROOBY, GAINSBOROUGH, AND BOSTON	9
III. THE PILGRIMS IN HOLLAND (*1608–1620*)	27
IV. SOUTH-EAST ENGLAND: THE HOME OF THE PILGRIMS	42
V. TIMBER HOUSES IN SOUTH-EAST ENGLAND	51
VI. THE PILGRIMS IN NEW ENGLAND (*1620–c.1635*)	116
VII. TIMBER HOUSES IN NEW ENGLAND (*c. 1635–c. 1685*)	142
APPENDIX: The Influence of Essex (England) on Early Brickwork in America	193
BIBLIOGRAPHY	199
INDEX	202

LIST OF ILLUSTRATIONS

1. The Master-Weaver's House, Dedham, Essex . . *Frontispiece*
2. Map of South-East England . . . . . . *page* 5
3. The Manor House, Scrooby, Nottinghamshire }
4. 'Wolsey's Mill', Scrooby, Nottinghamshire . } . *facing page* 10
5. 'Bradford's House', Austerfield, Yorkshire }
6. Broek-in-Waterland, Holland . . } . . ,, 12
7. Ceiling Construction . . . . . . *page* 14
8. Epworth, Lincolnshire . . . . . . ,, 15
9. A typical Lincolnshire Farmhouse near Boston . . ,, 21
10. Section of Boarded Shed at Spalding, England . . ,, 23
11. Stadstimmerhuis, Leyden, Holland (1612) }
12. Zaandam, Holland . . . } . . *facing page* 34
13. Czar Peter's Hut, Zaandam, View }
14. Czar Peter's Hut, Zaandam, Plan, &c. } . . *page* 39
15. High Street, Billericay, Essex . . . . . ,, 44
16. Near Epping, Essex }
17. Braintree, Essex . } . . . . . *facing page* 46
18. St. Osyth, Essex . . . . *page* 48
19. Kingsbury Green, Middlesex . . . . . ,, 52
20. Great Wakering, Essex . . . . . . ,, 55
21. Barns, Canvey Island, Essex }
22. Barn, Wethersfield, Essex } . . . . *facing page* 56
23. Netteswell Cross, Essex }
24. Near Takeley, Essex } . . . . . ,, 60
25. Ruined Barn, near Edgware, Middlesex . . . *page* 62
26. Ivy House Farm, Ickenham, Middlesex . . . ,, 64
27. Rochford Hall, Essex. An Old English Kitchen Fire-place . ,, 75
28. Toppesfield, Essex }
29. Potter Street, Essex } . . . . . *facing page* 78
30. Newark Mill, Ripley, Surrey }
31. The Old Mill, St. Osyth, Essex } . . . . ,, 80
32. Denny Gate, Cambridgeshire }
33. Thatching at Toppesfield, Essex } . . . . ,, 82
34. Doors from Chantry House, Billericay, Essex . . *page* 85

LIST OF ILLUSTRATIONS

35. Panelling in Chantry House, Billericay, Essex	page 87
36. (a) Iron Casement from Godalming, Surrey. (b) Wood Casement from Wethersfield, Essex. (c) Iron Casement from Suffolk. (d) Ditto from Geffrye Museum, London. (e) Lead Ventilating Quarry	,, 89
37. English Ironwork of the Seventeenth Century. Mostly from East Anglia	,, 93
38. 'Fishermen's Houses', Southwark (London)	
39. Mill Hill, Middlesex	facing page 96
40. Mill Hill, Middlesex	
41. Mill Hill, Middlesex	,, 98
42. Mill Hill, Middlesex	
43. Barnet, Hertfordshire	,, 100
44. West Blatchington, Sussex. Windmill and Barn	page 100
45. Eltham, Kent	
46. Eltham, Kent	facing page 102
47. Fordwich, Kent	
48. Sandwich, Kent	,, 102
49. Clayhithe, Cambridgeshire	
50. Mill near Wickhambreux, Kent	,, 104
51. Moor Mills, Hertfordshire	
52. Moor Mills, Hertfordshire	,, 106
53. The Windmill at Billericay, Essex	page 107
54. Much Hadham, Hertfordshire	
55. Sheering, Essex	facing page 108
56. Mill at Stisted, Essex	
57. Mill at Bocking, Essex	,, 110
58. Windmill at Bocking, Essex	
59. Putwell Farm, Brentwood, Essex	,, 110
60. Bambers Green, Takeley, Essex	
61. Great Oakley, Essex	,, 112
62. Wickford, Essex	
63. Vange, Essex	,, 114
64. Map of New England	page 117
65. Reconstruction (1930) of the Trading-House at Aptucxet	
66. Reconstruction (1930) at Salem, Mass., of the Houses built by the first Settlers in 1630	facing page 138
67. Windmills at Cataumet, Mass.	
68. Paine House and Windmill, Easthampton, Long Island	,, 140
69. Stone House, Guilford, Conn.	
70. Starr House, Guilford, Conn.	,, 152

LIST OF ILLUSTRATIONS

71. Plans of (a) Thos. Lee House, E. Lyme, Conn., before alteration, and (b) Older Williams House, Wethersfield, Conn. . . . *page* 153
72. Section of Older Williams House, Wethersfield, Conn. . . „ 156
73. Details of Posts and Framing . . . . . . „ 157
74. Detail of Chimney Girt, &c., Hubbard House, Guilford, Conn. . „ 160
75. Older Cowles House, Farmington, Conn.
76. Hyland-Wildman House, Guilford, Conn. } . . . *facing page* 162
77. Typical Gambrel Roof Framing . . . . . *page* 164
78. Harrison-Linsley House, Branford, Conn.
79. Older Williams House, Wethersfield, Conn. } . . *facing page* 168
80. Hathaway House ('Old Bakery'), Salem, Mass.
81. Paul Revere House, Boston, Mass. . . } . . *facing page* 170
82. Strong House, East Windsor, Conn., Framing and Panelling . *page* 171
83. Hart House, Ipswich, Mass. (c. 1640)
84. Paul Revere House, Boston, Mass (c. 1676) } . . *facing page* 172
85. Casement Windows from Connecticut . . . *page* 173
86. 'Parson' Capen House, Topsfield, Mass.
87. Hyland-Wildman House, Guilford, Conn. } . . *facing page* 176
88. Iron Latches from Connecticut Houses . . . . *page* 179
89. Boardman House, Saugus, Mass.
90. House of the Seven Gables, Salem, Mass. } . . *facing page* 180
91. Fairbanks House, Dedham, Mass.
92. John Ward House, Salem, Mass. } . . . . „ 182
93. 'Parson' Capen House, Topsfield, Mass. (1683). Exterior
94. 'Parson' Capen House, Topsfield, Mass. (1683). Interior } „ 190
95. St. Luke's Church, Virginia, 1632
96. Woodham Walter Church, Essex, 1563-4 } . . . *page* 197

Vignettes

Whipple House, Ipswich, Mass. . . . . . . *Title page*
John Ward House, Salem, Mass. . . . . . . *page* ix
Post-Mill at Torksey, Gainsborough (England) . . . . „ xii
Post-Mill at Bourn, Cambridge (England) . . . . „ 192

I. THE ORIGINS OF THE PILGRIM MOVEMENT

c. 1570–1608

THE story of colonial architecture in America begins almost simultaneously in New England and in Virginia. It is only with the former district that this book is concerned; and up to the date (*c.* 1685) which serves as a conclusion to my study of the homes of the Pilgrim Fathers, Virginia and New England were separate colonies.

The two Companies founded by James I in 1606 to colonize North America and to trade therewith were known by the names of their English head-quarters, London and Plymouth. The former occupied 'Virginia', so called in honour of Queen Elizabeth, in whose reign an attempt had previously been made to colonize that country by Sir Walter Raleigh. The London company's trading rights in 'Virginia' extended from latitude 34° to 41°, and its first settlement was established at Jamestown in 1607. In the following year a church was built. The oldest surviving building in Virginia, and perhaps in all the States, is the interesting brick church (1632) of St. Luke in Isle of Wight County, Virginia (Fig. 95), and it is remarkable that it is in the brick Gothic style that one finds in Europe at a rather earlier date, more especially in Essex (England) and parts of Holland (see Appendix, p. 193). By the year 1622 the population of Virginia exceeded 4,000, and by 1648 it had increased to 15,000.

Meanwhile the Plymouth company had been unsuccessful in its first efforts at colonization, and it was not until the arrival of the little band of 'Pilgrim Fathers' in 1620 that any permanent settlement was achieved in the concession hitherto known as 'Northern Virginia' and now to be named 'New England'. In the following year the Dutch occupied the district round modern New York, christening it the 'New Netherlands', with 'New

Amsterdam' as its capital; and Swedish colonists founded 'New Sweden' (comprising the modern state of Delaware and most of New Jersey) in 1638. The French territories in Canada adjoined New England on the north and reached to within 100 miles of the New England seaboard. Yet by 1640 the original little company of 102 persons (including women, children, and servants) who had arrived in the *Mayflower* twenty years before, had grown to 26,000 (about double the number of the Virginian colony at that time); they had driven back the Indians; and eventually they imposed their language, ideas, and system of government upon their neighbours, until the Dutch and the French and the Swedes were successively defeated, and at last the eastern shores of North America became entirely English in language and ways of life. One result of this really marvellous achievement was to establish the traditional architecture of south-eastern England in north-eastern America; and to understand the processes which led to that result one must study the previous history, in England and Holland, of the Pilgrim Fathers and their immediate successors.

That history begins about the middle of the sixteenth century, when little communities of people who disagreed with the doctrines and practice of the Church of England, in spite of the Reformation, began to assemble—usually in secret—in various parts of England, but especially in London and the eastern counties. These communities were then called Separatists, or 'Brownists' (after the name of their first notable leader, Robert Browne), and were the direct ancestors of the modern 'Congregational' churches. Without describing their articles of faith or entering into any controversial questions, it may reasonably be said that they consisted for the most part of law-abiding people with deep convictions, and included a considerable number of well-born and well-educated men. Robert Browne himself came from an aristocratic family in Rutlandshire, graduated at Cambridge in 1572, and went to London as a schoolmaster afterwards. It was apparently at Cambridge that he contracted unorthodox ideas, and soon after he reached London he began preaching to secret meetings in the open air. He then travelled through East Anglia, spreading his 'heresies' in Cambridge, Norwich, and Bury St. Edmunds. About 1581 he was joined in Norfolk by a former Cambridge friend and graduate, Harrison. Both were imprisoned for their preaching, and on release they and some of their followers fled to Middelburg in Holland, where they established a Congregational church and a printing-press. From Middelburg they issued a stream of politico-religious books and pamphlets, which had a wide circulation in England. In 1583 the first martyrdoms of Congregationalists took place at Bury St. Edmunds, already a noted centre of Separatism. The next prominent name in this connexion is that of John Greenwood, who graduated at Cambridge in 1581 and then became chaplain to Lord Richard Rich, of Rochford Hall near Southend in Essex.[1] His preaching there led him into prison, where he met a young lawyer, Henry Barrowe, son of a Norfolk squire, who had graduated at Clare Hall, Cambridge, in 1560-70. Somehow they managed to write and issue 'seditious' books while in prison, and both were executed at Tyburn in 1593. In 1592 another leader of the movement, John Penry, also a Cambridge man, was martyred.

This brief account of the origin of Congregationalism in Queen Elizabeth's reign is given here to substantiate certain theories of the origin of Pilgrim architecture to be stated later, and establishes the following facts. Firstly, the chief leaders of the movement were without exception well-born and well-educated men, every one of whom had graduated at Cambridge. Secondly, the seat of their preaching activities was mainly in London and the eastern counties, especially the latter. (Even

[1] This building is still standing, and is now used as the head-quarters of the local golf-club. As explained later, its ancient fireplace provided me with useful hints for the reconstruction of the fireplace of the Trading Post at Aptucxet.

before their time, Essex had furnished a notable list of Marian martyrs, and one reads of executions and burnings at Coggeshall, Brentwood, Braintree, Maldon, Horndon-on-the-Hill, Chelmsford, Rayleigh, Stratford, and repeatedly at Colchester.) 'The movement for freedom of worship spread through the eastern counties with startling rapidity,'[1] and in 1586 Sir Walter Raleigh said in Parliament that he feared there were 'near twenty thousand Brownists in England'. It is clear that the geographical position of the University of Cambridge may have played some part in this state of affairs. The third point to notice is that the early Congregationalists were already in touch with Holland, which later becomes important as the country where the Pilgrim Fathers lived for many years before they set out for America, and may have influenced the style of their first buildings in New England. There was a further exodus of persecuted Separatists to Amsterdam from about the year 1593, these being from the Congregational church in London (existing at least as early as 1567[2]), and when their minister Francis Johnson (another Cambridge graduate) was released from the Clink Prison in 1597 he joined them there. Johnson had been imprisoned nine years earlier, when he was only 26 years of age, for preaching a sermon in favour of the Presbyterian system, in the University church at Cambridge; but in a subsequent visit to Holland, where he became minister of the church at Middelburg, he came across some of Barrowe's writings and afterwards returned to London to join the Separatists. His visit to Holland in 1597 was therefore not his first experience of that country; and when he settled in Amsterdam he founded the Congregational church there. There was also a congregation of English and Scottish refugees in Antwerp before 1583, for William Davison, one of Queen Elizabeth's Secretaries of State who was living there at the time, became an elder of that church, and his children's

---

[1] C. S. Horne, *A Popular History of the Free Churches*, p. 35 (London, 1903).
[2] *Ibid.*, p. 62.

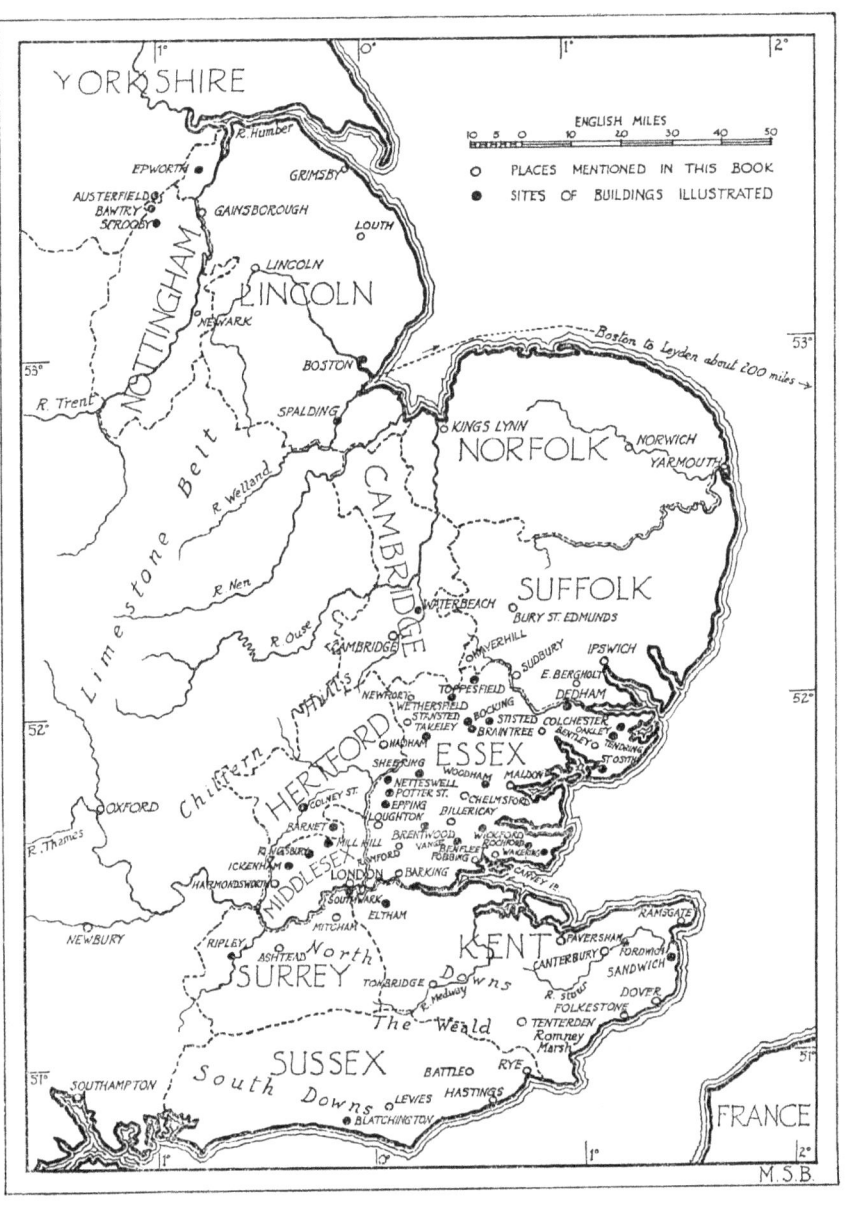

2. MAP OF SOUTH-EAST ENGLAND

names are still to be seen in the baptismal register. The next exodus took place in 1606, when the Separatist congregation from Gainsborough in Lincolnshire, which had existed as an organized community since 1602, took refuge in Amsterdam under their minister, John Smyth (who had graduated at Christ's College, Cambridge, in 1575–6), and there they formed a new church independent from Francis Johnson's. Yet a third foundation, though of the Presbyterian order, took place in 1607, when a company of British merchants were granted by the corporation the old nunnery (*Beguyn*) chapel near the Kalverstraat. The city actually paid the stipend of the first minister, a Scot, and the building is still in use as a Scottish Presbyterian church.

With the mention of Gainsborough we come to the district which in the popular mind has long been regarded as the cradle of the Pilgrim Fathers, but I hope to show here, as a result of personal investigation in the locality, that it was not the cradle of Pilgrim architecture in New England.

Up to 1842, the locality of the place where Governor Bradford and William Brewster met for worship, before they led the famous exodus via Boston and Amsterdam to Leyden in 1608–9, does not appear to have been known. Bradford's own description of the district referred to 'several towns and villages, some in Lincolnshire, and some in Yorkshire, where they bordered nearest together'; he adds that he and his friends 'ordinarily met at William Brewster's house on the Lord's day, which was a manor of the bishop's'. It was then discovered that Scrooby, a village on the Great North Road, about a mile and a half south of Bawtry, and about twelve miles west of Gainsborough, fulfilled the necessary conditions; and the subsequent publication in 1849 of Bradford's *Collections concerning the Early History of the Founders of New Plymouth* confirmed the discovery. Scrooby is now visited annually by large numbers of American pilgrims in consequence.

William Brewster, son of the Archbishop of York's bailiff at Scrooby, was born probably about 1566–7 in the old manor-

THE ORIGIN OF THE MOVEMENT (c. 1570–1608)   7

house there, already mentioned, which belonged to the Archbishop. He matriculated at Peterhouse, Cambridge, in December 1580 at the early age of 14 or less, but apparently did not take a degree at the University. In 1585 he was in Antwerp in attendance upon Mr. Secretary Davison, and in 1587 he was appointed 'Post' on the Great North Road in his native village of Scrooby. When the first 'Separatist' or Congregational church was founded at Gainsborough, in or about 1602, William Brewster and others who shared his religious opinions journeyed there from Scrooby every Sunday for three or four years. But in 1605 or thereabouts he and his neighbours formed a separate church[1] in Brewster's own house, under two ministers, Richard Clyfton and John Robinson. Clyfton had been ejected from a neighbouring rectory on account of his religious views, while Robinson, a Lincolnshire man by birth and a graduate of Corpus Christi College, Cambridge, had been driven from a Separatist congregation in Norwich. Among others who joined them at Scrooby, and afterwards lived to be Governor of the Plymouth Colony, was one William Bradford (c. 1590–1657), then a mere boy, who walked to Scrooby from his house, still standing, at Austerfield just over the Yorkshire border. Before long, even the secrecy that they observed in holding their meetings failed to protect them, and in 1607–8 several of them were heavily fined by the Ecclesiastical Courts at York for 'disobedience in matters of religion'. Continued persecution at last drove them to follow the example of their old associates at Gainsborough, in seeking a refuge in Holland, which since the close of the cruel Spanish wars offered a safe refuge to the victims of oppression; and in the autumn of 1607 they made their first attempt to escape from their own country. In so doing they were acting illegally, for there were laws to prevent men leaving the country as well as laws to prevent them worshipping in their own way while they

[1] The word is used here in the apostolic sense to denote a community of believers, not an ecclesiastical building.

stayed there. However, they chose the evil which appeared to them the less and took risks with their eyes open. Betrayed by the master of the ship which they had hired, they were all arrested, and imprisoned in those cells in the Guildhall at Boston (Lincolnshire) which every good American visits when he is in England, for two of the cells, as well as the beautiful room in which the Pilgrims came before the magistrates, still remain.

Boston was itself so partial to Separatism that the magistrates were lenient, and sent back the bulk of the prisoners to their homes in Scrooby. The ringleaders were detained and brought up at the next assizes, but in the following spring they made their second attempt at escape from a lonely point on the Humber estuary between Grimsby and Hull. Again they met with misfortune, half the party being caught by a large body of soldiers who were in pursuit of them, but after a long series of trials and hardships they finally reached Amsterdam in instalments during the summer of 1608. In that city, as previously stated, were already established two different Separatist churches; the Gainsborough congregation who had come over with their minister John Smyth in 1606, and the older London church under Francis Johnson, which had arrived in 1593–7. The Scrooby community did not stay long in Amsterdam—the church there being torn by a serious schism regarding the high-heeled shoes and other vanities affected by the parson's wife—but moved on to the university town of Leyden, where their petition to settle down as citizens was duly accepted by the Burgomaster on 12 February 1609. Here we may leave them for a time, but only to return in a later chapter to consider how far their sojourn in Holland influenced them as house-builders in New England a few years later, for it was from the Leyden church that the bulk of the Pilgrim Fathers came. Meanwhile, we may examine the possibility that the district round Scrooby, Gainsborough, and Boston provided the architectural tradition which inspired the colonists in their first attempts at building in New England.

II. PILGRIM HOMES IN SCROOBY, GAINSBOROUGH, AND BOSTON

A GLANCE at a geological map of England shows that the villages of Scrooby, Austerfield, and Bawtry, as well as the town of Gainsborough, are situated in a district where excellent building-stone is ready to hand, while Boston lies in marshy country by the sea and is therefore accessible for barges bringing stone from elsewhere. Unfortunately for the scenery of the Scrooby neighbourhood, rich coal-measures are now being developed within a few miles and its rural charm is being disturbed by this means as well as by the endless stream of motor-vehicles that roar along its edge on their way between London and the North. The district contains at least three buildings associated with the Pilgrim Fathers: the Manor House at Scrooby, William Bradford's old home at Austerfield, and the Old Hall at Gainsborough. All these have been frequently illustrated in books about the Pilgrim Fathers, and all are shrines for American visitors.

Scrooby Manor House (Fig. 3) is a small but substantial building standing in a little lane on the east side of the village, which itself lies to the east of the Great North Road. The house is built of brick and stone, and, as we now see it, appears to be decidedly later than Brewster's time. Parts of it certainly date back beyond the beginning of the seventeenth century, but considerable alterations and additions have been made since. The roof is covered with the pantiles that are common in the neighbourhood, the brick chimney-stacks are of the plainest possible kind, and most of the windows are sash-windows. But Dr. Dexter, as a result of lengthy and frequent examination of the buildings, seems to have proved conclusively that it is a mutilated relic of the archbishop's palace described below.

Behind the Manor House, on the village side, lie the

comparatively modern farm-buildings and stables, surrounding the usual farmyard. These buildings, too, are mainly of brick, roofed with pantiles, and are certainly not of early date. There is, however, an old hay-loft where Brewster and his friends are reputed to have hidden when the ecclesiastical officers were hunting for them, and a cow-shed containing fine carved beams of late Gothic date, illustrated in a popular book on the Pilgrim Fathers as a 'probable place of meeting in 1607'.[1] But these beams should not be used as evidence that the building in which they now stand is of Gothic date, for it is obvious to any trained eye that they have been removed from some other and much older building. They are 'notched' for struts and braces as part of a roof of quite different type.

Probably they were brought here from the old palace of the Archbishops of York, the remains of which are now buried in a field near the Manor House, which almost certainly formed an integral part of them. Cardinal Wolsey spent three months there in 1530, after he had fallen into disgrace, and King Henry VIII slept a night at the palace in 1541. It is curious that the Pilgrim Fathers should have hatched the scheme which eventually led to the foundation of New England under the shadow, if not actually within the house, of that archbishop who urged his royal master 'to have a vigilant eye to depress this new pernicious sect of Lutherans'. Leland the antiquary wrote of the place in 1541: 'In the meane townlet of Scrooby I marked two things—the parish church, not big but very well builded; the second was a great manor place, standing within a moat, and longing to the Archbishop of York; builded in two courts, whereof the first is very ample and all builded of timber, saving the front of the house that is of brick, to the which *ascenditur per gradus lapideos.* The inner court building, as far as I marked, was of timber building, and was not in compass past the fourth part of the outer court.' From another source it appears that the palace

---

[1] Dr. John Brown, *The Pilgrim Fathers of New England*, Fig. on p. 109.

contained thirty-nine rooms in all, and that the dining-hall had panelled walls and an oak ceiling. Some time afterwards, and probably before the time when Brewster and his friends began to hold their secret meetings, the greater part of the palace fell into disuse and then into decay. Thoroton wrote in 1677 that: 'Here *within memory* stood a very fair palace, a far greater house of receit and a better seat for provision than Southwell, and had attending to it the North Soke, consisting of very many towns thereabouts; it hath a fair park belonging to it. Archbishop Sandes caused it to be demised to his son Sir Samuel Sandes, since when the house hath been demolished almost to the ground.'

The interest to us of these quotations lies in the fact that this palace was largely 'builded of timber'; that is, of timber framing filled in with bricks ('half-timber work') or with plaster, or covered with weather-boarding ('siding' in America), as are most of the oldest houses in New England. In my own opinion, the last alternative is the least likely; for, as subsequent pages show, this method of covering is to-day very rare indeed in Lincolnshire and in the Bawtry district; whereas a few buildings survive in which the framing is of timber and the filling of plaster (see pp. 18–19). Thus, though Brewster, Bradford, and their friends may have taken over to Holland in 1608, and afterwards to America in 1620, some recollection of timber construction in the palace at Scrooby, it is unlikely that they obtained any familiarity with weather-boarding from that source.

Of the surviving seventeenth-century buildings in New England, there are, however, two or three structures in brick or stone, such as Governor Cradock's House at Medford, Mass. (1677–80). And although this book is mainly concerned with the wooden houses of New England and their English (or English and Dutch) ancestry, some reference will be made to the less common buildings in brick and stone (see Appendix, p. 193).

In this connexion, Scrooby Manor House has nothing much to tell us; nor is there anything very suggestive about the so-called 'Wolsey's Mill' (Fig. 4), the chief building in the village apart from the church. It is a brick building, said to have been erected in 1722, though part of the stone substructure is evidently much older than that. The roof is of pantiles, with a pitch of less than 50°, and there is no special feature of distinction in any part of the design.

Evidently the oldest surviving house in Scrooby is the 'Old Vicarage', a little brick building adjoining the parish church, with a steep pantiled roof and casement windows. There are other cottages, probably later than Brewster's time, where brickwork is pleasingly and skilfully handled. The chimneys are plain in design, and the roofs pantiled.

Austerfield, where Governor Bradford lived, lies some three miles north of Scrooby and is a straggling village which is losing its rustic air as the collieries creep up towards it. It contains a house of medium size known, to American rather than English visitors, as 'The Bradford House' (Fig. 5). For a long time it has attracted American pilgrims as the home of William Bradford, whose birth is recorded clearly enough in the register of the little Norman church close by, under the date 19 March 1589 O.S. (1590 N.S.). Dr. Dexter explodes the legend by his calm refusal to credit this local tradition, but doubtless the visitors' book will continue to enrol a list of American names. However, even if we are not allowed to be certain that Bradford was born here or lived here, there is nothing to prove the contrary; and the house is old enough to serve as an example of a typical yeoman's dwelling in the district at the beginning of the seventeenth century. It is now divided into two cottages, so that the arrangements of the entrance have almost certainly been altered. On the left of the entrance is the main living-room, a large and cheerful apartment known in this district as the 'house' or 'house-place', with a great open fireplace and baking-oven.

3. THE MANOR HOUSE, SCROOBY, NOTTINGHAMSHIRE

4. 'WOLSEY'S MILL', SCROOBY, NOTTINGHAMSHIRE

Photo: Author

5. 'BRADFORD'S HOUSE', AUSTERFIELD, YORKSHIRE

Photo: Author

6. BROEK-IN-WATERLAND, HOLLAND (see p. 35)

On the right is another large room which served as a scullery or working kitchen. From this room a short flight of stone steps leads down into a cellar with a vaulted roof, labelled on the picture-postcards as a 'secret meeting-place'. Dr. Mackennal, who is inclined to swallow the legend of 'The Bradford House', draws the line at 'the secret meeting-place', pointing out that the entrance to the cellar is far too obvious to afford any secrecy whatever, and refuses to recognize it as 'the place where the Pilgrims used to worship for fear of the persecutors'.[1]

Apart from these sentimental associations, the house has some architectural character. It is two stories high, long and low, with a pantiled roof of medium pitch. The walls are of good brickwork, likewise the massive chimneys capped by a simple oversailing course or 'cap.' The window-frames and casements are of wood, divided into small panes by means of wooden bars. In the living-room, which is very low, the ceiling is of wooden beams 12 in. deep and 8 in. wide, with massive joists 5 in. deep and 6 in. wide, spaced only 13 in. apart. The upper floorboards seem to rest directly upon these with only a thin layer of plaster beneath them, but in the neighbouring town of Bawtry I found a similar construction in a floor from which some of the plaster had fallen, and it could be seen that there was a thin layer of rushes running in the same direction as the boarding (i.e. across the joists) which served as a primitive lathing or backing for the plaster (Fig. 7).

In the autumn of 1929 I made a pilgrimage round the district in search of such old houses as may have influenced the colonists from Scrooby; but nowhere could I find any trace or any record of old buildings covered with weather-boarding. Even the windmills, of which there are a few, are of brick tarred over. The old barns, the old cottages, and the old farmhouses are nearly all built of red brick, though occasionally one finds examples in the good local stone, of which all the churches are

[1] A. Mackennal, *Homes and Haunts of the Pilgrim Fathers*, p. 46 (London, 1920).

built. At Epworth (a little town famous as the home of John Wesley), not far from Scrooby, are some brick cottages with a curious treatment at the gable-ends known as 'tumbling', and consisting of triangles of bricks set at right angles to the slope of the gable, which I have seen not only in Lincolnshire and Norfolk, but in Holland. These particular cottages (Fig. 8) had

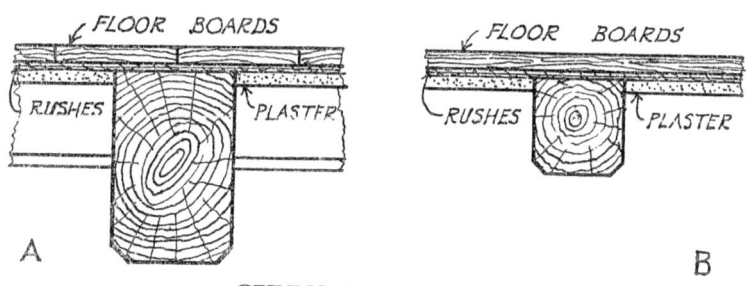

7. CEILING CONSTRUCTION
A, 'Bradford's House', Austerfield, Yorks;
B, Bawtry, Notts.

at one end, on the gable, three out of four iron figures of a date, '16–9'. The date was sufficiently interesting to arouse my curiosity. An intelligent little girl told me that she could remember the missing letter falling, and that it was '1'. A date of 1619 would have given me a building practically contemporary with the landing of the Pilgrims, but when I found a row of figures on the corresponding gable at the other end of the row of cottages, unmistakably '1793', my confidence was shaken. Nevertheless, it is conceivable that the first part of the row was erected in 1619, and additional cottages built on identical lines in 1793. The fact is that very few of these humble dwellings are dated at all, and one would welcome more precise inscriptions. The cottages at Epworth, if one accepts the date of 1619, show tricks of brick craftsmanship which may have come over from Holland or Flanders, a frequent occurrence in the eastern counties of England. (Chapter III deals with the possibility of Dutch influence on Pilgrim architecture in America. See also Appendix.)

HOMES IN SCROOBY, GAINSBOROUGH, BOSTON

The bricks used in the district in the seventeenth century are dark or bright red, about $2\frac{1}{4}$ in. thick, laid in lime-mortar with rather wide joints. The end of the roof, at the beginning of that

8. EPWORTH, LINCOLNSHIRE

century, invariably finished in a pointed gable, not a 'gambrel' gable or a hip, and was carried up as a parapet just above the level of the pantiles with which the roof was covered. The eaves, at 'Bradford's House' as well as in most buildings in the neighbourhood, had a very slight projection. Beneath the eaves there is often a projecting course or courses of bricks, known in England as 'oversailing courses', and nowadays there is often an iron gutter resting upon them. It is uncertain whether any of these houses originally had wooden gutters, or whether the water dripped from the pantiles of the eaves direct on to the ground.

Occasionally one finds a band of bricks forming a string-course at a point half-way or so up the walls, but such cases probably date from the latter part of the century.

Chimneys of the ordinary dwelling-houses in this district are invariably plain and solid, the only relief being two or three oversailing courses of slight projection to form a cap, and perhaps one course, a little lower down, to serve as a 'necking'.

The roofs at the beginning of the seventeenth century were of steep pitch, say 50° to 55°. The pitch decreased to about 45° to 47° towards the end of the century, and often a 'lean-to' addition was made to a house with a steep pitch, the addition being of a lower pitch (see Fig. 8).

The construction of floors and ceilings has already been described, in reference to the 'Bradford House' at Austerfield, and this massive framing in oak probably applied generally in the locality, for roofs as well as for floors. The absence of timber-framed buildings, filled with brick or with plaster, is singular; but some may have escaped notice, and probably some have been demolished in modern times.

If any doors of the period survive, they probably present no peculiar features. As regards windows, my casual journeys did not reveal more than one example of leaded panes. This was in Bawtry, where the panes were rectangular, not diamond-shaped. In the Trading Post at Aptucxet (1627, see Preface and p. 136), diamond panes were restored on the strength of a fragment found in the ruins, but it seems likely that rectangular panes were almost as commonly used in England at that date. In the Scrooby-Bawtry-Austerfield area, the older houses nearly all have the type of wooden window-frame known as 'Yorkshire lights'. These consist of two or three 'lights', of which only one can be opened. But instead of swinging outwards on hinges, as a 'casement', it slides in grooves formed in the head and sill of the frame. Nothing seems to be known as to the date when this type of window came into use. The 'lights' are usually narrow, and about twice their width in height, divided into small panes with wooden bars.

The result of this brief summary of characteristics of old

houses in the district (including Scrooby, Bawtry, Austerfield, Blyth, Barnby Moor, Finningley, Haxey, and East Retford) is to prove that old weatherboarded houses appear to be unknown; that even timber-framed houses are now scarce or non-existent; that the normal building materials are brick (occasionally stone) for walls and pantiles for roofs; and that all the old domestic buildings are devoid of any ornamental forms. It may be added that the local scenery is varied, with sluggish streams and fenland round Scrooby, woods and undulating country round Blyth, bare hills and long views near Epworth; but the roar of motor-coaches on the Great North Road and the slow creeping of colliery shafts towards these homes of the Pilgrims is gradually eliminating their charm.

Gainsborough is the next place to examine as a possible source of inspiration for Pilgrim architecture. It is a very ancient town on the river Trent, and played a prominent part in English history as far back as the times of Alfred and Canute. Its aspect seventy years or more ago is supposed to be faithfully depicted in George Eliot's *Mill on the Floss* (published in 1860) under the name of 'St. Ogg's'....

... 'That venerable town with the red-fluted roofs and the broad warehouse gables, where the black ships unlade themselves of their burthens from the far North.... It is one of those old, old towns which impress one as a continuation and outgrowth of nature...: a town which carries the traces of its long growth and history like a millennial tree.... Many honest citizens lost all their possessions for conscience' sake in those times, and went forth beggared from their native town. *Doubtless there are many houses standing now on which these honest citizens turned their backs in sorrow*: quaint-gabled houses looking on to the river, jammed between newer warehouses, and penetrated by surprising passages, which turn and turn at sharp angles till they lead you out on a muddy strand overflowed continually by the rushing tide. Everywhere the brick houses have a mellow look.'

The lines which I have italicized seem to indicate that in 1860 or so, unless the gifted authoress was using her imagination in this passage, one might have found many buildings at least as old as the time of the Pilgrims. But since those days Gainsborough has developed into a manufacturing town with engineering works employing thousands of hands, and has lost most of the picturesqueness and antiquity which it evidently once possessed. There is, however, one notable exception, the famous 'Old Hall' which ranks among the historic and beautiful homes of England quite apart from its sentimental association with the Pilgrims in their earliest days. It is illustrated in Garner and Stratton's *Domestic Architecture of England during the Tudor Period* (vol. i), and is believed to have been built in three stages, the first in *c.* 1480–4 and the third in 1600. The owner of the house when the third instalment of it was built came of a family already conspicuous for religious nonconformity, his father and mother having been exiled for allowing conventicles to be held here. Hence it has been inferred by some writers that he likewise encouraged the Separatist congregation which existed in the town from 1602 to 1606 and which migrated to Amsterdam in that year as already mentioned. The building forms three sides of a quadrangle, the south side remaining open, though once there was a gatehouse there, now demolished. The north side, which contains the Great Hall, is the oldest, the west wing was probably added during the reign of Henry VII, and the east wing was erected in 1600 by Thomas Hickman, who had recently purchased the house and whose descendants still own it. The Great Hall is a magnificent room, entirely constructed of timber framing, with an open roof containing a louvre through which smoke escaped from a fire on a central hearth. The west and east wings are partly framed in timber, but mainly of brickwork with stone-mullioned windows filled with leaded lattice glazing.

But neither in Gainsborough itself, nor anywhere in North Lincolnshire, was I able to find old houses covered with weather-

HOMES IN SCROOBY, GAINSBOROUGH, BOSTON

boarding. Inquiries made among several photographers in the district who have made a hobby of photographing old houses produced an invariably negative answer, a search of topographical prints and books revealed nothing, and architects who have practised in the district all their lives could tell me of no local examples. A leading architect in Lincoln informed me that probably there were once many old buildings of timber framing, filled with plaster panels, but that these have fallen down or have been rebuilt in more durable materials. Surviving examples are the fine old gabled houses on Castle Hill at Lincoln, and an inn with an overhanging timber front and pantiled roof at Newark in the neighbouring county of Nottinghamshire. But there is a somewhat dilapidated boarded windmill at North Hykeham near Lincoln which may be as old as the seventeenth century. Grimsby, a great town devoted to fish, has nothing to show in the way of ancient domestic architecture in its squalid streets; and neither Louth in Lincolnshire nor Worksop in Nottinghamshire furnishes anything useful for our quest. Coming farther south, I have heard of a boarded barn at Corby, near Grantham, but have not been able to visit it personally.

In the southern part of the county the chief town and port is Boston, closely connected with New England as the place where the fugitive Pilgrims from Scrooby were imprisoned in 1608 (see p. 8), and in later years the source from which so important a contingent crossed to Massachusetts that its new capital was named after their home-town in 1630. In Boston, if anywhere, one would look for old buildings of the type which the early colonists reproduced in their first building ventures overseas. The strength of the Puritan movement in the district depended mainly upon two important men: Lord Lincoln of Tattershall Castle (who never emigrated himself but whose two sisters married men who did, and crossed to America with their husbands), and John Cotton, vicar of Boston Church, now perhaps the finest parish church in England. Cotton was born in

1585, went to Cambridge at the early age of 13, became a fellow and tutor of Emmanuel College, and in 1612 began his ministry at Boston, which lasted twenty years. His broad and advanced views brought him into conflict with his bishop, and in 1633 he followed many of his parishioners across the Atlantic. In Boston, Mass., he became co-pastor of the church there, and died in 1652.

Tattershall Castle, built c. 1440, is a magnificent brick house of semi-fortified type, in the form of a keep. It contains much fine late-Gothic detail, but can hardly have had any influence upon the humble cottages and homesteads erected in wood by the first settlers of New England. The town of Boston, besides its lovely church, contains a few noteworthy buildings, including the Guildhall where the Scrooby pilgrims were imprisoned, a brick building of the fifteenth century with a fine traceried window; Shodfriars Hall, a much-restored but fine timber-framed house of the fifteenth or sixteenth century with traceried bargeboards, overhanging stories, and shops beneath; and the little brick building known as the 'Church House'. The last-named is evidently a work of the seventeenth century, possibly of its first half, and, in spite of much later alteration, it is interesting on account of its curved 'Dutch' gable and its bold chimneys. Boston is one of the many places on the east coast of England where Dutch influence is marked (and in attempting to locate the source of Dutch elements in New England one has always to remember this fact, as explained in Chapters III and V). Near the parish church is a quaint little timber-framed building filled in, as is Shodfriars Hall, with plaster, and known as 'The Church Key', but in Boston itself I was unable to find any timber-framed houses covered with weather-boarding.

Just outside the town is a large and most attractive house, Burton Hall, of late sixteenth- or early seventeenth-century date, with brick walls, long low mullioned windows, curved gables crowned with stone finials, lofty chimney-stacks, and—like

HOMES IN SCROOBY, GAINSBOROUGH, BOSTON

the other houses in Boston previously mentioned—plain tiles. (There is another house of Elizabethan style near the station at Bourne in Lincolnshire.)

Near Butterwick, about five miles east of Boston, is an

9. A TYPICAL LINCOLNSHIRE FARMHOUSE NEAR BOSTON

isolated farmhouse that is very typical of the local building tradition (Fig. 9). It probably dates from the late seventeenth century, and alterations to the windows have evidently taken place since, but its long pantiled roof, with a pitch of about 50° to 52°, terminating at each end in a gable with a brick parapet, is probably original. There is a plain brick chimney with brick necking and oversailing courses, and a plain brick string-course half-way up the walls. While it is not old enough to have inspired the Pilgrim builders, it presents an interesting comparison with the few New England houses built in brick or stone in the seventeenth century, and at any rate shows the sort of house that the Lincolnshire farmer of 1680 or 1700 occupied.

Wandering about the countryside between Boston and the

Wash, I came across several old boarded barns of uncertain date, at Wrangle Tofts and elsewhere. There is a small one behind Burton Hall, close to Boston, with a pantiled roof, but it is of no great interest and may not be more than a century old. At Friskney, between Boston and Wainfleet, there is a very fine boarded windmill, and another near Butterwick.

The town of Spalding, however, in the south part of Lincolnshire, possesses a building which, though insignificant in itself, is the only one in that county—so far as my own researches go—that resembles in design and construction the early boarded houses of New England (Fig. 10). It is interesting, too, because it served to some extent the same purpose as the old Pilgrims' trading station at Aptucxet, mentioned in the introduction to this book. It is known as 'Birch's cattle-cake warehouse', and stands on the bank of the river Welland near the centre of the town. It is a building of three stories including the attic in the roof, the two lower stories being each about 7 ft. high, floor to floor. The whole structure is of oak framing, the main 'walls' being formed of posts 8 in. by 9 in., with sills and heads about 8 in. by 8 in. Intermediate posts 10 in. by 5 in., spaced at wide intervals, help to carry the floor, which is also of solid construction. Braces stiffen the angles between the outer posts and the head. The rafters of the roof are 5 in. by 5 in., and about 16 in. apart. The roof is now covered with modern corrugated iron sheets. An old man told me that it was formerly slated, but there is little doubt that the original roofing was either pantiles or thatch, for slates were not much used in the eastern counties before the nineteenth century.

The exterior is covered with oak boards about 7 in. wide overlapping 1 in., so that the 'gauge' or exposed width is 6 in. These boards are feather-edged and tarred, and are now fixed with iron nails, but the original fixing may have been by means of oak pegs.

Spalding contains many other old buildings of interest, but no others, so far as I could learn, of weather-boarding.

HOMES IN SCROOBY, GAINSBOROUGH, BOSTON 23

I have assumed hitherto that readers of this book are already acquainted with the state of domestic architecture in England

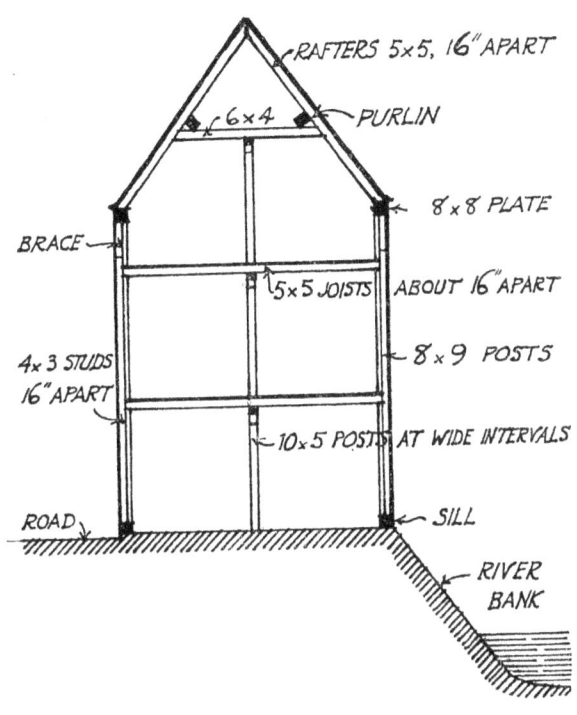

10. SECTION OF BOARDED SHED AT SPALDING, ENGLAND

in the first quarter of the seventeenth century. But certain passages in Professor Fiske Kimball's excellent book *Domestic Architecture of the American Colonies and of the Early Republic*, to which I have constantly had recourse in preparing these pages, lead me to believe that there is some misapprehension on this point.

On his page 3 he writes: 'It is little realized that few of the old cottages now standing in England antedate the seventeenth century, and that they represent a general rise in the "culture stage" of the English yeomanry which took place at that time, bringing to them, as of right, things which had before appertained only to the gentry, and involving the destruction and replacement of the cruder dwellings which had been used hitherto. In his recent and fundamental study, Innocent has shown that the usual dwellings of agricultural labourers in England down to this period, and in remote districts long afterward, sometimes nearly to the present day, were not of stone or brick, or even of frame, but of much more rudimentary construction—of branches, rushes, and turf, of palings and hurdles, of wattle, clay, and mud.'

Taken literally, and enhanced by quite modern photographs of woodmen's wigwams in Yorkshire and Lancashire, this passage would lead an unwary reader to believe that in 1600–20 the normal residence of the peasantry of these English counties was in huts no better than those of primitive savages, and that even to-day parts of these northern shires are in the same state of development as Patagonia or the Andaman Islands. In all my travels over England, including my native county of Yorkshire, I have never seen or heard of such huts as are described and illustrated in Professor Kimball's book. They may exist in remote forest areas, as shelters for the woodmen, but not as normal places for family habitation.

It is undoubtedly true that a large proportion of the old cottages of England have given place to more modern substitutes; it is equally true that up to the seventeenth century the majority of them were made of timber, but that is not all the truth. Wealth was pouring into England during the fifteenth and sixteenth centuries, owing to the prosperity of the cloth trade, and during this period the shocking conditions of life suffered by the lower classes and even the newly created middle-class improved enormously. This improvement applied especially to certain favoured districts, but the rest of the country benefited indirectly too. Of all parts of England, the Cotswold district stands out most prominently as the locality where conditions changed for the better at this time. 'Stone villages of the noblest Tudor architecture', writes the chief modern historian of the English people, 'encircled for miles round by Tudor farms built in the same lavish style, tell the tourist on Cotswold the tale of the ancient prosperity of the loom. And the history of the Kendal cloth trade can still be read in the stout stone walls and oak furniture of Westmorland and Cumbrian sheep-farms. . . . The farmer of Lincolnshire was growing fine wool for looms in Yorkshire, while the merchants and seamen of Hull and London were finding new markets for it. . . . In the fifteenth and sixteenth centuries, East Anglia, with Norwich for its capital, was greatly enriched by the cloth trade.'[1]

It was, in fact, during the fifteenth, sixteenth, and early seventeenth centuries that the smaller homes of England attained their greatest beauty, a beauty fully appreciated by American visitors. And while one cannot pretend that the medieval miseries of the English peasant had vanished in the age of Shakespeare, it remains true that the small squires, the prosperous farmers, and the higher ranks of craftsmen and agricultural workers had attained a condition of comparative comfort, according to the standards of the day, by the time when the Pilgrims set out for Holland between 1593 and 1608.

For they were not, for the most part, of the peasant class. They were mainly hard-working and thrifty middle-class folk, and the homes that they left were not, as a rule, huts built of turf or of wattle-and-daub. At that time chimneys were something of a novelty in small houses, glass was a rarity reserved for the homes of the prosperous classes, and the ground floor of a small dwelling too often consisted of beaten earth, while thatch was in common use for cottage-roofs. But the Pilgrims were not living like beasts of the field when they made their great venture for the sake of their faith.

Yet, as subsequent chapters show, most of them lived in great

[1] G. M. Trevelyan, *History of England*, pp. 280–2 (London, 1926).

poverty during the years of their exile in Holland; and on reaching New England they were faced with the stern necessity of providing immediate shelter against a rigorous winter climate and hostile tribesmen. This, and this only, was the reason why their first temporary homes were mere wigwams; not because their former English homes had been of such a kind.

As a matter of fact, Professor Fiske Kimball is fully aware of all this, as appears from other passages in his book. 'To the gentlemen who were the leaders and chroniclers, their first abodes in the new world were mean enough compared with those to which they were accustomed.' . . . But the conclusion of the sentence needs to be taken cautiously: . . . 'To many farm servants and poor people the rude shelters meant no more than a perpetuation of conditions at home.'

In a later part of this book it will be shown not only that the timber-framed houses (which so quickly followed the temporary huts and wigwams erected in the first hectic years of settlement) are of English type—as Professor Fiske Kimball himself generally admits—but that they are derived directly from the very district of England whence the bulk of the *Mayflower* colonists came, a district which was nowhere near Scrooby.

III. THE PILGRIMS IN HOLLAND
1608–1620 et seq.

As we have seen, the English Separatist refugees arrived in Holland at various times from 1593 to 1608 and afterwards. The first party of whom there is any definite record, who left England in 1593 from London and elsewhere, 'tarried a while at Campen and at Naarden, but at last they settled at Amsterdam'. The next organized exodus was from Gainsborough in 1602, and this body formed a church or congregation under their minister John Smyth, quite distinct from the London church under Francis Johnson; while neither group was connected with the church of English and Scottish Presbyterians in the Begijnen Hof at Amsterdam, founded under municipal patronage in 1607, and still existing. Lastly came the large party of refugees from Scrooby and district who arrived at Amsterdam in instalments during 1608, and finally settled at Leyden early in the following year. It was from Leyden that the famous voyage of the *Mayflower* to New England in 1620 was organized, and therefore Leyden takes the foremost place in the story of the Pilgrim's sojourn in Holland.

Three questions naturally arise in connexion with this period in Holland: (i) were any of the refugees employed there in the building or woodworking crafts; (ii) what was the style of architecture then in vogue in the Netherlands, and to what extent can it have directly influenced them in their buildings erected in New England after 1620; and (iii) could Dutch influence have affected their architecture indirectly by means of the hold that it had already obtained in the eastern counties of England?

In spite of the vast amount of research devoted to the lives of the refugees in Leyden and Amsterdam, especially by American scholars, during recent years, very little is definitely known about their doings. This is not to be wondered at. Even the most prosperous of them had sacrificed everything when they fled secretly to Holland, and practically all of them had to turn to some employment, often menial employment very different from their previous occupations, when they settled in these Dutch towns. In some measure they lived a communal life, the more prosperous among them aiding the weaker brethren. But entries in baptismal and marriage registers have enabled scholars to form a vague picture and estimate of their occupations. The Dutch seem to have offered no objection to the settlement of all these foreigners in their midst; in fact, as Brandt says of the arrival of the Scrooby contingent at Amsterdam, the authorities actually favoured them—'knowing these people to be very industrious, and that by their propagating all sorts of Manufactures, and Handicrafts, they brought great advantage to the said City'.[1]

But this was not entirely the case. The Pilgrims were a very miscellaneous community, and though certainly some of them were skilled artisans, a much larger number were farmers or agricultural labourers or tradesmen who had to acquire a new occupation on entering a large town like Amsterdam or Leyden. Evidently they intended from the outset to stick together in Separatist congregations, and that decision necessarily involved town-life. For they were foreigners, the language and manners of the Dutch were strange to them, and it is probable that many of them never contemplated permanent settlement there. If they had scattered themselves as hired labourers over the farms of Holland, they would have cut themselves off from the communal religious life for which they had made such sacrifices.

So it may be assumed that for some time, 'probably some suffered actual distress, while clearly all endured more or less privation'.[2] Then, after migrating as a body to Leyden, the

---

[1] Quoted in H. M. Dexter, *The England and Holland of the Pilgrims*, p. 419 (Boston, 1905).   [2] *Ibid.*, p. 428.

THE PILGRIMS IN HOLLAND (1608–1620)

Scrooby Separatists gradually began to find employment, and by the year 1613 most of them were comfortably settled. 'They had become so far identified with its life as to feel measurably at home. The struggle for a living still was severe. But their increasing familiarity with the language and customs of the people and their unfailing good repute had removed, or modified, some early hindrances of their prosperity.'[1]

About half the entries in official documents which mention the occupations followed by members of the English colony in Leyden refer to various branches of the wool trade and the weaving industry, perhaps because these required only a short initiation or because these Englishmen had practised them previously in their own country. Many were engaged as merchants or tradesmen, but not all of those were necessarily Separatist refugees. It is estimated that between 1609 and 1620 some 400 to 500 people were resident in Leyden, and of these only a small number arrived from Scrooby in 1609, and barely 100 sailed in the *Mayflower* in 1620, the latter number including many women and children. The number residing in Amsterdam, after the Scrooby contingent had gone to Leyden, is uncertain also.

But of 102 English refugees in Amsterdam, mainly from London, whose occupations are recorded in documents, the following were occupied in the building crafts: 3 masons, 3 smiths, 2 hodmen, 1 carpenter, 1 cooper, 1 painter, and 1 woodsawyer; 12 in all. Of 131 Englishmen working in Leyden between 1609–20, there were 2 masons, 1 carpenter, 1 cabinetmaker, 1 cooper, 1 smith, 1 lockmaker; 7 in all. The carpenter was William Jepson, who arrived from Worksop in Nottinghamshire in 1609, aged 26, with the Scrooby pilgrims. He married a fellow-refugee, Rosamond Horsfield, of his own town, in Amsterdam just before setting out for Leyden; and took some part in the purchase of the site on the Kloksteeg there

[1] *Ibid.*, p. 548.

in 1611, perhaps helping to build some of the twenty-one houses subsequently erected there for the colony. But he did not go to New England with the Pilgrims, and, of the lists of workers in the building trades just quoted, we have no knowledge as to how many were refugees, though probably most of them were. All we can infer from these figures is that if nineteen Englishmen in Holland, out of 233 whose occupations are known, were employed in one or other of the building crafts, those of the Pilgrims themselves who made their great adventure in 1620, and those who left Holland in their wake within the next few years, may have acquired some special methods or fashions from the Dutch craftsmen among whom they plied their craft during the years they spent in Holland.

But it is unlikely that the selection of persons to form the *Mayflower* party was ever made on the grounds of vocation. The younger and stronger members of the community were undoubtedly chosen, for it was known from the outset that their venture would be hard and hazardous, though probably the hardships of the first terrible winter were not foreseen. Yet though long research has been devoted to the personal antecedents of the Pilgrims, even now we know very little as to their actual callings. Of the forty-one men who signed the famous covenant on arrival in New England on 11 November 1620, four joined the *Mayflower* at Southampton and most of the rest came from Leyden. Of all the forty-one, only one is known to have been employed in anything approaching a building craft, and he was John Alden—the hero of Longfellow's poem *The Courtship of Miles Standish*—who was taken on at Southampton as a cooper. Many of the others were personal servants of the more fortunate members of the community, and the rest were a motley band of weavers, schoolmasters, and so on. Half of the company died during the first winter in America. Of the five men who arrived on the *Fortune* in 1621, the *Anne* and the *Little James* in 1623, the only one associated with building was

William Bassett, a master-mason of Sandwich in Kent, who came from Leyden. This is the meagre result of much investigation on my part into the question of the Pilgrims' technical knowledge of building up to about 1623. (Cf. p. 131.)

But the fact remains that during their long exile in Holland they may have assimilated some ideas from the buildings which surrounded them in their daily life. Leyden, which is estimated to have had a population of about 50,000 at that time, was a thriving industrial city, and its University—established in 1575—was enhancing the town's importance. Partly because of its commercial prosperity, but probably also because the sympathies of its learned professors would be with the revival of Roman tradition, Leyden was one of the cities where the Renaissance in architecture was eagerly welcomed.

It may be recalled that the real beginning of this Renaissance movement took place in Florence early in the fifteenth century. About a hundred years later it made its appearance in France, at first only as a new fashion in the ornamental details of architecture; and later still its influence began to be definitely felt in England. Holland, although much occupied with the Spanish wars and other troubles, was infected with the new Renaissance ideas a little later still, and it is not until about 1590 that one finds any definite change of style in architecture. Even then the change was very gradual, and medieval forms—such as steeply-pitched gables and mullioned windows—continued in use, as also in England. It has been claimed for the old brick church of St. Luke, in Isle of Wight County, Virginia (Fig. 95), that it is not only 'the oldest church in America' but also 'the last of the Gothic', though built as late as 1632. Not one Englishman in ten thousand realizes the surprising fact, and probably few Americans are aware, that their continent possesses a real Gothic building; yet the claim is perfectly justified. A brick church of this type in the Gothic style can be matched in only three other places—Holland, Prussia, and certain districts of eastern

England—and almost certainly the few brick buildings in the Gothic style that survive in Essex and elsewhere are derived from Holland or Flanders. But, just as the unknown designer of St. Luke's Church in Virginia used 'crow-stepped' gables, and windows with pointed heads containing somewhat rude tracery and mullions of brickwork, ten years after Inigo Jones had completed his full-blown Roman Banqueting-House in Whitehall (London), so the architects in Leyden and other Dutch cities persisted in using the familiar old forms of the Middle Ages even though they introduced the fashionable Orders of architecture from Rome into their designs. Dutch Gothic is nearer to French than to English, and it is sometimes said that it is hardly worth notice; but such great churches as the Cathedral of Utrecht and the 'Groote Kerk' (St. Bavo) at Haarlem belie that statement, while Leyden itself has Gothic churches of no little importance in the fine 'Hooglandsche Kerk' (St. Pancras) and St. Peter's.

Under the shadow of the latter dwelt the little colony of English Separatists in the Kloksteeg, but these great stone churches can have had no influence upon the humble dwellings which they afterwards erected in New England. It is rather in the secular buildings of the period 1590–1630 that we must look for any evidence that Holland affected their architectural outlook.

The Renaissance in Holland, as in other countries, produced what Sir Thomas Jackson[1] has acutely called 'the architecture of the book'. 'The Book' to which he refers is the manual written by Vitruvius (probably in the first century B.C.); and elsewhere he describes it as 'the architect's Bible'. He means by this that architects began to use Roman rules for proportion and design, as laid down by Vitruvius, in buildings fifteen hundred years later in date. (It is hardly necessary to remind the reader that modern architects in both England and America still make

[1] Sir T. G. Jackson, *Architecture*, p. 302 (London, 1925).

11. STADSTIMMERHUIS, LEYDEN, HOLLAND (1612)

12. ZAANDAM, HOLLAND

Photo: *Author*

copious use of Roman forms in design.) In this artificial revival by means of books, Flemish architects played a prominent part; and some of their folios of illustrations (or caricatures) of the ancient buildings of Rome were freely used in England, until England herself began to cater for this new literary market. Jan Vrederman de Vries published one such book at Antwerp in 1577.

The appearance of books synchronized with the recognition of the architect as a professional man competent to expound the mysteries they contained. There had been architects in the Middle Ages, all over Europe, but now they began to adopt the Latin title in harmony with their use of Roman forms. The chief architect in Leyden at this time was one Lieven de Key (pronounced 'Kay'), who was born about 1560 and died in 1627. He was the city architect of Haarlem, a few miles away, where he built the Meat Market in 1602-3, also the Old Weighhouse in 1598 and an almshouse in 1608. In Leyden his principal works are the Town Hall (*c.* 1597), almost completely destroyed by fire in 1929; the Gymnasium in Lokhorst Straat, close to the Pilgrims' houses in Kloksteeg; the Stads Timmerhuis in 1612; and probably the Gemeenlandshuis in Breestraat in 1596-8.

All these buildings have many characteristics in common, and perhaps a description of the Stads Timmerhuis on Smidssteeg (Fig. 11) will serve for the rest; especially as it was built while the Pilgrims were in Leyden, and stands near their headquarters. For anything we know, Jepson the carpenter and Bassett the master-mason may have assisted in its erection; at all events we can safely assume that all the Pilgrims must often have paused to watch its progress. It is a delightful building, Dutch to the core, and is in excellent preservation. Like all Dutch buildings of the period, it is of brick with stone dressings. The bricks are very small, averaging 7 to $7\frac{1}{2}$ in. long and $1\frac{1}{2}$ to $1\frac{3}{4}$ in. thick, of a rich red colour, with mortar joints about $\frac{3}{8}$ in. thick. The whole façade of the building, which overlooks a quay on the Galgewater, is formed into a single stepped gable as at St. Luke's Church in Virginia, and this gable is divided horizontally into tiers by projecting cornices—almost the only classical details in the whole design. There are three windows in each of the two lower stories, two in the third, and one in the attic. Windows play a considerable part in the external appearance of Dutch buildings, because they have massive wood frames which, being generally painted cream colour in the seventeenth century, provided a contrast to the dark red of the bricks and enhanced it. Anybody who is familiar with the beautiful architectural paintings of Pieter de Hoogh (1630–c. 1677) and Jan Vermeer (1632–75) knows how those two great artists found wonderful colour-schemes in these very house-fronts, and often they depicted buildings older than their own day. The windows of the period had mullions, and transoms, for the sash-window did not make its appearance in Holland till about 1630,[1] and even then probably only the lower part was made to slide and open. The frames of the windows at the Stads Timmerhuis at Leyden are 5 in. wide. Each window is divided by a mullion and transom into four lights, and each light (about 4 ft. high by 2 ft. wide) is subdivided, into panes measuring on an average $8\frac{1}{4}$ by $6\frac{1}{2}$ in., by wooden bars about an inch wide. Judging from contemporary paintings, most of the windows originally contained lead glazing, but those at the Stads Timmerhuis have wooden bars, and they—as usual—are painted white. The steps of the gables have none of the frisky ornaments and finials such as their architect used on his Meat Market at Haarlem, and elsewhere. As a result, the plain façade of this modest little civic building depends for effect partly on its gaily painted wooden shutters, possibly modern copies of the originals.

Speaking in general of the seventeenth-century brick houses of Holland, it may be said that they depend very largely for

[1] Dr. Slothouwer, in introduction to Yerbury's *Old Domestic Architecture of Holland* (London, 1924).

their charm on colour, and that the colour-scheme consists mainly in the contrast of cream and white woodwork and brightly painted shutters with the warm red of the small Dutch bricks. Their picturesqueness is chiefly due to bold and fanciful gables. Almost every house has a narrow gabled front facing a street or a quay, for most Dutch towns contain a network of canals. One of the most beautiful and complete streets in the whole country is Groot Heiligland at Haarlem, which has an unbroken row of houses with stepped gables of brick.

In subsequent chapters some reference will be made to the influence of Flemish and Dutch architecture upon the smaller domestic architecture of the eastern counties of England, including the Kentish port of Sandwich, from which came William Bassett the master-mason who crossed to New England from Leyden in 1621.

My own researches in the track of the Pilgrims in Holland next led me to look for boarded houses of the type erected by them all over Massachusetts and Connecticut in later years. At first the quest seemed fruitless. Dutch architects could not point me to early examples, but I was informed that a visit to the towns of the Zuyder Zee would provide me with many specimens later than the seventeenth century. My time was limited, but at Broek-in-Waterland, between Amsterdam and Volendam, I came across a number of charming boarded houses of uncertain age (Fig. 6). All had pantiled roofs and boarded sides, but no indication of date. The boarding of the sides was horizontal, and differed in no way from the English examples described in the next chapter. But some of the gables were covered with vertical boarding in narrow widths. The tourist-ridden village of Volendam is full of boarded houses, but none of those which I saw were of any considerable antiquity. On the neighbouring island of Marken, however, I found one cottage with 'Anno 1607' over the doorway. It had a brick front surmounted by a gable of vertical boarding with scalloped bargeboards of wood. This work was probably modern, and might or might not be a copy of the original. But the main structure of the cottage was probably contemporary with the doorway. The sides were covered with tarred horizontal boards of uniform thickness, not 'feather-edged', about 9 in. gauge and $1\frac{1}{4}$ in. thick. The rainwater ran off the steep pantiled roof into a gutter, formed of a single board about 6 in. wide and $2\frac{1}{2}$ in. deep, scooped out in the middle. This gutter was fixed about 6 in. away from the face of the 'wall' on shaped wooden brackets, made out of wood $1\frac{1}{4}$ or $1\frac{1}{2}$ in. thick, spaced on an average about 6 ft. apart. Most of the older cottages on Marken had gutters of this type, which is also found on Czar Peter's cottage on Zaandam, described below (p. 37). A violent thunderstorm prevented me from obtaining a satisfactory photograph of this cottage.

In Amsterdam the only seventeenth-century boarded house of which I could hear is situated in the Begijnen Hof, close to the Scottish Presbyterian Church already mentioned, but though it appears to be of the period and has an overhanging front, it has been so obviously restored in recent years that its original form can only be imagined. Leyden, Delft, Haarlem, and The Hague provided nothing. I was unable to visit Naarden, the little town near Amsterdam where the London Separatists 'tarried a while' on their way to that city in 1593 (see p. 27), but Dr. Alexander Mackennal, in his *Homes and Haunts of the Pilgrim Fathers*, p. 88, describes it as 'a pleasant little spot, whose *pretty wooden houses*, standing among fine trees, bordering broad and dusty roads, remind one of the rural suburbs of Boston and the villages of New Jersey'. This comparison provides a justification, if one be needed, for the present chapter.

It was at Zaandam, however, that at last I found the evidence for which I had been seeking. Zaandam is a small town situated on the Zaan, some five miles north-west of Amsterdam. It is noted chiefly for its windmills, though these seem to be

THE PILGRIMS IN HOLLAND (1608–1620)

disappearing rapidly, and for its rows of one-story houses, many of which are of wood painted a cheerful green. One building, on the quay known as Krimp, appeared to be of considerable age (Fig. 12). It is a tall three-story structure with a pantiled roof and a gable-end towards the canal, standing on a brick plinth. The sides are all covered with weatherboarding, the boards being of considerable width, with wooden angle-fillets at the corners. There is a solid wooden gutter on brackets at the eaves, as in the cottage at Marken previously described. Farther along the same quay is another cottage, of only one story, which may be of seventeenth-century date, but the gable-end has chamfered horizontal boarding below and narrow flush boarding in the gable itself. The sides are of wide boards fixed horizontally. The roof is covered with pantiles, and there is a plain square brick chimney in the centre of the roof. There is a wooden gutter carried on shaped brackets.

The chief attraction to visitors to Zaandam is the queer little building (Figs. 13–14) known as 'Czar Peter's Hut' (*Czaar Peterhuisje*). Its celebrity arises from the fact that Peter the Great, Czar of Russia, spent a week here in 1697 when learning the trade of shipbuilding. Because a king once lived for one week in a small house, snobbery has made this insignificant wooden shack a place of pilgrimage for many years, and ugly tablets and framed inscriptions record the visits of Russian and other crowned heads. But this regrettable sycophancy has had one useful result for the purpose of my inquiry, by preserving the little building to this day. Some forty years ago it suffered from a serious flood, so was re-erected and completely protected within a particularly hideous red-brick building at the expense of His Imperial Majesty the Czar, to whom it belonged until the recent collapse of Czardom. The new building prevents one photographing the old hut, but my own drawing, made on the spot, is an accurate representation of its present appearance. Before its re-erection in 1897, another and somewhat larger cottage adjoined it (at the right-hand end of the building as shown in my sketch), and a brick chimney-stack served them both. Against the boarded 'wall' on the left of the doorway shown in my sketch there was a small lean-to shed, now removed. As appears from an old painting of the original building, the original gable-end had only a central doorway, so that the present wide windows (divided into square panes) on each side of the doorway must be later additions. The present brick plinth is obviously modern but probably replaces a similar arrangement, as the damp soil of these waterside towns renders such a precaution desirable. In spite of renovation, the whole structure is rickety and is propped up all round. For the sake of clearness, I have omitted the props in my drawing.

If the only distinctive fact about this house had been its occupation by Czar Peter in 1697, it would have less interest for us in relation to the question of Dutch boarded houses of Pilgrim times. But fortunately documents exist to show that it was built by one Gerret Kist, a Dutchman, in 1632. It is therefore very nearly contemporary with the departure of the Pilgrims from Holland to America in 1620, and proves conclusively that, at that time, Dutch people, as well as Englishmen in Essex and elsewhere, were building wooden houses and covering them with weatherboarding, in the style which became so familiar in Massachusetts and Connecticut within a few years.

Czar Peter's cottage, as we now see it, is about 30 ft. long and between 14 and 15 ft. wide, externally. It is divided into two rooms, with an attic or loft upstairs, to which access is obtained by means of a hinged ladder. The right-hand room is entered direct from outside, through the door shown in my sketch, and it contains a brick fireplace. The hearth is (now) covered with red 'quarry' tiles, and is considerably higher than the floor-level. That level is uncertain, because the whole building has warped and sunk, with the result that one cannot be sure of its original level at any given point, but apparently the hearth may always

13. CZAR PETER'S HUT, ZAANDAM, VIEW

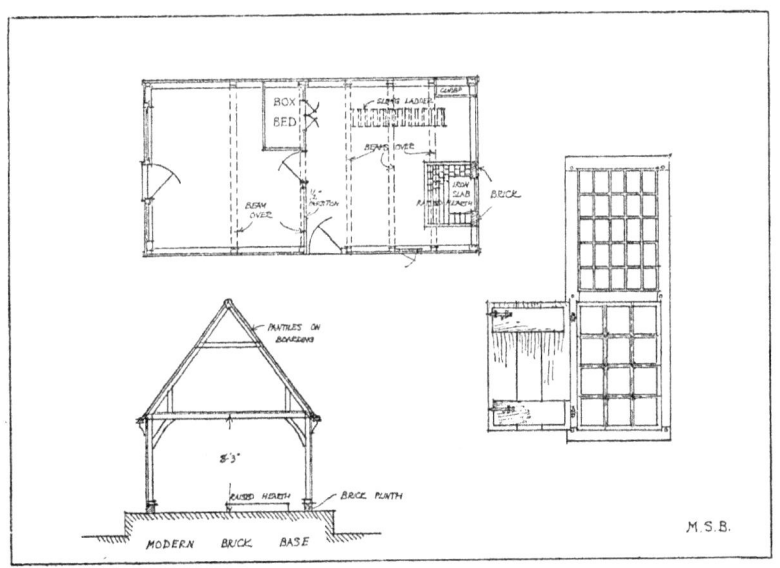

14. CZAR PETER'S HUT, ZAANDAM, PLAN, ETC.

have been 9 in. higher than the floor of the room. The actual fireplace has an iron hearth and an iron fire-back. The jambs are lined with Dutch blue-and-white tiles.

The roof is of pantiles and is of a fairly steep pitch. The tiles are laid on boards about 12 in. to 15 in. wide, running from eaves to ridge (not parallel with eaves and ridge in the usual way). The gutter is of solid wood, hollowed out as in the Marken cottage previously described, and is fixed on brackets.

The main timbers of the framing are about 7 in. by 5 in. and are covered externally with horizontal boarding in wide widths. At the angles is a cover-fillet about 3 in. by $1\frac{1}{4}$ in. Internally there is a lining of vertical boarding. The partition between the two rooms is of feather-edged and tongued boards only half an inch thick, a wonderful bit of joinery. Similar boarding encloses the 'box-bed', a typically Dutch fitment. The front door and the other doors are of plain boarding with ledges but no braces, and the front door is hung in two heights as shown in my drawing. The boards of the door between the two rooms are only $\frac{3}{8}$ in. thick.

The fanlight over the front door, and the window adjoining it, have leaded lights, almost certainly original. The window has a boarded shutter over its lower part, but a sash of later date with wooden bars has been added since. The leadwork of the window and fanlight is about $\frac{3}{8}$ in. wide and is rather rough, as is the glass.

The posts of the main framing are let into a sill-piece resting on the brick plinth. The ceiling consists simply of the boarded floor of the attic, carried on square wooden beams which are indicated by dotted lines on my plan. The ladder which leads to the attic is about 20 in. wide and is slung from the ceiling and hinged at its upper end. The steps and rails are about 4 in. wide. The present ladder is apparently modern, but may replace an older one of similar type.

The foregoing description, with the accompanying illustra-

16. NEAR EPPING, ESSEX

17. BRAINTREE, ESSEX

THE PILGRIMS IN HOLLAND (1608–1620) 41

tions, will enable the reader to trace a close parallel between this Dutch boarded cottage of 1632 and approximately coeval examples in the eastern counties of England and in America. The extent of English and American borrowing from Dutch architecture in sundry other details will appear in later chapters. But a visitor to Holland should not fail to see the domestic furniture of the early seventeenth century in the Rijks Museum at Amsterdam, where he will inevitably recognize many features as characteristic of contemporary work in New England as in the Old Country. Dutch influence continued to permeate English architecture and English furniture-design in the time of William and Mary, and made itself felt across the Atlantic right into the eighteenth century.

In conclusion, it must be remembered that Protestant refugees from both Belgium and Holland poured into the south-eastern counties of England during the religious wars of the sixteenth century. As many as fifty thousand are said to have come from Antwerp alone after its capture by the Duke of Parma in 1585. Norwich contained nearly 4,000 Dutch and Walloons in 1571, and in 1587 they numbered 4,679. A few years later London contained over ten thousand foreigners, mostly Walloons, out of a total population estimated at 130,000. Sandwich, Canterbury, Maidstone, and Dover were in like case. It is hardly possible to exaggerate the influence—social, religious, and artistic—exerted on south-eastern England in Elizabeth's reign by this stream of refugees from the Low Countries.

IV. SOUTH-EAST ENGLAND: THE HOME OF THE PILGRIMS

Having now considered in some detail the claims of the Scrooby–Gainsborough–Boston district of England, and the parts of Holland in which many of the Pilgrims lived from 1608 to 1620, it remains to justify the statement made at the end of Chapter II: that we must look to another part of England for the sources of their architecture.

That district, as will now be explained, comprises the south-eastern counties of England, and especially Essex, Cambridgeshire, Hertfordshire, Middlesex, Surrey, and Kent. It is in these six counties that one finds nearly all the surviving examples resembling those of seventeenth-century New England, and it is from them that practically all my illustrations are taken. For reasons which will appear later, these counties are, in fact, the natural home of the weatherboarded house. They are also, as it happens, the spiritual home of English Nonconformity and therefore the cradle of the American nation.

This last statement is confirmed in a simple and surprising way by a careful study of any large-scale map of the modern states which formed New England. It has interested me to collect from such a map the English names of 115 cities and towns in Massachusetts, Connecticut, Rhode Island, and adjacent parts of Maine and New Hampshire, and then to classify those names under English counties. Nearly half are derived from ten eastern and south-eastern counties, while the remainder are drawn from all the rest of England—thirty counties including Yorkshire and Lancashire. Further analysis reveals another interesting fact, that Essex alone accounts for twenty names, one-sixth of the whole: and, curiously enough, Essex in England is *par excellence* the county of boarded houses, as it once was the county most marked for its dissenting fervour. These twenty

THE HOME OF THE PILGRIMS

names occur frequently in the history of English Nonconformity, and many of them will be mentioned in subsequent pages as places where good examples of boarded houses, mills, and barns are still to be found. They are Stepney, Stratford,[1] Romford, Epping, Easton, Hatfield,[1] Braintree, Newport,[1] Billerica,[2] Wickford, Chelmsford, Springfield, Danbury, Malden,[1] Wethersfield, Topsfield, Colchester, Dedham, Harwich, and Waltham.[1] The adjoining county of Hertfordshire presumably suggested the name of 'Hartford' (Conn.) and Ware; while Middlesex contributed Acton, Chelsea, Enfield, Hadley, and Uxbridge. Kent is recalled by Ashburnham, Canterbury, Chatham, Dover, Greenwich, Rye, Rochester, Sandwich, and Southborough; and Surrey by Guilford (Guildford), Kingston, and Petersham. Suffolk accounts for Groton, Haverhill, Ipswich, Newmarket, Sudbury, and Wenham; Cambridgeshire for Cambridge and Wilbraham; Norfolk for Attleborough, Hingham, Lynn, Norwich, and Yarmouth; Bedfordshire for Bedford, Dunstable, and Woburn; and finally Lincolnshire for Boston and Lincoln. There is also a fair sprinkling of English names from Dorset, Devon, Somerset, and Hampshire—where Nonconformity flourished but boarded houses were practically unknown. Yet the outstanding feature of this brief survey is the predominance of Essex names.

And this commonsense test is supported by history. Dr. H. M. Dexter[3] has made a careful study of the provenance of all those who arrived in America in the *Mayflower* in 1620 and in the *Fortune* in 1621. Yorkshire, Nottinghamshire, and Lincolnshire —the three English counties which converge near Scrooby— provided 22; Norfolk, Suffolk, and Essex 46; Kent 17; London 17; all other counties 21; and 14 of whom nothing is known make up the total of 137 souls. Here again, the south-east of

[1] Other English counties contain towns of this name.
[2] Spelt thus in America and formerly in England, but the modern English spelling is Billericay.
[3] *England and Holland of the Pilgrims*, pp. 601-41 (Boston, Mass., 1905).

England accounts for two-thirds of the immigrants. But too much importance should not be attached to the fact. A number of women and children are included in the figure of 137, and a great many of the 53 men who arrived in the *Mayflower* died

15. HIGH STREET, BILLERICAY, ESSEX

under the hardships of the first winter. Indeed it does not appear that more than 21 men were still living when the *Fortune* brought a few more to swell their small number in 1621. To generalize about so slender a total is obviously unfair. But there was a steady stream of arrivals from England up to the year 1640, when the Civil War put an end to religious persecution, and up to that date it may be said that nearly all the immigrants were Nonconformist refugees. For the purpose of our study, it is reasonable to describe this much larger body of people, estimated to number about 25,000 in 1640, as 'Pilgrim Fathers'; and this figure affords a more adequate basis for argument.

'The great majority of the first Anglo-Americans', writes

THE HOME OF THE PILGRIMS

Professor G. M. Trevelyan,[1] 'came from the south-east of England and represented her most pronounced Nordic stock. Of about 25,000 English settled in New England in 1640, it has been calculated by some statisticians and genealogists that 50 per cent. came from Suffolk, Essex, and Herts.; 20 per cent. from Norfolk, Lincolnshire, Nottingham, Yorkshire, Middlesex, Kent, Surrey, and Sussex. The counties on the Welsh and Scottish borders supplied only scattered individuals. These original 25,000 to whom collectively may be extended the term "Pilgrim Fathers", were a prolific stock and their descendants were the men who did most to set the political and social tone of the United States in its great developments west of the Appalachian Mountains in later times, until about 1870.'

Briefly, then, in 1640 about two-thirds of the population of 25,000 people inhabiting New England came from the group of south-eastern counties of Old England already mentioned; and before that date some of the surviving houses illustrated and described in the last chapter of this book had already been erected.

The reason for this disproportionate emigration from a few counties is not to be accounted for by the supposition that they were at that time densely populated as compared with those northern and midland shires which are now the most busy and crowded parts of England. It is true that parts of the eastern counties were then comparatively flourishing owing to the prosperity of the wool trade, but so were other counties which produced few 'Pilgrim Fathers'.

Even after making all allowance for social changes of this sort, we are faced with the undeniable fact that south-eastern England provided the backbone of New England for the first and most vital twenty years of its history. This circumstance is readily and completely explained by a reference to religious history, to which we may profitably turn for a moment before proceeding to examine its traditional domestic architecture.

[1] G. M. Trevelyan, *History of England*, p. 437 (London, 1926).

Right back to its very beginning, the whole miserable story of religious persecution contains indications of the gradual growth of dissent in the south-eastern counties. A 'conventicle' at Chesterton near Cambridge is mentioned as early as 1475, others at Amersham and Newbury in 1507 and 1518 respectively, while complaints reach the authorities of unorthodox preaching at London, Uxbridge, Burnham, Henley, Stratford, 'Billerica', Chelmsford, Colchester, Witham, and Braintree. The last six of these places are in Essex. In 1550, according to Strype the historian[1] (1643–1737), congregations were in existence at Bocking near Braintree in Essex and at Feversham (=Faversham) in Kent. 'The members of the congregation in Kent went over unto the congregation in Essex, to instruct and join with them, and they had their meetings in Kent in divers places besides Feversham.' The congregation at Bocking numbered sixty persons, and the clerical historian gains some satisfaction in noting that nine of them who were arrested were 'cowherds, clothiers, and such mean-like people'. Nevertheless, they probably contributed to the foundation of the United States, for three separate places in New England bear the Essex name of Braintree, of which Bocking almost forms a part. During the persecution of Protestants under Mary (1553–8) the number of Essex martyrs burnt at the stake is remarkable, and it may be presumed that some of these were the spiritual ancestors of the Pilgrim Fathers. The names of their homes may be repeated here, for they show the close connexion that the Essex centres of 'heresy' have with the Essex architectural tradition: Stratford, Brentwood, Chelmsford, Rayleigh, Horndon-on-the-Hill, Maldon, Braintree, Coggeshall, and Colchester.[2]

---

[1] *Ecclesiastical Memorials*, ii (1), 369.

[2] It may be added that even the Peasants' Revolt of 1381 was fomented in the same district. It appears that either Essex or Kent took the first steps in the agitation, and that the subsequent revolt began with the attempted prosecution of fishermen from Fobbing, Corringham, and Stanford-le-Hope for failure to pay the poll-tax. These villages are in South Essex, a centre of Lollardry. While it is

THE HOME OF THE PILGRIMS

It is not until 1567 or 1568 that any record appears of an organized Congregational church in London, with its own minister and officers; and Dr. R. W. Dale holds[1] that this was 'the first regularly constituted Congregational church', its predecessors already mentioned having been informal assemblies. Many members of this church fled to Holland about 1593 (cf. p. 4), and it was apparently distinct from the so-called 'Pilgrim Church' in Southwark, still existing, and founded, according to Dr. Dale,[2] in 1616. (In speaking of a 'church' in this book, I use the word in the apostolic sense, and not referring to the building.) By a curious coincidence, Southwark, the birthplace and early home of John Harvard, still possesses the only good example of a boarded house in all London (see Fig. 38).

The progress of 'Brownism' or 'Separatism'—or 'Congregationalism' as it has been known since about 1640—during Elizabeth's reign has already been sufficiently outlined for our purpose in Chapter I (pp. 2–6) of this book. But it is worth while to pause here to consider whether, as has been implied already, there is evidence that it was specially prevalent in southeastern England. To that end, I have examined with some care the year-books of the Congregational and Baptist bodies, each of which contains a full list of existing churches with the dates of their original foundation. Up to the year 1640, when the rush of religious refugees to America ceased and a more cosmopolitan type of settlement ensued, nine of the present

perhaps too much to claim this revolt as a precursor of modern Nonconformity, the underlying spirit was there; and the peasants attacked some of the chief abbots and priors, though rather in their capacity as great nobles than as clerics. When the revolt was finally quelled, severe punishment was meted out to the rebels at Billericay, Chelmsford, Colchester and other Essex towns which appear constantly in the pages of this book. Professor G. M. Trevelyan, from whose book *England in the Age of Wycliffe* (pp. 202–47) these facts are taken, says that the movement was infused with the spirit of 'Christian democracy'.

[1] *History of English Congregationalism*, p. 95 (London, 1907).
[2] *Ibid.*, pp. 220–1.

Congregational churches had been founded, and of these six were in the south-eastern counties of England, viz. at Cheshunt, Herts. (1600); Southwark, London (1616); Box Lane, Herts. (1622); Epping, Essex (1625); Sudbury, Suffolk (1631); and Poultry

18. ST. OSYTH, ESSEX

Chapel, London (1640). Earlier in date than any of these is Horningsham, Wiltshire, for which a date of 1566 is seriously claimed! Inquiry from its minister has produced a small history[1] of the church, including an illustration of the building, a thatched meeting-house which is said to have served its present purpose continuously since 1566. In that case, it is unquestionably the oldest Nonconformist place of worship in either England or America. There may be some in East Anglia, but I know nothing there older than Friar Street Chapel, Ipswich (1699), a fine example. Another very early Congregational foundation is at Troedrhiwdaler in Wales (1590). From 1641 to 1659 forty-

[1] The Rev. H. M. Gunn, *History of the Old Meeting House at Horningsham* (Warminster, N.D. recent).

THE HOME OF THE PILGRIMS 49

one more Congregational churches were founded, and of these twenty-eight—a very high proportion—were in the south-eastern counties. The list includes Ilford and Colchester in Essex; Halesworth, Bury St. Edmunds, Wrentham, Beccles, Woodbridge, Rendham, and Wattisfield in Suffolk; Deptford, Canterbury, Dover, Sandwich, and Staplehurst in Kent.

The Baptists have a much longer list of early churches, but these are far more evenly distributed over England, and out of seventy-one in all, only fifteen are in the south-eastern counties. These include Braintree (1550) and Ilford in Essex; Tring in Herts.; Ashford, Chatham, Eythorne, and Smarden in Kent; 'Bunyan Meeting' at Bedford; and two churches in London. There are also seven churches in Lincolnshire, including Crowle, (1599), Epworth (1599), Spalding (1646), and two names very familiar in Massachusetts—Boston (1635) and Bourne (1645).

Summing up this rapid excursus into early Nonconformist church history, it may be said that while the origins of Congregationalism are predominantly to be found in the south-eastern counties from which the bulk of the Pilgrims set out for America, the statistics of early Baptist churches show no such bias, but that the earliest Baptist church of all was founded in 1550 at Braintree, a very 'hotbed of dissent'. It is significant that out of some 120 Congregational and Baptist churches founded before 1660, not one occurs in the great modern centres of population outside London—viz. Manchester, Liverpool, Leeds, Sheffield, and Birmingham.

Lastly one may recall another fact bearing on every aspect of seventeenth-century life in New England: the preponderance of Cambridge graduates among the early settlers, for that is yet a further link with East Anglia. Not only were the founders of Congregationalism—Browne, Harrison, Greenwood, Barrowe, John Smyth, Johnson, Penry—all Cambridge men; but so was William Brewster who went over in the *Mayflower* to New England; so was the Rev. John Cotton, the vicar of Boston in Lincolnshire, who followed his parishioners to their new township overseas in 1633; so was John Winthrop, the first governor of Massachusetts; and finally, so was the Rev. John Harvard, who, at his death in 1638, left half his estate (£780) and three hundred books to the newly founded 'seminary in the wilderness' which has since become one of the most famous seats of learning in the world. The new town where it was established was christened 'Cambridge' in that same year; partly, it may be presumed, in honour of John Harvard himself, but also partly because some seventy of the leading men of the colony were Cambridge graduates. The other ancient English university whose Press has published this book will not resent the emphasis that I have laid on this feature of early life in New England, and Oxford swelled the quota of educated men, mostly ministers, among the new settlers. But the foregoing chapter has so far stated the case for the predominance of natives of south-east England among the Pilgrims that we may now proceed to study the methods of building that prevailed in that part of the Old Country early in the seventeenth century.

V. TIMBER HOUSES IN SOUTH-EAST ENGLAND

c. 1600–1700

THE south-eastern part of England with which we are now concerned comprises the counties of Norfolk, Suffolk, Essex, Cambridge, Hertford, Middlesex, Surrey, and Kent. Together they form only about one-sixth of the whole area of England, yet it is from this limited area that some two-thirds of the Pilgrims came, and they derived their style of domestic architecture from an even more restricted field, as will now be explained.

The map on page 5 is drawn to the same scale as the sketch-map of New England on p. 117. It shows the county boundaries, the principal places mentioned, and the sites of most of the buildings illustrated. But unfortunately on so small a scale it is not possible to indicate adequately the physical and geological features which have produced the various 'regional' and traditional forms of building in the different parts of this limited area. However, even this map may be made to illustrate a verbal description of the salient characteristics of the district.

In the first place, there is practically no building-stone of any importance in all these eight counties. There is a small patch of ferruginous sandstone, 'carstone', near Hunstanton in Norfolk. A few miles south of the line of the North Downs is a ridge of rough sandstone, unsuitable for fine carving or moulding, though it forms a pleasantly warm-toned material for rubble walling. The fine oolitic limestone of which the Cotswold cottages, the Oxford colleges, the city of Bath, and many of the noblest churches of England are built runs from the Isle of Portland in Dorset up to the north of Lincolnshire, and its situation in regard to the south-eastern counties is indicated by the word 'Limestone' on the map. The magnificent churches of north and west Norfolk and south Lincolnshire were built of stone from this belt, floated down to the Wash from the nearest quarries in Northamptonshire. The principal churches built during the Middle Ages in London and Kent, such as Canterbury Cathedral and Westminster Abbey, were largely constructed of stone from Caen in Normandy.

But one result of this shortage of stone in the eastern counties

19. KINGSBURY GREEN, MIDDLESEX

is to be seen in the wide use of flint for walling. In Norfolk especially, but all along the line of the chalk hills which run diagonally across East Anglia (marked 'Chiltern Hills' on map) and also across Kent and Surrey (marked 'North Downs' on map) there is a belt of clay containing an ample supply of such flints. The chalk itself is, for the most part, unsuited for building, though it is naturally largely used to produce lime for mortar; but at St. Alban's Abbey and elsewhere certain varieties of it have been used for internal work and carving with marked success.

The shortage of stone in these counties naturally led also to the introduction of brick manufacture, which remained one of the lost arts in England from Roman times until it was revived in the fourteenth or fifteenth century, in East Anglia first of all. Probably the Flemish weavers who had settled so freely in that part of the country were responsible, for Flanders is another district where there is a shortage of building stone. There is no part of England where Dutch and Flemish influence is so apparent in architecture as in Norfolk, Suffolk, and Essex, though some places in Kent and Sussex, such as Sandwich and Rye, are close competitors. Holland and Flanders lie opposite our eastern shores, and for some years after brickwork was introduced (or re-introduced), it seems probable that most of the bricks were imported into this country. An appendix at the end of this book deals briefly with the possible connexion between the brick building tradition of Holland and Flanders, East Anglia and New England.

But this brick architecture was never adopted in all parts of the south-eastern counties. In Norfolk it is found in profusion, but often combined with flint walling to give strength at angles and to frame the openings. In Suffolk, Essex, and Kent its use is mainly confined to buildings of the more expensive sort, such as manor-houses and churches, and even for the larger houses its use was by no means common at the beginning of the seventeenth century. In Hertfordshire and Middlesex especially brickwork was seldom employed at so early a date. London at the time of the Great Fire (1666) was still mainly a timber-built city, as may be seen from the excellent models in the London Museum.

Timber-framed houses may be divided into four groups according to the material with which the timber-framing is filled or covered, for the principles of their construction remain invariable (or practically so) whatever be the covering medium. The panels or spaces between the timbers may be filled in with bricks laid horizontally or diagonally; this practice is confined to parts of Surrey, Sussex, Hampshire, and a few other comparatively small areas. Or they may be filled with a kind of basket-work of laths or twigs, over which plaster is spread. Sometimes the plaster covers the whole face of the building, hiding the stout timber framing. This method is favoured in Suffolk especially, in parts of Essex and Cambridgeshire, and in a few other places. The plaster may be used only to fill the 'panels' between the framing; a method known as 'black and white work'. This was a popular method in the time of the Pilgrims in many parts of England, but especially in the West Midlands, Cheshire, and South Lancashire. It must have been familiar to Edward Winslow, whose ancestral home was at Droitwich, where there are many fine examples of this style of building; and probably also to Captain Miles Standish, whose home at Duxbury Hall near Chorley in Lancashire was not very far from such famous half-timbered buildings as 'Hall-in-the-Wood', standing only a few miles away. Yet there are no examples of this 'black-and-white' work, nor, so far as I am aware, of half-timbering filled with brickwork, in New England, though there may be a few where the plaster covering or 'parging' (sometimes called 'pargetting') is carried over the framework, thus concealing it. It is not generally known that this latter method was usually adopted in the seventeenth and eighteenth centuries in certain parts of England, and especially in East Anglia, for strictly utilitarian reasons, viz. to protect the timber framing and to prevent the passage of damp and draughts at the junction of frame and filling. Its removal by modern enthusiasts who desire to display 'ye olde woodworke' is therefore often a dangerous proceeding quite unforeseen by the original builders. The consistency of this plastering or 'parging' is extremely tough, due partly to the great care taken in preliminary kneading and mixing, and partly to the generous admixture of cow-hair and dung with the lime and sand—these ingredients giving increased tenacity and resistance to cracking. In composition as well as in workmanship, this old East Anglian plastering is very different from the material we use to-day.

IN SOUTH-EAST ENGLAND

The third method of finishing a timber-framed house is to cover it with 'tile-hanging'; that is, with plain roofing tiles, or with ornamental roofing tiles, hung from battens fixed horizontally across the 'studding' or 'framing'. This produces a very

20. GREAT WAKERING, ESSEX

attractive effect and at the same time acts as a most efficient protection against the weather. It is widely used in Kent, Surrey, and Sussex, but not very much elsewhere; and does not appear to have become common in New England. One explanation may be that the popularity of tile-hanging, in those counties where it eventually became traditional, was of comparatively late date, and may not have been familiar to the Pilgrim Fathers.

We have now eliminated, from the various wall-building methods available at the commencement of the seventeenth century, the following materials: stone, brick, flint, timber-framing filled with brickwork or plaster, timber-framing covered with plaster or tiling. This leaves us with that method which became so characteristic of the early homes of the Pilgrims in New England, the use of timber-framing covered with 'weatherboarding' (or 'siding'), usually fixed horizontally across the vertical posts or studs of the framing.

Houses so constructed are found over the greater part of Essex, as the map shows, in Hertfordshire, in Middlesex, and in parts of Cambridgeshire, Surrey, and Kent. They were once very numerous in and round London, but have been almost completely swept away with the march of 'civilization' and suburbia. (It is only too easy to demolish a wooden house when a road needs to be widened to comply with the clamant demands of modern motor traffic.) Outside this very small area—certainly not more than one-tenth of the whole extent of England—they are seldom found. But boarded barns are distributed over a rather wider field. Thus there are occasional examples in Lincolnshire (see p. 22), Norfolk, Oxfordshire, Buckinghamshire, and other counties east of the limestone belt marked on the map. But it is presumably of the little tract north and east of London—the counties of Essex, Middlesex, and Hertfordshire —that Professor Trevelyan is thinking when he writes[1] of the Pilgrims' first homes in New England that: 'Their houses were built of wood as universally as those of the early Saxons in the old English forest.' For this part of England was at one time densely wooded, and at Greensted, a village near Ongar on the west side of Essex, there still stands a Saxon church built entirely of timber, unique of its kind in England, though 'there is documentary evidence that in the non-stone districts of England they were not infrequent at the time of the Conquest'.[2] As the most remote known ancestor of the timber houses of New England, its construction may be briefly described here. It is 'the oldest building with wooden walls in England. . . . It has been cited as an English example of the so-called "block-house construction", but in true block-house construction—the

[1] G. M. Trevelyan, *History of England*, p. 439 (London, 1926).
[2] A. W. Clapham, *English Romanesque Architecture before the Conquest*, p. 105 (Oxford, 1930).

21. BARNS, CANVEY ISLAND, ESSEX

22. BARN, WETHERSFIELD, ESSEX

block bau of the Germans—the timbers are laid horizontally, and at Greensted, on the contrary, they are upright. . . . The church at Greensted has its walls formed of half trunks of trees set upright, with the split faces inwards. The upper end of each half trunk originally was roughly tenoned into a plate and the lower end into a sill. There were two pegs to each tenon and both the plate and the sill were tenoned. The sill was laid upon the ground, but in the course of time it rotted, as did the lower portions of the trunks, and in one of the various "restorations" which the church underwent in the nineteenth century, the sill and the rotted parts of the trunks were removed, and a low dwarf wall built, on which a new sill was placed. The roof was also renewed at one of the "restorations". Each half trunk is connected to its neighbour by a grooved and tongued joint, and at the angles of the building three-quarter trunks are used in order to keep the continuity of the walls, inside and out'. The timbers of the walls were dressed with an adze internally, after they had been split. 'The Greensted church wall is similar to the stockaded ramparts of the English boroughs and the Norman *mottes*, from which the walls of their timber superstructures were copied.'[1] The date of this church is unknown. Another church in East Anglia, at Bury St. Edmunds in Suffolk, was built of 'wooden boards' either in the reign of Alfred or in that of Canute.[2] These buildings have a more specific interest to students of early American architecture because it is thought by some that the first homes of the Pilgrims in New England were similarly constructed of tree-trunks, and the introduction of horizontal boarding fixed to vertical framing did not come till many years after 1620. This question is discussed in Chapter VI.

The next stage in timber-construction is the gradual development of the framed house from the stockade type of wall just described. The plate at the upper end of the wall remained,

[1] C. F. Innocent, *Development of English Building Construction*, pp. 108–10 (Cambridge, 1916).   [2] *Ibid.*, p. 177.

as also the sill at the lower end. But in place of the continuous line of connected tree-trunks, upright trunks or posts were placed some distance apart, tenoned at head and foot as before. Such a form of construction may conceivably have been in vogue as early as the time when Greensted Church, naturally a more important structure than any peasant's shack, was erected. In any case, timber churches, which were sometimes built during Saxon times, were never common; whereas the first huts or cottages of the serfs must have been mainly built of timber, at any rate outside the stone districts and probably even in those areas too. What is more difficult to determine is whether the timber-built homes of the East Anglian families from which the Pilgrims came were, so late as the reign of James I, mere wigwams or shacks of mud and branches, or whether they were comparable, as regards accommodation, appearance, and other amenities with the brick and stone cottages then being erected in other parts of England (see pp. 23-4). The difficulty arises from the fact that few of the surviving boarded houses of East Anglia bear any definite date. One can only hazard a guess as to their probable age. In most cases the boarding has been renewed, in many instances new windows and doors have been inserted, while the thatch has almost certainly been replaced more than once—perhaps in these latter days by corrugated iron. The framing itself is concealed, and often the only clues to the date of the building are to be found in the pitch of the roof, and the general proportions of the structure; but one gradually develops a sixth sense or instinct enabling one to attribute a probable age to the design.

Even allowing for the fact that many of the small houses originally built for yeomen and small tradesmen came into the possession of labourers as the constant drift from country to town proceeded, it is evident that the south-eastern counties of England were especially prosperous in Elizabethan times (see p. 25), and it is reasonable to assume that even the agricultural labourers and the artisans in the towns were living under far better conditions than prevailed locally in the Middle Ages. The boarded cottages illustrated in this book are, for the most part, of unknown date, but most of them may be assumed to be of the seventeenth century. Their timbered sides are obviously less permanently built than the stone walls of the cottages in the Cotswolds or Yorkshire, or the brick walls of similar buildings in Norfolk and Kent. Their roofs, again, are generally covered with thatch, which is liable to catch fire, to harbour vermin, and—with the lapse of time—to let in the rain. It is not to be compared for permanence with the beautiful golden 'stone' slates of Gloucestershire (of which a fine and authentic example is to be seen in Mr. Edsel Ford's new house near Detroit), with the heavier Yorkshire slabs, or with the lovely sandy tiles of southern and eastern England. But so far as mere creature comforts go, the farmers and merchants and tradesmen who formed the bulk of the 'Pilgrim Fathers' (i.e. the settlers in New England from 1620 to 1640) were probably quite comfortably housed in this country in their timber homes, and soon established comparable conditions in their American habitat. Their rooms were low and often dark, usually either stuffy or draughty. Sanitary conveniences were most primitive, baths unknown, and personal cleanliness perhaps at a low standard. But change in these respects only came late in the nineteenth century, and there seems to be no need to assume that English people of any but the very poorest class were not comfortably and adequately housed, according to their lights, three hundred years ago.

The timber-framed house is not to be regarded as an ephemeral construction. England contains many substantial barns that have a recorded history of at least five hundred years, all built of wood; and although many of her smaller houses could prove an equal antiquity, some perished during the nineteenth century before the cult of the picturesque became fashionable, far more have given way to the juggernaut of progress, and of the remainder only a fraction are dated. Every suburb of London would be able to show seventeenth-century boarded and timber houses of the seventeenth century had they not been swept away to make room for multiple stores, tramways, and villa-residences. These things are inevitable, but we must award honour where honour is due, and the disappearance of so many of our wooden buildings is no evidence of their instability; on the contrary, they stand surprisingly well when reasonably treated.

The durability of such structures as the seventeenth-century houses and mills of the south-eastern counties is due partly to the nature of the timber employed—usually oak for framing, and elm or oak for boarding—and to the solidity of the framework. For although the 'scantlings' (the dimensions of the various members) are flimsy in comparison with the stockade-like arrangement at Greensted, yet they are very sturdy compared with modern practice. In fact, the strength of each oak member is several times more than is necessary for the purpose it has to meet, as defined by modern building by-laws where it is assumed that fir and not oak will be used. In other words, the seventeenth-century builders adopted a very high 'factor of safety', as the engineers say nowadays, the factor of safety being the number of times the calculated breaking load of the beam or post exceeds the load that has actually to be supported.

It is becoming increasingly well known to-day that timber structures suffer from parasites and diseases, the 'death-watch beetle' and 'dry rot', to give them their common English names, being the most familiar. The former pest seems to have become much more prevalent in recent years, and its increase is attributed to the warmer atmosphere produced in our old churches by improved methods of heating, which seem to stimulate the activity of the beetle. Dry rot is a fungus which most commonly attacks unseasoned wood in damp and unventilated spaces, but old and seasoned timber is not necessarily immune. Both these troubles are only too common in England, and doubtless the old cottages and barns and mills of Essex suffer from them as well as the churches of which one hears more. But here the high 'factor of safety' comes in. A wooden house which is, perhaps, five times as strongly built as it need be theoretically, will remain standing until four-fifths or more of the thickness of its timbers is eaten away.

The principles of the framing may be understood by a reference to the photograph (Fig. 24) of the interior of a barn in Essex, or to Fig. 25, which shows a partly ruined timber barn in Middlesex. (For obvious reasons it is impossible to photograph the framing of a house which is intact, because the framework is completely concealed by boarding or by plaster.) In the former illustration the sill and head are clearly seen, and the roughly hewn posts between them, strengthened by diagonal braces. In this case the sill is about 7 by 7 in., and the posts, which are about a foot apart, average 4 by 4 in. in section, though they vary greatly. The sill rests on a brick plinth 9 in. thick. Like many other barns of this size, this example has an 'aisle' with a roof continuing the main slope and resting on a stout post with curved struts or brackets at the top, to distribute the weight of the beam carrying the roof. The external boarding can be clearly seen in the photograph.

The other illustration (Fig. 25) shows a derelict and half-ruined barn at Edgware in Middlesex. The massive framing can be seen, the sizes or scantlings of several of the members being figured on the drawing.

According to Mr. C. F. Innocent,[1] the use of 'crucks' is unknown in the south-eastern counties of England. A 'cruck' is a curved tree-trunk which is made to serve the dual functions of a roof-truss and its supports. Thus, a row of pairs of crucks, spaced several feet apart, could and did form the whole main

[1] *Development of English Building Construction*, p. 35 (Cambridge, 1916).

framework of a building, being connected one to another by horizontal sill, plates, and purlins. In the various districts of south-east England, the posts were not one with the roof, the plate forming a definite line of division and connexion. The

25. RUINED BARN, NEAR EDGWARE, MIDDLESEX

same method appears to have prevailed in New England from the beginning; indeed it is unnecessary here to give more than a brief description of the framing methods adopted in south-east England, for they resemble precisely the early American practice (except the 'hewn overhang' mentioned on p. 161, a distinctively American innovation); and every detail of such work has been most admirably described and illustrated by Mr. Kelly in his monograph on the early houses of Connecticut.

English methods differed in various parts of the country, and the following paragraph applies particularly to Essex, Kent, Surrey, and the neighbouring counties. The framing always begins with a heavy sill, which almost always rests on a plinth or dwarf wall of brickwork, rising a foot or so above ground-level. Sometimes this sill is concealed by weatherboarding carried over it. At each of the four corners of the building a massive angle-post 8 or 9 in. square was tenoned into the sill. Such posts were formed of tree-trunks with the bole set upwards, to provide enough timber for the double corner joint. Another reason advanced for this method is that the sap was allowed to run out thereby, a practical and possible explanation. Such posts are said to be 'flared' or 'shouldered' (cf. p. 158). Stout intermediate posts were used at structural points as necessary in the case of a long frame, and studs, stronger and more closely spaced than in modern practice, formed the remaining vertical members. At the upper floor-level and the upper ceiling level were plates all round the building, corresponding to the sill beneath; the heavy joists being tenoned into them. Diagonal or curved braces or struts were occasionally used to give additional strength where necessary. All tenoned joints were secured with oak pins about ¾ in. in diameter, usually two pins to each ordinary tenon joint. The roof formed an integral part of the framing.

Perhaps the most attractive feature of some of these old houses is the overhanging upper story, which may overhang on any or all of the four sides. Among the boarded houses now under consideration only a few possess this feature, and then it is generally confined to one side. As already explained, a stout tapered post was generally used at the angles of framed buildings to allow of the making of a double corner joint. From the head of this post a heavy beam known as a 'dragon beam' was run diagonally across the building, and into it on either side were framed the joists of the upper floor. These joists were carried over the head of the ground-story framing to project a foot or two beyond it, and their outer ends were rounded off. Fig. 26, a drawing of my own of a barn at Ickenham in Middlesex, shows joists projecting in this way; but sometimes, frequently in East Anglia, the 'soffit' (underside) of the overhanging story was plastered or boarded. In that case, brackets are often used at each end of the overhang, and perhaps intermediately also,

Ivy House Farm. Ickenham
28th December 1930.

26. IVY HOUSE FARM, ICKENHAM, MIDDLESEX

to support the overhanging portion. My other drawing of a cottage at Kingsbury in Middlesex (Fig. 19) shows the joist-ends exposed, and also brackets. Such brackets were not moulded, were usually about 3 in. thick, and were tenoned at each end into the post and joist respectively. In some East Anglian buildings, the feet of the angle-posts of the overhanging portion are worked into ornamental pendants or 'drops', like the drops at the feet of seventeenth-century newel staircases. But though this very pleasing fashion reached New England (see p. 161), I have encountered no examples of its use on boarded houses in this country.

There seems to be a good deal of doubt as to the object of the projecting story, which must have greatly complicated construction. It is quite credible that in the narrow streets of an old

23. NETTESWELL CROSS, ESSEX

24. NEAR TAKELEY, ESSEX

town, the extra foot or two of space in the upper rooms would be welcome, and in many of the old English, French and German towns, where timber used to be the chief material for construction, there still remain narrow streets where the tall houses of many stories nearly meet at the upper stages. But in remote villages or isolated farmsteads in Essex, this consideration can never have arisen, and the only possible explanation is that the projecting upper story was so constructed to protect the lower part of the building from the weather. Even that seems rather fanciful, and no more likely to apply in New England than in Old England; for in any case the upper story was unprotected. Still, it is just conceivable that the idea of sheltering the important joints at the top of the corner-posts, at first-floor level ('second floor' in America), may have appealed to the practical mind of the seventeenth-century builders. Moreover, the overhang did afford some cover to the entrance door and the windows on the ground-floor.

But those who have previously discussed this question seem to have overlooked another possibility: that the projecting story or the projecting gable was intentionally used as a means of enhancing the effect of the design. We have become so accustomed to the theory that builders of three hundred years ago and more were hard-headed utilitarians, concerned only to solve functional and structural problems in the simplest and most direct way, that the attribute of beauty, consciously sought, is completely omitted. But is that reasonable? The 'practical' theory breaks down in the case of most church buildings, where carving, tracery, and other ornaments were clearly superfluous from a strictly utilitarian point of view. Similarly, the mansions and palaces of Queen Elizabeth's noblemen—the Cecils and their kind—were lavishly and even extravagantly decorated, far beyond any functional need. Can we believe that the prosperous farmers and tradesmen, and their wives, in the seventeenth century had no ambition to emulate the pretensions of their social superiors? If so, human nature was strangely different in that class and at that period from what it is to-day. There is nothing in history to support such a view. A modern architect who is instructed by a patron to design a house in 'ye olde fashioned manner' makes no bones about such things. If his employer can afford the expense in these straitened times, the architect utilizes overhanging stories and gables, when it suits his main conception, with the sole object of producing an attractive group.

This brings us to the vexed question of the training and status of the men who designed the smaller houses of England at the time when the Pilgrims left our shores. Were they 'architects' as we understand the term, or were they country builders with no comprehension of the principles of design? In a recent book[1] I have examined the history of the architect-designer in all ages, whether he bore that title or any other, and have proved that a personage corresponding to the architect, though not necessarily known by that name, can be definitely associated with the design and erection of many of the great medieval churches; moreover, the presumption is that all the greater buildings were so designed. But the adventure of the Pilgrim Fathers occurred at a time when the Latin (originally Greek) title of the architect had been consciously revived. It was, in fact, in 1563 that John Shute, 'Paynter and Archytecte', published his book—*The First and Chief Groundes of Architecture*—which brought the Roman Orders of architecture for the first time within the reach of the English reader and builder. John Thorpe is described as a 'surveyor', but the fact remains that his book of drawings, preserved in the Soane Museum in London, contains hundreds of illustrations of houses known to have been built between *c.* 1570 and *c.* 1600, and now presumed to have been mainly designed by him and erected under his supervision. Then there was Robert Smithson of Nottinghamshire, whose epitaph in Wollaton

[1] M. S. Briggs, *The Architect in History* (Oxford, 1927).

Church[1] describes him as 'gent, architector, and survayor unto the most worthy house of Wollaton with divers others of great account'. He died in 1614, and the Library of the Royal Institute of British Architects in London contains a large collection of his drawings. But the first architect of whom we have any considerable biographical information was Inigo Jones (1573–1652), who visited Italy to study Roman and Renaissance architecture before 1603 and again in 1613–15. He was definitely 'in practice' as an architect in London from 1616 to 1643, and again from 1646 to 1651; and is believed to have designed the Queen's House at Greenwich in 1617 and the Banqueting House at Whitehall in 1619. All these dates precede the sailing of the *Mayflower* in 1620. Under the curious title of 'mason-architects', that is, men who undertook both design and contracts for building, may be included Ralph Simons and Gilbert Wigge, who carried out a good deal of work at Cambridge (*c.* 1593–1619), and Robert Grumbold, who designed Clare Bridge at Cambridge in 1638–9. It is quite certain that the larger houses of Elizabeth's and James I's day must all have been built from careful plans, and equally certain that the many novel features of decorative design that they contain must have entailed study of classical architecture, for in no sense are such details derived from the preceding English tradition. But it seems probable that many of these buildings, as well as the Oxford and Cambridge colleges of the period, were erected by master-masons, carpenters, or bricklayers who had obtained a smattering of the new Italian fashions by patient study of various pattern-books. John Shute's work is one of this type; others came from Antwerp and the German printing-presses. The quality of 'picturesqueness' that distinguishes Elizabethan and Jacobean architecture from the more scholarly (or pedantic) work of the mature and late Renaissance is due mainly to the artless grafting of these second-hand Italian details

[1] Illustrated in *The Architect in History*, Fig. 36.

on to a Gothic stock by men who were not fully-trained designers.

The result of this excursus is to show us that the greater brick and stone mansions of south-eastern England—such houses as Hatfield in Hertfordshire (1607–11), Audley End in Essex (1603–16), and Blickling Hall in Norfolk (1602)—must have had builder-architects or mason-architects, or architects of some kind to bring them into being. But there is no reason to suppose that any of the earlier examples of small boarded houses illustrated in this book required professional skill in their design, and one may assume that, during the first half of the seventeenth century at least, they were the unaided work of the country builder. On the other hand, the country builder had certainly begun to buy books on architecture before the close of the century, and in some of the later examples illustrated in this chapter the effect of his studies may be discerned. In the next chapter, reference will be made to the probable conditions under which the first houses of New England were erected.

It may be observed that the occupation of the modern 'master-builder' or 'contractor', that is, a person who undertakes all branches of the building-trade and employs workers in every craft, is a comparatively recent innovation in England, not more than a hundred years old or thereabouts, and thus of about equal antiquity with the professions of the engineer and the quantity surveyor. In some parts of the North of England the separate crafts still work independently. Certainly there was nothing in the shape of a 'general contractor' in the seventeenth century. The greater part of the work on houses of the kind that we are considering would be directed by the master-carpenter. At a later stage he would be followed by the plasterer, the thatcher, the joiner, and the glazier. The bricklayer's work would be confined to the chimney and the dwarf-wall or foundation on which the wooden sill of the framing rested. The plumber would have little or nothing to do, and the smith's field would consist of a few latches and locks, perhaps an iron fire-back, and the simple equipment of the kitchen fireplace. It is therefore probably the carpenter rather than the 'builder' proper to whom we owe the design of these little buildings and to whom we must ascribe any beauty, intentional or unintentional, which they may possess.

The carpenter and the joiner, whose work is now combined as one craft, were then separate tradesmen, as appears from the existence among the City Companies of London of two distinct companies. But prior to the seventeenth century, when industrial disputes as to 'demarcation' of duties began to arise between carpenters and joiners, the work of the former trade—that is, the construction of the framework of the timber houses—was commonly executed by a craftsman known as the 'wright', a carpenter in all but the name; hence our old words 'shipwright' and 'wheelwright' to denote specialized branches of the trade. The appearance of the joiner as a rival to the carpenter in the minor details of domestic woodwork synchronized with the greatly improved standard of comfort which prevailed in the late sixteenth and early seventeenth centuries, for by that time a demand had arisen for more and better furniture, and this led to a development of the craft in general. A writer of the third quarter of the seventeenth century observes that 'Joynery is an Art Manual, whereby several Pieces of Wood are so fitted and joined together by straight Lines, Squares, Miters or any Bevel, that they shall seem one intire Piece'.

Mr. C. F. Innocent[1] gives a list of the tools possessed in 1597 by one Will Hobby, a 'wright' of Leicester, and doubtless a similar outfit would be at the command of those who erected the boarded houses of East Anglia. 'The yard attached to his shop was occupied by wood for carts, etc., and in the shop were two "blocke sawes", a whipsaw, seven axes, three hatchets, three adzes, six "beerezees", one great hammer and two little

[1] *Development of English Building Construction*, pp. 96-7 (Cambridge, 1916).

ones, two pairs of pincers, an "yron dogge", four spoke shaves, twenty-one augers, and other "trinketes", worth altogether thirty-three shillings and four pence. This gives an indication of the stock of tools kept by a provincial carpenter in the days of Queen Elizabeth.'

Still more detailed information of the tools used in England about 1678 is to be found in a scarce and most interesting little book, *Mechanick Exercises*, written by one Joseph Moxon, and first published in serial parts in London in that year. It is really a manual of building construction, and deals successively with the various trades. Two plates illustrate the tools then in use by the carpenter and the joiner respectively, and show that they are surprisingly like modern patterns. As this work is not generally accessible, though I have a copy in my own possession, I may mention that one of these two plates is illustrated as Fig. 151 B in my book, *A Short History of the Building Crafts*, published at Oxford in 1925.

The same author, Moxon, deals in great detail with the various materials and processes in vogue in his day. Evidently he was not a craftsman himself, but rather a compiler of technical and scientific manuals on various subjects, including printing and 'dialling'. But his book forms by far the best record that we have of the building crafts in the time of Sir Christopher Wren.

There is one small book of slightly earlier date, *The City and Country Purchaser and Builder* (1667) by Stephen Primatt,[1] of which more than half deals with building construction. He is, however, concerned with the measuring and cost of buildings rather than with methods, and the various plans which he prints are mainly for town houses with brick walls.

Perhaps the most interesting thing in Moxon's chapter on carpentry is his detailed description, with a plan and section to

[1] The copy in the British Museum bears an amusing pencil note on the flyleaf, 'Scarce, only 2s. 6d.' The book is now very rare and expensive.

scale, of the actual construction of a timber-framed house measuring 50 ft. by 20 ft.;[1] for this closely approximates to the type of dwelling which the New England colonists erected in the years immediately following the initial hardships of their arrival. Some of this description may now be quoted for purposes of comparison with the surviving homes of the Pilgrims in America. Moxon tells us something of the way in which a carpenter set to work on such a building in 1678, and for a small house of this kind he evidently assumes that no architect is to be consulted.[2] 'Being now come to exercise upon the *Carpenter's* trade', he begins, 'it may be expected by some, that I should insist upon *Architecture*, it being so absolutely necessary for Builders to be acquainted with: But my Answer to them is, that there are so many Books of *Architecture* extant, and in them the Rules so well, so copiously, and so compleatly handled, that it is needless for me to say any thing of that Science: Nor do I think any Man that should, can do more than Collect out of their Books, and perhaps deliver their Meanings in his own Words.... Yet because Books of Architecture are as necessary for a Builder to understand, as the use of Tools; and lest some Builders should not know how to enquire for them, I shall at the latter end of *Carpentry* give you the Names of some Authors, especially such as are Printed in the *English* Tongue.'[3]

He then describes the use of the various tools, and next the procedure '*to measure and describe the* Ground-plot'. This is done by the master-carpenter himself. 'And thus you are also to describe by your Scale your Front, and several sides of the Carcase;

[1] Moxon, *Mechanick Exercises*, pp. 126–42 (London, 1678).
[2] *Ibid.*, p. 117.
[3] But Moxon seems less inclined to trust the design of a brick house to a bricklayer. This is what he says (on his p. 253) in that connexion: 'The drawing of Draughts is most commonly the work of a Surveyor, although there be many Master Workmen that will contrive a building, and draw the designs thereof, as well, and as curiously, as most Surveyors: Yea, some of them will do it better than some Surveyors: especially those Workmen who understand the Theorick part of Building, as well as the Practick.'

allowing the *Principal Posts, Enterduces, Quarterings, Braces, Gables, Doors, Windows,* and *Ornaments,* their several Sizes, and true Positions by the Scale: Each side upon a Paper by it self: Unless we shall suppose our Master-Workman to understand *Perspective*; for then he may, on a single piece of Paper, describe the whole Building, as it shall appear to the Eye at any assigned Station.'

The next step, he tells us, is to dig the cellars, if such be required. 'But if the House be designed to have no Cellars (as many Country-Houses have not) yet for the better securing the Foundation, and preserving the Timber from rotting, Master-Workmen will cause three, or four, or five course of Bricks to be laid, to lay their *Ground-plates* upon that Foundation.'

The dwarf wall or plinth, 9 to 15 in. high, which Moxon has suggested for country houses, is exactly what one finds as a rule among the timber-framed cottages of the seventeenth century in south-eastern England. The material is nearly always brick, though flint is very occasionally found in certain districts, and the thickness is usually one brick ($=9$ in.). In many of the illustrations to this chapter the brickwork of the plinth is clearly visible; in others it is difficult to see as it has been cemented or tarred, or because the boarding is carried down over it, nearly to the ground.

The 'ground-floor', as we call it in England ('first floor' in America), was generally, in the smaller houses which we are now considering, level with the surrounding ground or even below it. Cellars are very seldom found. Ground-floors in English cottages at this period were simply made of earth or mud, beaten hard. Such a surface naturally absorbed the filth of a not particularly clean generation of people, and this filth contained nitre, a substance useful in the manufacture of gunpowder. Hence was evolved the 'saltpetre man', a most unpleasant and unpopular functionary whose duty it was to dig up the nitre-

29. POTTER STREET, ESSEX

28. TOPPESFIELD, ESSEX

sodden earth of the floor. His activities included not only houses, stables, and the like, but even town-halls and churches—a sad comment on the habits of city fathers and pious worshippers. His glory seems to have reached its apogee in the reign of Charles I, after which his powers were limited. Sometimes bullocks' blood was used, mixed with the mud, to give floors a dark surface when polished. This fashion appears to have been introduced from Italy, with other 'quaint conceits', about 1594.[1]

The timber-framed house described and illustrated by Moxon (1678) has, however, a ground-floor of wooden joists (7 by 3 in. and 11 in. apart for a bearing of only 8 ft.) framed into the main sill-pieces at ground-level. It does not seem probable that this practice was common in small houses and cottages at the beginning of the century, for the ground-floor. Stephen Primatt, in his book already quoted (p. 70), writes of 'Ten inch tiles' laid in mortar for the 'Pavements for Cellars and Kitchens'. That was in 1667, and such floors were frequently used in those rooms throughout the century, even in small houses and country cottages of the better sort.

Although the brickwork of south-eastern England had reached a really high standard in the time of the Pilgrims, it was only used in the boarded houses for plinths and for chimney stacks; and because these houses were invariably of simple design and inhabited by people of no great wealth or social importance, the chimney-stacks were simple too. In Essex and Kent and Suffolk there are still numbers of examples of richly moulded and spiral brick stacks, but a study of the photographs in this chapter will reveal no such flights of fancy. Nevertheless, compared with modern work, they are expensively constructed because of their very massiveness. This generous treatment was conditioned by the ample width allowed for the great fireplace, which occupied one end or side of the living-room. The houses which I have photographed for this book are all occupied, and

[1] Innocent, *op. cit.*, pp. 158–9.

I have been unable to explore their interior arrangements. But there is a fine old fireplace in Rochford Hall, Essex, which may have had some associations with the founders of Congregationalism who set the Pilgrim movement in motion. As I have already mentioned (p. 3), Rochford Hall was the meeting-place of a Separatist congregation in 1580, and was built *c.* 1540-50. The fireplace in the kitchen there, though stated in a recent and authoritative publication[1] to be a later addition, has an opening 6 ft. 6 in. wide, 3 ft. 3 in. deep, and 5 ft. high. The opening is spanned by a great oak beam or 'bressummer', 11 in. deep and 8 in. thick, supporting the partition-wall between the flue and the kitchen (Fig. 27). The vast chimney recess is 'gathered in' behind this wall till it diminishes to the size of the smoke-flue. Two iron bars run across it, built into the brickwork at the front and back of the flue, and from them is hung by chains a long iron bar bearing a number of hooks for roasting purposes. From these bars stock-pots and kettles were also hung. A piece of wood near the ceiling is said to have supported, many years ago, one end of a pole from which wool was hung and weighed. This practice may or may not be as old as the time of the Pilgrims. The recess now contains two ranges, probably of the nineteenth century: and there is also an iron door opening into a baking oven about 6 ft. long, 2 ft. 6 in. wide, and 1 ft. 6 in. high, but an examination of the exterior of this feature leads me to think that it is later than the house itself. On either side of the great fireplace is a recess containing a window. Beneath the left-hand window is a 'copper' used for brewing, and under the other are two more coppers, all set in brickwork. There is nothing to indicate the date of these coppers, which have flues which enter the main stack at the side. The hearth of the fireplace is of stone, and the floor of the kitchen (which has no cellar beneath) is of red bricks set on edge without any skirting round the whitewashed walls. This is, of course, the

[1] *Royal Commission on Historical Monuments (England), Essex, S.E.*

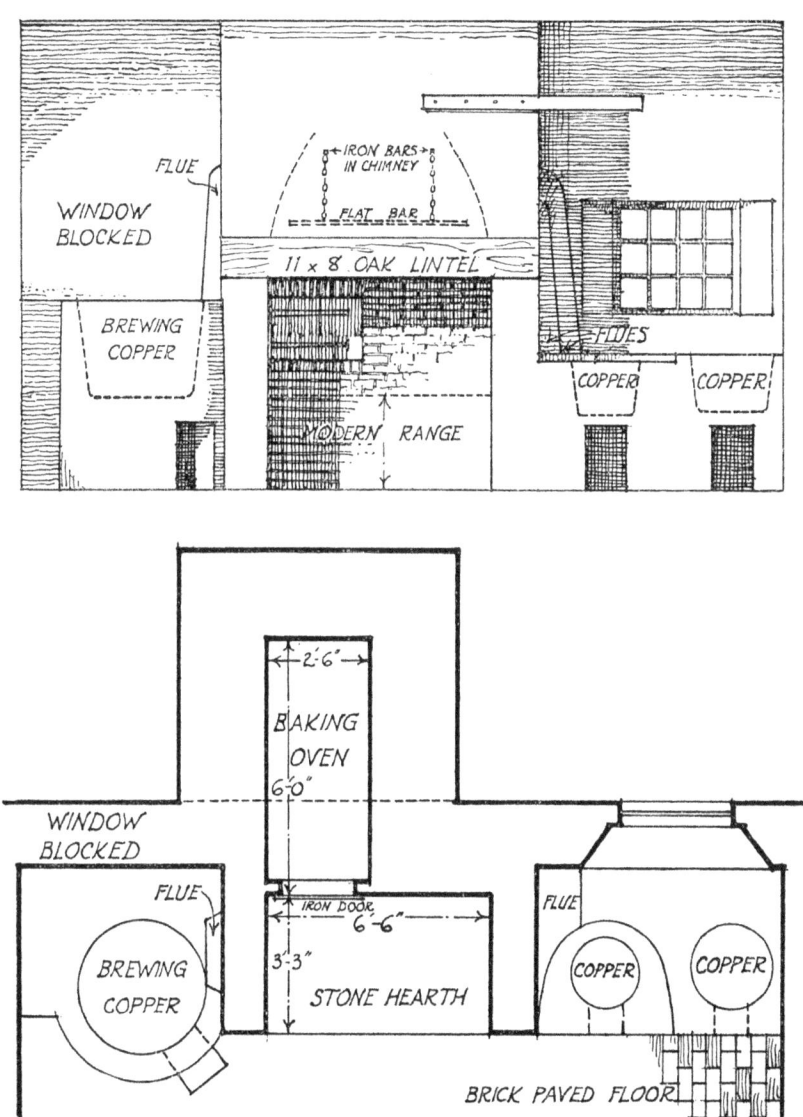

27. ROCHFORD HALL, ESSEX
AN OLD ENGLISH KITCHEN FIREPLACE

kitchen equipment of a nobleman's house; but the same type of open fireplace, on a smaller scale, was generally used in the less pretentious houses and cottages of the seventeenth century. The great size of these old fireplaces is due to three causes: the prevalent use of wood fuel, sea-borne coal first coming into use about 1600; the large amount of meat consumed in the diet of the day; and the number of servants and retainers to be provided for. Andirons were used to support the ends of the logs. From the early sixteenth century onwards, cast-iron fire-dogs and fire-backs from the Weald of Sussex came into fashion.

Chimney flues in the old houses are never less than 14 in. by 9 in., and often more. These measurements are excessive, and help to account for the great solidity of the chimney caps. It will be noticed that a number of the boarded houses illustrated in this book have thatched roofs, which are obviously very liable to take fire, but it is believed that many old cottages were without brick chimneys until the seventeenth century, clay serving as a substitute.

The inhabitants of Clare, Suffolk, held a court in 1621 and decided that every chimney in that village should be built of brick, 'above the roof of the house fower feete and a halfe upon the paine for every such offence to be hereafter committed the summe of vl.'[1]

The capping of the chimneys of the houses illustrated in this chapter is, without exception, of the simplest possible character, consisting of a series of projecting and receding courses of plain bricks, without any sort of mouldings or dentil courses. But great judgement is required, as every architect knows, to get the best effect from these 'oversailing' courses. If the projection of each is even half an inch too great, the capping looks top-heavy. If, on the other hand, the projection is too slight, the effect is weak. On one example (Fig. 61) there are two courses of bricks below the capping, each of which projects slightly. This

[1] Innocent, *op. cit.*, p. 271.

practice, intended to throw rain water clear of the face of the stack, is not so common in the eastern counties as in Surrey and Sussex. Mr. Nathaniel Lloyd's monumental work, *A History of English Brickwork*, is full of examples showing the traditional treatment of these niceties of brick construction, and contains many specimens from south-eastern England.

But though these counties abound in beautiful brickwork, there is nothing remarkable about the bricks used in the humble boarded buildings now being described. In the seventeenth century such bricks were locally made, and are somewhat rough and sandy in texture, usually from 2 in. to $2\frac{1}{4}$ in. in thickness. The lime-mortar joints are at least half an inch thick, and often more. The colour of bricks varies in the different districts according to the composition of the clay from which they are burned; where red bricks are used they are of a warm tint with a good deal of variety in the shades.

The material for covering the external 'walls', more precisely the timber framing, is either the plaster or 'pargeting' already described (see p. 54), or weather-boarding. Although a few examples of the former method are to be found in New England, weather-boarding was more generally adopted by the Pilgrim settlers, for the simple reason that suitable timber was plentiful.

The *locale* of this craft in England has also been defined in a previous passage (p. 56). Although I have examined a large number of examples to obtain exact information of the material used and the size and method of fixing of the boarding, such data are not to be relied upon as evidence of original workmanship. It cannot even be assumed that a house now covered with boarding was not formerly parged, or that the boarding now existing is original. Although the concealed framing may be old, it stands to reason that the exposed boards are more subject to the ravages of the weather, and as a rule they have been renewed because renewal is easy and cheap. The only way to be certain that the boarding now existing is part of the original structure is to strip it bodily from the framing. If only one set of nail-holes in the framing is then revealed, it may be assumed that the boards are part of the original fabric. But because an Englishman's house is—in theory at any rate—his castle, it is obvious that an inquiring architect would not be allowed to prosecute his researches to the extent of stripping the castle walls.

The usual material employed for boarding in south-east England was oak or elm in the seventeenth century. Both these timbers were plentiful, and it was not until the import of softwoods—fir and pine of various kinds—from the Baltic countries began that the old materials were displaced. The shortage of English oak was due to the periods of naval expansion, at first in the time of Samuel Pepys in the latter half of the seventeenth century, but much more during the Napoleonic wars. Nowadays, deal boards from the Baltic are largely used in the renewal of old weather-boarding, though their resistance to weather is far inferior to that of oak or elm. On the other hand, these latter woods are apt to warp and so lift from their nails. So long ago as 1641, a Yorkshire writer quoted by Mr. Innocent[1] alludes to that defect as follows: 'Firre deales are accounted better for bordeninge with then oake that hath not had time for seasoninge, because that when oak cometh to dry it will shrink, cast, draw a nayle, and rise up at an ende or a side.' But this writer lived near Hull, then as now the nearest port in England to Norway and the Baltic countries, so that he is more likely to have had experience of imported timber than the builders of cottages in the forest-clad counties of south-eastern England.

The photographs illustrating this chapter show boarding of widths varying from 4 in. to 8 or even 9 in., this being the exposed width, to which must be added the concealed portion over which the next board overlaps, technically known as the 'lap', whereas the distance from edge to edge or from one horizontal row of nail-holes to the next is known as the 'gauge'.

[1] *Development of English Building Construction*, pp. 103–4.

But a gauge of so little as 4 in. indicates modern work, and the beaded edges which are sometimes run, by machinery, on these narrow boards supply an additional indication of a late date. Thus if one finds boarding of 5 or 6 in. gauge, with or without a beaded edge, one may assume that it is modern. The old boarding was usually of oak or elm, with a gauge of 6 to 8 in. and a lap of 1 to $1\frac{1}{2}$ in. There seems to be no certainty as to when 'feather-edged' boarding (that is, a board, diminishing in thickness from, say, 1 inch on the lower edge to $\frac{1}{4}$ in. or $\frac{3}{8}$ in. on the upper edge) was introduced. Those experts in the matter whom I have consulted appear to think that either plain or feather-edged boards may be original. Mr. Nathaniel Lloyd, who is our chief authority on the history of brickwork and a keen student of all the old building crafts, writes to me that 'there is a practice, not a modern one, in this district [Kent and Sussex] of weather-boarding with 1 in. boards, not feather-edged as is the usual $7 \times \frac{3}{8}$ to $\frac{1}{4}$ in. board. Personally I like this, which may also be done in the $\frac{3}{4}$ in. parallel board. The thick edge throws a nice shadow, just as that of the feather-edged board. The usual way of nailing weather-boarding through the framing—through both boards—causes them to split when they shrink, and this is particularly bad when oak or elm are used. Nails should go through the thick edge of the upper board, so as just to clear the thin edge of the board below'.

The boarding was nailed to the 'studs' (intermediate posts) of the framing at intervals of 15 to 20 inches with wrought-iron nails rather roughly made. In all but two of the old buildings which I have examined the boarding is horizontal. One exception is the huge barn at Harmondsworth in Middlesex, described later, where the boarding of the 'walls' is fixed vertically to framing which is certainly medieval. The other occurs in a cart-shed at Netteswell Cross (fig. 23) in Essex, where the boundary of the site is curved, so that the builder may have found it more convenient to bend his framing in short lengths than to bend the external boarding. I have also observed a few cases of quite modern vertical boarding, and two or three of diagonal boarding as sometimes used in America to give extra rigidity. But such boarding is not overlapping, and therefore is not, strictly speaking, weather-boarding. I may add that weather-boarding is called 'wash-boarding' in Lincolnshire.[1]

Although it is now often tarred, the original boarding was frequently left untreated, so that with the lapse of time the oak or elm bleached to beautiful grey tones.

The practice of tarring, only too common in Essex and elsewhere, greatly spoils the effect of these buildings, which are far more attractive if painted some light cream or stone colour, as is often done in the Kentish villages between Tonbridge and Rye. At the angles, the usual method is to fix a vertical 'fillet' or strip of wood, 2 to 4 in. wide, but there are rare examples where the boards at the angles are mitred.

The floors of these timber-framed houses are always massively constructed. Sometimes the thick floor-boards are exposed beneath, as in 'Czar Peter's Cottage' at Zaandam (see p. 40), or a ceiling may be plastered on to rushes between the joists and the boards as at Austerfield and Bawtry (see fig. 7), or the rooms may have the modern type of plastered ceiling. This latter type, on laths, came into general use during the second half of the seventeenth century, except for small cottages.

The roofs of the older houses are invariably of steep pitch, and in fact a lower pitch than 50° is usually an indication of a date in the latter part of the seventeenth century. The normal pitch for the Pilgrim period was from 50° to 55°. The general form of the roof was of the simplest possible type.

---

[1] A modern specification for weather-boarding runs as follows: 'Sawn fir rebated weather-boarding, cut feather-edged (two out of 1¼ in. by 7 in.), lapped 1½ in., and bottom nailed with 2 in. cut nails to each stud, so that nails pass through each board singly just above lap. Lowest board to lap 1½ in. over brick or concrete base. All external faces to be underlined with approved asphalted sarking felt below the boarding, lapped 4 in. at horizontal joints and neatly fitted to openings.'

Photo: 'The Times'

30. NEWARK MILL, RIPLEY, SURREY

31. THE OLD MILL, ST. OSYTH, ESSEX

The normal plan of the smaller houses being oblong, there was a gable at each end, a ridge running parallel with the two longer walls, and no intersections, hips, or other complications, the slope running straight up on each side from eaves to ridge. The brick chimney was usually at one end in a one-roomed house (i.e. one room on each floor), or in the centre for a two-roomed house. But dormers, which were used in England at least as early as the fourteenth century, occur in many of the examples illustrated, and create a picturesque note in the grouping. Some of the houses have projections with gables, and these do complicate the otherwise simple roof-construction.

The hipped gable type of roof, that is, a roof with the gables hipped back above the level of the collar (see Figs. 15, 29, &c.), is a familiar and attractive feature, especially in the barns and cottages of Kent and Surrey. Mr. A. R. Powys, of the Society for the Protection of Ancient Buildings, informs me that this practice was common in the period 1580–1620. Hipped roofs, that is, roofs which slope up from all four sides towards the apex (Figs. 17, 40, &c.), were certainly in use in England as early as the date (1636) when Raynham Park in Norfolk was built, and possibly even before that.

Another remarkable type of roof found very frequently in New England from the third quarter of the seventeenth century onwards is that known as the 'gambrel', which is stated by Mr. J. E. Chandler[1] to be 'almost unknown in England'. It is certainly not very common in all parts of this country, but reference to the various illustrations to this chapter, which may be taken as typical of the normal examples in south-east England, reveals gambrel roofs at Barnet (Herts.), and at Great Wakering, Wickford, Toppesfield, St. Osyth, and Stisted (all in Essex). I have noted other examples at Leigh, Benfleet, Horseley Cross, Rochford, Clacton, Chelmsford, and Barking (all in Essex); and the photograph (Fig. 30) of the mill at Ripley, Surrey, shows a

[1] J. E. Chandler, *The Colonial House*, p. 47 (New York, 1924).

good example. This kind of roof has two slopes, and is similar in contour to the French 'mansard' roof which was widely used in France in the seventeenth century. English examples include the Great Hall (1530-2) of Hampton Court Palace. The purpose of the gambrel roof, to which further reference will be made in the next chapter, was of course to provide better accommodation for attic bedrooms.

The roofing materials mainly used for the weather-boarded cottages of south-east England in the seventeenth century were, in order of frequency, thatch, plain tiles, and pantiles. To-day one has to add to that list, unfortunately, slates and corrugated iron (or galvanized sheeting as it is more correctly described). For although Sir Balthazar Gerbier, in his little book *Council and Advice to all Builders* (1663)—which contains forty dedications and an approximately equal length of text—recommends 'blew slates' as an ideal material for roofing, their export from Wales and Westmorland to other parts of England did not become considerable until the early nineteenth century. Economic stringency or mere obtuseness has caused any number of old boarded cottages, barns, and mills to be re-roofed with slates or iron during recent years. It must be admitted that in some parts of England the art of the thatcher has been lost or is becoming so. That applies to the part of North Middlesex where I live, and where London is now stretching its tentacles of 'distinctive homes', each exactly alike and utterly devoid of soul but full of labour-saving gadgets. It applies to the nearer parts of Essex and Hertfordshire where the suburbs are trampling out the farms.

But a friend of mine who practises as an architect in Canterbury tells me that a family of competent thatchers still continues to practise the craft in Kent and is kept very busy, while the number of newly-thatched cottages and barns that one sees in the remoter parts of Essex shows that the craft still lingers there. It is a question whether either the plain tiles or the pantiles now seen on the roofs of some of the boarded houses illustrated in this chapter were originally intended when the houses were built; some examples were probably altered at a later date. But plain tiles are well suited to the gambrel type of roof. Pantiles appear to have been mainly imported from Holland, and Moxon in his *Mechanick Exercises* (1678) writes of them thus: '... *Pan-Tiles*, being about thirteen Inches long, with a Nob or Button to hang on the Laths, and are hollow or circular breadthways, being eight Inches in breadth, and about half an Inch in thickness, or somewhat more. The best sort of these are brought from *Holland* into *England*, and are called *Flemish Pan-Tiles*, we having such Tiles made here in *England*, but not so good: Which *Flemish Tiles* are sometimes glazed, and are of a Lead, or Blewish colour, and being glazed they are very durable and handsom.'

Fig. 29 shows an example of the use of pantiles at Potter Street near Epping (Essex), and Fig. 40 another example from Mill Hill (Middlesex). The latter is a good instance of a 'hipped' roof, the former of a 'hipped gable'. Wood shingles, so largely used in New England, are now, at any rate, almost unknown in this country, and are certainly not employed on any of the buildings illustrated in this chapter. Mr. Innocent says quite categorically[1] that 'the use of shingles hardly lasted after the fourteenth century. ... In England the use of shingles is now confined to such structures as church spires, and these only in the south-eastern counties'.

The craft of thatching was at one time practised all over England, but it was in the eastern counties that it reached its greatest perfection. Both straw and reeds were used in that district, and fig. 33, a photograph taken near the remote village of Toppesfield in Essex in 1931, shows modern thatchers at work. Fig. 28 shows an adjoining cottage where the thickness of the thatch and its projection at the eaves can be clearly seen.

[1] *Development of English Building Construction*, p. 185.

TIMBER HOUSES

Mr. Innocent devotes thirty-five pages of his book[1] to an admirable study of the thatcher's craft in England and elsewhere.

The rain drips from the projecting eaves of thatched roofs direct to the ground, no gutter being either necessary or possible. The gutters now found on those houses which have tiled roofs are presumably later additions, required by the building by-laws of most villages and towns, and useful, even on isolated houses, in districts where the water-supply is unreliable or non-existent, so that the rain-water may be collected in 'butts' (barrels) or tanks. These statements, however, must not be regarded as absolutely definite. It is conceivable that wooden gutters may have been used occasionally on certain parts of thatched roofs; and it is known that they were sometimes used on tiled roofs, even in the seventeenth century.

We have now considered the chief elements in the 'carcass' of the typical wooden house, and there still remain such details as doors, windows, and ironwork.

The use of framed or panelled doors became general during the seventeenth century, but was not common at its beginning, except where the door formed part of a scheme of interior panelling, when its panelling and mouldings followed those of the whole scheme. Such doors were very thin, sometimes not more than an inch, and the styles and rails—to comply with those of the panelling—were only about 3 in. wide. They were delicately moulded, and always made of oak. In the 'Old Neptune' inn at Ipswich is a beautifully panelled room of this type.[2] Although the date is so late as 1639 and although some of its ornament shows distinctly the influence of the Italian Renaissance, the panelling is of the 'linen-fold' pattern so popular in late Gothic ('Tudor') buildings of the sixteenth century. But one does not expect to find work so rich and decorative as this in the humble boarded houses of the period. Doubtless

---

[1] *Development of English Building Construction*, pp. 188–222.
[2] Illustrated in B. Oliver's *Old Houses in East Anglia*, Figs. 70–1. (London, 1912.)

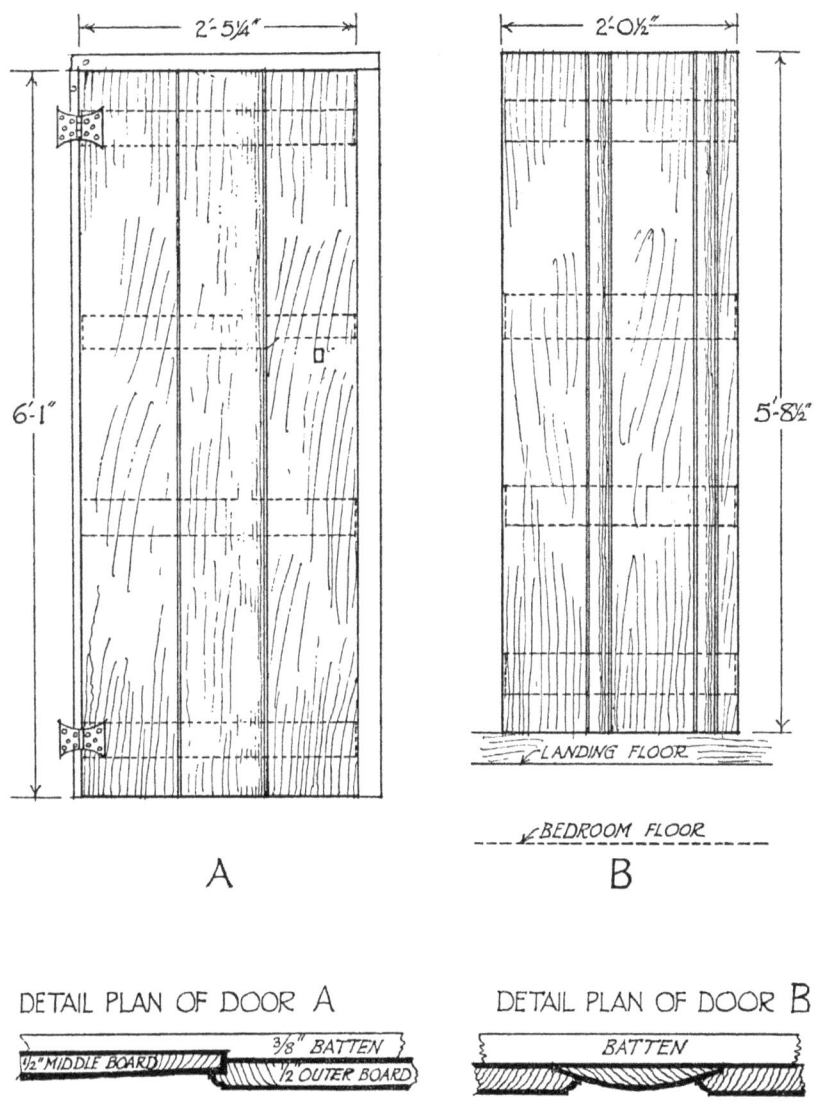

34. DOORS FROM CHANTRY HOUSE, BILLERICAY, ESSEX
(Reputed home of Christopher Martin, one of the Pilgrims)

some of them are panelled, but for the most part their doors, now largely replaced by modern substitutions, must have been 'batten' doors of one form or another. Such doors, of which several types still exist in New England also, consisted in essence of two thicknesses of boards, vertical and horizontal respectively. In the case of external doors, the vertical boards were placed on the outside, and behind them were either three 'ledges' (horizontal boards) or a series of horizontal boards from top to bottom of the door. For any such important position, the edges of the vertical boards (which were usually tongued or rebated into one another) were often moulded, or sometimes moulded strips were fixed to cover the vertical joints. These doors were hung to the posts by wrought-iron strap hinges made by the local blacksmith, and if vertical strips—as just described—were used, they were rebated to allow the strap-hinges to pass beneath them. The face of the door was liberally studded with the large heads (about an inch square) of iron nails which passed through both thicknesses of boarding and were clenched on the inside.

The internal doors of the smaller houses were also formed of battens, but usually had only ledges instead of continuous horizontal boarding on one side. They were very thin and light. Fig. 34 illustrates two such doors still existing in the 'Chantry House' (the reputed home of Christopher Martin, one of the passengers in the *Mayflower*) at Billericay, Essex. My drawing clearly shows, in the detail plans, the incredibly light construction, the boards being only half an inch thick and the battens $\frac{3}{8}$ in. thick. The central board of door 'A' is slightly convex, and the two strips of door 'B' (which appears to have been cut down in width) have a decided convex curve. The small size of both doors (cf. p. 172) and the hinges remaining on door 'A' are worthy of notice.

Fig. 35 is a sketch of the corner of a room of the ground-floor (American 'first floor') of the same house. The panelling is of

35. PANELLING IN CHANTRY HOUSE, BILLERICAY, ESSEX
(The reputed home of Christopher Martin, one of the Pilgrims)

the sixteenth century, before Christopher Martin's time, but the fine cupboard must have been inserted late in the seventeenth century, for it displays classical details. The interior of this cupboard has curved shelves, is of niche form, and has a domed head vaulted in wood with ribs, a finished piece of craftsmanship.

At the time time when Moxon published his *Mechanick Exercises* (1678), it is evident that the new type of panelled door with its deep rails had come into fashion for the front entrance but not for the minor rooms and back entrance: 'They consider what sort of *Hindges* are properest for the *Door* they are to *Hang*. When they have a *Street-door* (which commonly is to take off and lift on) they use *Hooks* and *Hindges*. In a *Battend-door*, *Back-door*, or other *Battend-door*, . . . they use *Cross-Garnets*. If a *Framed Door, Side Hindges*.'

Windows at the very beginning of the seventeenth century were invariably of the casement type (Fig. 36). Sash windows (that is, 'double-hung' sashes or 'guillotine' windows) were first used in England about 1630 (e.g. at Raynham Park, Norfolk, 1630–6, and by John Webb in houses at Great Queen Street, London, 1640). Still earlier is the Banqueting House, Whitehall (1619–22); but there the windows, which always looked like sashes, were originally fixed, and were only replaced by sliding sashes at a later date. At first only the lower sash of such windows was made movable, being kept up by a series of notches and a catch to hook into them. Late in the century, and probably introduced from Holland, came the modern method with weights, pulleys, and cords. The English word 'sash' is derived from the French *chassis* (frame), and Moxon, at the end of the seventeenth century, spells it as 'shas'. We may assume, then, that the existence of a 'fixed sash', with wooden bars, indicates in these wooden houses a date after 1620, and that a double sliding sash (that is, with both sashes sliding up and down) denotes a date late in the century.

Casement windows, on the other hand, persisted all through

32. DENNY GATE, CAMBRIDGESHIRE

33. THATCHING AT TOPPESFIELD, ESSEX

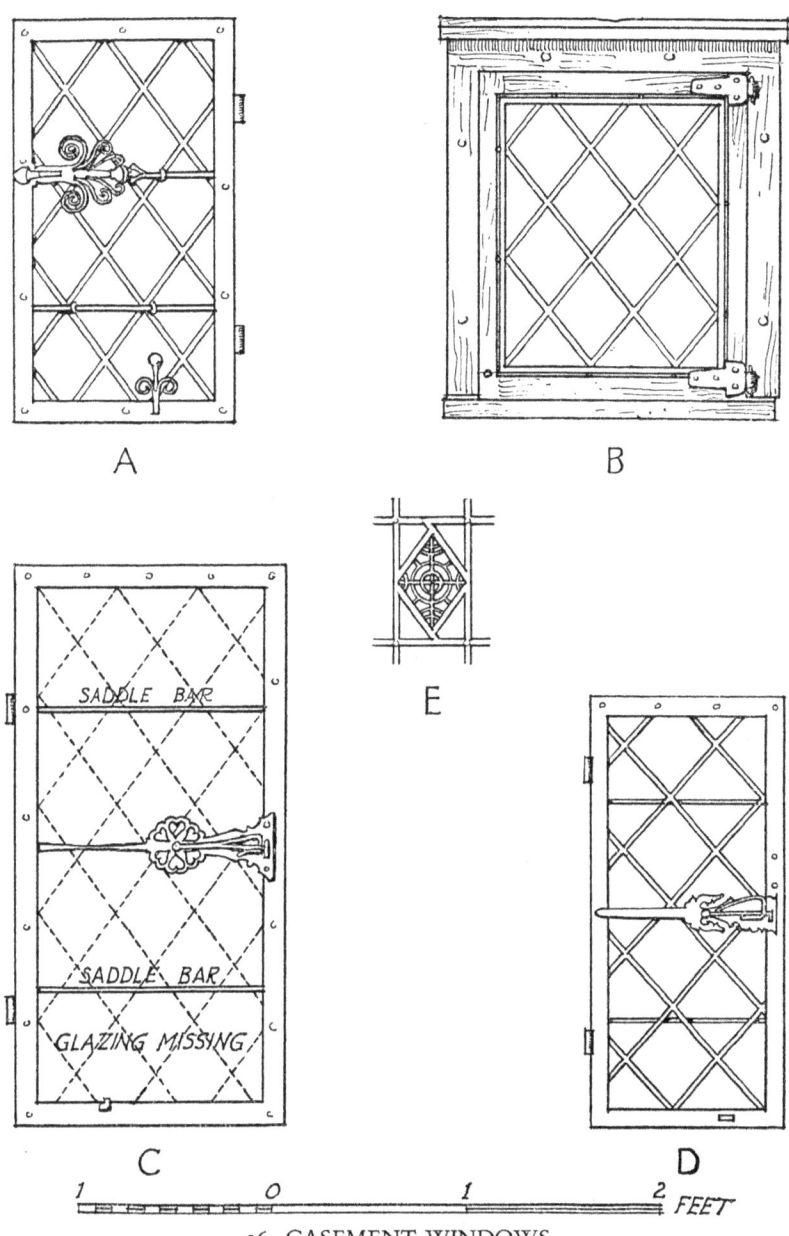

36. CASEMENT WINDOWS

A. Iron casement from Godalming, Surrey (V. and A. Museum); B. Wood casement from Wethersfield, Essex; C. Iron casement from Suffolk (V. and A. Museum); D. Ditto from Geffrye Museum, London; E. Lead ventilating quarry (V. and A. Museum).

the century. At first they were invariably small and narrow with leaded glazing in diamond patterns, commonly called lattice windows, and in fact rather stupidly copied from the diagonal arrangement of interlaced wattle or laths or bars which preceded the introduction of glazing. Examples are here given of a small wooden casement with diagonal lead glazing, measured and drawn by myself in the little Essex village of Wethersfield (fig. 36 B), and several iron casements of the early seventeenth century now preserved at the Victoria and Albert Museum in London (Fig. 36, A, C), and elsewhere. The use of horizontal saddle bars will be noticed.

Rather later than these came the use of rectangular lead panes, and again Wethersfield furnished examples. I measured a number of such windows in that village, and found that the panes in these varied in width from 4 to 5 in., and in height from 5¾ to 8 in. A proportion of 5 to 8 gives a pleasing result. The width of the 'lights', that is, of each casement between its upright posts or mullions, is usually from 13 to 18 in. But besides wrought iron casements with leaded glazing, wooden casements with wooden bars are frequently found, and their date is uncertain. Still more puzzling is the type of window commonly known as the 'Yorkshire light', where the opening casement (instead of being hung at its side on hinges) slides horizontally in grooves between the head and the sill. In spite of its name, this window occurs all over Essex and elsewhere, as may be noticed in many of the photographs. Recourse to a well-known work of reference produces the following helpful definition—'YORKSHIRE LIGHT: a term used in Lancashire for a sliding sash'! At all events, such sashes were in use by the end of the seventeenth century, abreast of all the various forms of casement and the double-hung sash. But very few casements were made to open, and by way of relief, one or more panes of glass were sometimes replaced by a pierced lead ventilator, as in the charming example from Dedham in Essex—a name very familiar in New England—illustrated by Mr. Oliver.[1] Fig. 36, E, shows an almost identical specimen from the Victoria and Albert Museum.

The casement-fasteners and stays used with these windows, like the ironwork of the doors, are often of great delicacy and beauty (Fig. 37), although they must have been made as a rule by the local smith.

Apart from the locks, latches, and hinges of the doors, the stays and fasteners of the windows, and the simple accessories of the fireplace, there were few examples of the smith's art in the smaller houses, where cooking utensils and a few lamps comprised the remaining metal-work. Many skilful smiths came into the south-eastern counties from Flanders during Elizabeth's reign, some fine specimens of wall-anchors of Flemish type still surviving in Sandwich, Yarmouth, and Canterbury.

Furniture, too, was of the simplest kind. Chairs had only just come into use even in large houses, and in cottage homes stools and forms were generally found. The more fortunately situated of the Pilgrim Fathers, men like Brewster and Bradford, came from houses of a larger size where chairs would be used, and indeed some of the furniture now jealously preserved in American museums is said to have been brought over in the *Mayflower* and other early ships. A cradle was another feature in these Jacobean homes. Tables were changing from the medieval trestle-type to the framed type, and draw-tables had just come into use. Chests or coffers were found in practically all the houses, and sideboards occasionally. Upholstery was scarce in cottage furnishing, hard seats being the rule. All this furniture was of oak, simple in design and massive in construction, treated with wax or oil and fitted with mounts of hammered iron. The Metropolitan Museum in New York possesses a magnificent collection of seventeenth-century furniture, some of which is displayed in 'period rooms.'

[1] B. Oliver, *Old Houses in East Anglia*, fig. 69.

From the foregoing general account of the characteristics of boarded houses in the south-east of England it will have been gathered by the reader that it is by no means easy to attribute an exact date to any example merely on the strength of its individual details. This is the more unfortunate because documentary evidence of the date of erection is practically always non-existent. In the stone houses of the Cotswolds or of the Yorkshire dales, a date is often carved over the door or one of the windows. In other types of house, even on the pargeted houses of Suffolk, a date is sometimes found, but the boarded houses are almost always lacking in any such record. Nor has any detailed study ever been made such as the recent research into the old houses of New England, which, numerous as they are and neglected as many of them have hitherto been, have lately found themselves in the spot-light of American learned criticism. England itself is so rich in great monuments of the past that this by-path of rural building has almost escaped the keen eye of the architectural scribe. But the fine series of volumes now appearing under the aegis of the Royal Commission on Historical Monuments has already covered three of the counties—London, Hertfordshire, and Essex—with which we are concerned, and Middlesex and Kent will have their turn in the fullness of time. Yet even these handsome and meticulously complete volumes can find little space for describing boarded cottages, barns, and mills—such is the wealth of ancient buildings in this land, and especially in its south-eastern shires.

The last part of this chapter may well be devoted to a rapid survey of the various districts where boarded houses are found and to a brief description of those selected for illustration here.

London itself is the natural point from which to begin. A century ago, or even less, the capital city of England[1] must have contained hundreds of examples, but now not more than

---

[1] It may be interesting to note here that its population has been estimated by Dr. Creighton as 123,034 in 1580, 272,207 in 1622, and 460,000 in 1661.

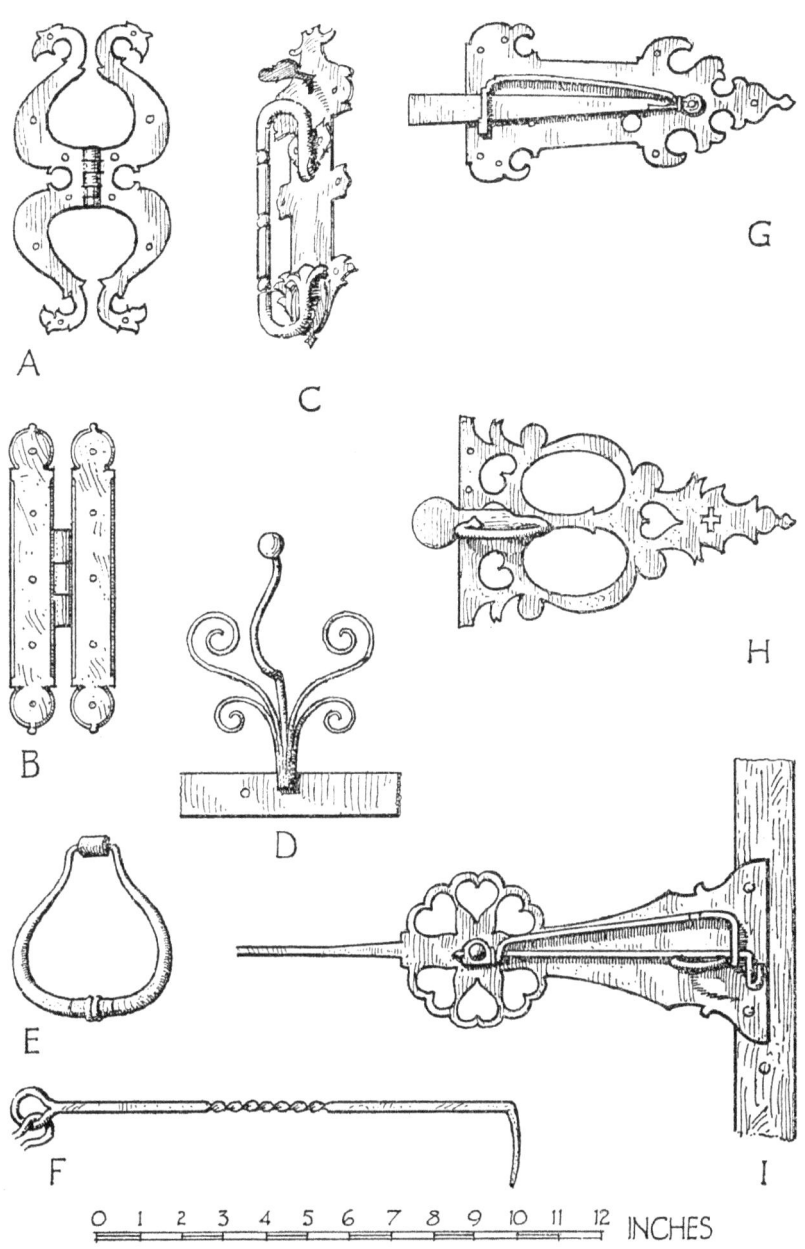

37. ENGLISH IRONWORK OF THE SEVENTEENTH CENTURY
A, B, hinges; C, door latch; D, casement pull; E, door handle; F, casement stay;
G, H, I, casement latches. (Drawn by the Author from examples, mostly from
East Anglia, in the Victoria and Albert Museum, London.)

a dozen survive, and most of these are either sadly neglected or much altered from their original state. Indeed there are very few timber-framed houses of any kind left in London, the most important being the magnificent half-timbered Staple Inn (1581) in Holborn, and the half-timbered front of the Inner Temple Gatehouse (c. 1611) in Fleet Street, both in admirable condition. The reason for this dearth of timber houses in the centre of the City is plain enough. The beautiful models in the London Museum show that Westminster, the City itself, and Southwark were all mainly built of timber, except the larger buildings and the churches, in the time of James I and even later. But the Great Fire of 1666 destroyed the whole of the City proper, and led to stringent regulations against the erection of any more timber structures. The two examples mentioned lay just outside the area of the conflagration, hence their survival. Other fires destroyed most of the timber buildings round Whitehall, and the remaining parts of central London, which were not laid out until after the time of the Fire, were mostly built in brick or stone from the outset.

It is therefore not surprising that the best example of a boarded building still surviving is to be found in Southwark, the district which grew up as a sort of 'bridge-head' where the old Roman roads from Dover and Chichester crossed the Thames at London Bridge, itself covered with picturesque wooden houses at one time. Southwark, the place where Shakespeare's theatre and other famous places of amusement had their location at the time when the Pilgrims set forth on their great venture, has many associations with their early history. Here was born John Harvard (1607–38) in Borough High Street, where the old coaching inns with their timbered galleries recently stood, though now only one (the 'George') still remains, and here he was baptized in Southwark Cathedral. Here is the so-called 'Pilgrim Church', a modern successor of the first organized Congregational church in London (see p. 47). And in

Southwark Cathedral is a tablet to the memory of one William Emerson (*d.* 1575), tersely but adequately described as 'an honest man', and probably an ancestor of Ralph Waldo Emerson. Hence the name given to Emerson Street near by.

Southwark's surviving boarded building is a group known as 'Fishermen's Houses' (Fig. 38), erected late in the seventeenth century in Collingwood Street, a narrow thoroughfare adjoining a church in the busy Blackfriars Road. The latter road was not laid out until 1760, and it appears that the 'Fishermen's Houses' must have been planted in the midst of fields and gardens bordering on the Lambeth marshes. They are difficult to photograph, as they face north and are obscured by the trees of the churchyard. The block consists of six houses, two stories high with a tiled roof. One of them (No. 78) contains the original staircase with turned balusters and some of the original batten doors. The present boarding, which may not be original, is ¾ in. thick and 4 in. gauge with a beaded edge. The condition of the building is good, and the bold projection of the eaves is worth notice. The general appearance would be greatly enhanced if the exterior were to be painted a light stone colour.

Elsewhere in South London there are a few remaining boarded houses in Bermondsey and Rotherhithe. A visit to the four examples mentioned in the *East London* volume of the Historical Monuments Commission (England), published in 1930, revealed the fact that two have already been demolished to allow of much-needed housing improvements, viz. the five cottages Nos. 302–310, Rotherhithe Street, and also No. 2, St. Paul's Lane. The house numbered 37 St. Mary-Church Street, Rotherhithe, is dilapidated; and the fourth example, in Jacob Street, Bermondsey, though still standing, is unoccupied and appears to be doomed. It is a small building of two stories plus attic and cellars, with a pantiled roof, sash windows, and shutters. It appears to be of the late seventeenth century.

The East End of London can now show only a few dilapidated boarded houses in Bow Road and High Street, adjoining Bow Church, and another at 195 Mile End Road, none of which is of any interest. But the London Museum contains a large collection[1] of charming water-colour drawings, mostly executed by Mr. J. T. Wilson between 1850 and 1871, which prove that all the surrounding villages, such as Merton, Edmonton, Edgware, Stockwell, Leyton, Mile End, and Clapton—since absorbed by the ever-extending growth of the city—contained boarded houses of some interest. Examples from Westminster, Bankside, and Holborn, show that similar buildings existed half a century ago in inner London. Most of the libraries and art-galleries of the London boroughs contain numbers of drawings and photographs of old boarded houses which have been demolished during the past fifty years.

The process which has led to their disappearance may be understood with painful clearness by a study of the changes that have taken place recently in the neighbouring county of Middlesex. Up to the time when the County of London was formed in 1888, Middlesex included the most important part of London, the remainder lying within the boundaries of Surrey, Kent, and Essex. In that year the new boundaries brought in a considerable area of Middlesex, and portions of Surrey and Kent, though the Essex suburbs were not absorbed. But although the suburban areas of Middlesex were then brought into London, there has been such an enormous development during the last thirty-five years that now 1,638,521 people are living in Middlesex in places that were rural areas or small villages in 1888. The normal procedure in this development includes the driving of wide arterial roads through the villages, the felling of trees everywhere, the building of innumerable 'distinctive homes' in dreary rows, and the erection of shops and garages at every focus of traffic. It is this last process in particular

[1] 'The P. A. S. Phillips Collection.' See also the Norman Collection.

39. MILL HILL, MIDDLESEX

38. 'FISHERMEN'S HOUSES', SOUTHWARK (LONDON)

which has obliterated so many of the timber houses which existed in these former picturesque villages and winding elm-clad lanes even in my own boyhood.

A group of boarded cottages which used to stand in North End Road, Hampstead, have recently disappeared; and many others could be mentioned. The village of Mill Hill, about nine miles from the centre of London, retains a number of examples (Figs. 39 to 42) on the Ridgeway, a wide and beautiful road which has been saved from standardization and development because its frontages are owned by a great public school and some Catholic institutions, while much of the surrounding country is completely absorbed by suburbia. For this reason I have been able to collect several excellent illustrations of old boarded houses within a hundred yards of my own door. Fig. 42 shows the earliest in date of these, a group of cottages on 'Milespit Hill', with boarded sides, tiled roofs, and dormers. Fig. 39 illustrates the corner of a house known as Rosebank, built in 1678, and originally erected as a Friends' Meeting House. Fig. 40 shows a cottage adjoining with a hipped roof of pantiles and a brick chimney. The date of this is uncertain. The boarding is tarred. In the autumn this cottage is a blaze of colour, being covered with 'Virginia creeper' (*Ampelopsis*). Fig. 41 illustrates one of the surviving farms.

In the north-east part of Middlesex there are a few surviving examples, such as the 'Fallow Buck' Inn at Enfield and a group of houses in a backwater in the crowded industrial area of Ponders End. Most of those in Tottenham and Clapton have now perished.

West of Mill Hill is another village, Kingsbury, that has been submerged by suburbia during the past few years. On the old village green, now a busy thoroughfare, are a quaint boarded inn of uncertain date[1] and the cottages illustrated in Fig. 19 from a sketch of my own. The chief interest of these unassuming

[1] Demolished during the past year.

cottages lies in the overhanging front, with the ends of the floor-joists and the supporting brackets revealed. The roof is tiled.

The march of progress has swept across a much more remote village at Ickenham near Uxbridge, fourteen miles from the centre of London, where the barn with overhanging front, illustrated in Fig. 26, seems to be in daily peril of disappearing before the advancing tide of shops and villas which have now reached it on either side. At Hayes, in the same district, orchards and barns are giving way to vast factories where gramophones are made. A similar process is obliterating most of Middlesex. At Harmondsworth, at the west end of the county, is a barn which is reputed to be the largest in England. Originally a part of the buildings of a Benedictine priory, its vast aisled interior is like a great wooden church and is certainly medieval; but there is nothing to indicate the date of its external boarding, part of which, as already noted (p. 79), is fixed vertically.

Surrey also contains a sprinkling of examples of boarded architecture. At Mitcham, for instance, there are three cottages, Nos. 48 to 52 in Church Street, with boarded sides and tiled roofs; and in London Road is a large gabled house now known as Ravensbury School, also with a tiled roof, boarded gables, and bay windows. Adjoining the latter is a charming group of boarded houses standing near a bridge over the little Wandle river and surrounded by gardens. The National Trust (a body for the preservation of historical and beautiful buildings and sites) has acquired the neighbouring meadow, so it is to be hoped that this group of cottages will be saved from destruction. There are other boarded houses of interest at Ashstead, Merton, Capel, and Streatham, but these are of the eighteenth century.[1]

Near Ripley in Surrey is one of the finest boarded mills in

---

[1] All are illustrated in Stanley Ramsey's *Small Houses of the Late Georgian Period* (London, 1919).

England (Fig. 30), Newark Mill, on the site of the Abbey of that name, since vanished. It stands on the banks of the river Wey, a tributary of the Thames, and has a fine tiled gambrel roof. Its date is unknown.

Sussex has not been included for our purpose among the group of south-eastern counties, but it contains a certain number of boarded houses, mills, and barns. Most of these are in the eastern corner of the county nearest to Kent. Mr. Basil Oliver, in his recent book *The Cottages of England* (published in 1929), illustrates attractive cottages at Northiam and near Battle, both in that district. Hipped gables are particularly favoured in the county.

Sussex still possesses a number of boarded windmills, though these picturesque and once indispensable buildings are fast disappearing. Recently several books on this subject have appeared,[1] so that some record will be kept of their situation and their design, even if the actual structures, like so many of those in Holland, are doomed to decay and destruction. Fig. 44 shows one such mill at West Blatchington near Brighton, with the boarded barns which surround it. The old county town of Lewes contains at least three groups of boarded houses. Two of these seem to be of a later date than the seventeenth century, but the third sports an unmistakable '1699' on its façade. This group is of the greatest interest even apart from its scholarly design, because here the boarding of the upper story has grooves worked upon it simulating brick joints. The rusticated quoins are also of wood. One of the other groups has a lower story of flintwork, banded with bricks, and a boarded upper story—an unusual combination. The quaint boarded net-houses or 'Fishermen's Shops' at Hastings may be mentioned, and at

[1] Batten, M. I., *English Windmills*, vol. i (London, 1930); Hopkins, R. T., *Old Watermills and Windmills* (London, 1930); Hughes, H. C., *Windmills in Cambridgeshire and the Isle of Ely*, in Cambridge Antiquarian Society's Proceedings, vol. xxxi (1929-30); Mais, S. P. B., *England of the Windmills* (London, 1931); also three small books on Windmills in Surrey and Sussex by J. B. Paddon (Oxford, 1925-6).

Wartling Hill, not far away, are some charming boarded cottages.

The lovely county of Kent is the 'garden of England', the cradle of our race and of our Christianity. Mr. Basil Oliver has

44. WEST BLATCHINGTON, SUSSEX. WINDMILL AND BARN

said that it is '*facile princeps* in architectural interest in the whole of England',[1] and that is no exaggeration. Moreover, it has a special interest to students of architecture because it has always been the first part of the country to feel foreign influences, and hence has formed the field for many new ventures in building methods of alien origin. From its white cliffs the shores of France can clearly be seen, and Flanders lies not much farther away. It was a stronghold of Nonconformity in the time of the Pilgrims, in spite of the powerful tradition of Canterbury, and it furnished a strong contingent to their settlements in New

[1] B. Oliver, *Cottages of England*, p. 57 (London, 1929).

40. MILL HILL, MIDDLESEX

41. MILL HILL, MIDDLESEX

Photo: Author

Photo: Author

England, including William Bassett of Sandwich, the only one among the early colonists described as a 'builder'. It contains a large number of boarded houses, but not quite so many as Essex.

Kent includes several very different types of landscape. The line of the North Downs, a range of chalk hills (see map on p. 5), approaches the shores of the Thames estuary near Dartford, and here for miles there are huge quarries where chalk is obtained for mixing with the clay to make Portland cement in great works close to the river. The north-east of the county is very flat between Canterbury, Sandwich, and Herne Bay, and across the marshes of the Stour rises the former Isle of Thanet, now an island only in name, also formed of chalk and mainly occupied to-day by famous pleasure-resorts, such as Margate and Ramsgate. Between the North Downs and the Sussex boundary is an attractive district with plentiful woods and uplands known as the Weald, where formerly the fringe of the Sussex iron industry extended; and the southern tip of the county includes the flat area known as Romney Marsh, extending to the picturesque old towns of Rye and Winchelsea on the banks of the sleepy little river Rother. Great fruit-orchards and hop-fields cover the central area, and within the last twenty years the development of the Kent coal-field has greatly changed the aspect of the triangle of country between the old towns of Canterbury, Sandwich, and Dover.

A part of rural west Kent, now rapidly becoming suburban, was included in the new administrative area of the County of London in 1888, and here there are a few boarded houses, such as Bostall Farm near Woolwich. But the finest example of such buildings is the group of houses at Eltham (Figs. 45 and 46) which originally formed part of the 'Green Courtyard' of the medieval palace there, and are now known as 'Nos. 32, 34, and 36, The Courtyard'. They are described as follows in the magnificent Inventory of the Royal Commission on Historical

Monuments (*London: East*), with ample and excellent photographs and plans:

'The S.W. part of the building, Nos. 36 and 34, has a weather-boarded S.E. front with a projecting gabled wing at the end [Fig. 45]; this wing has a square bay-window standing on a brick plinth with three chamfered offsets and finished with a low seventeenth-century pediment. The rest of the front has a projecting upper storey, broken by a small gabled projection, now a porch [Fig. 46] but probably retaining the structure of the 'oriel' of the original Hall, shown on Thorpe's plan [late sixteenth century]. At the junction of the main building and the wing is a chimney stack with original bases. The windows, generally, have solid frames, mullions and transoms, and are probably of late seventeenth-century date.'[1]

In the picturesque High Street of Eltham, formerly a quaint old market-town, is another group of boarded buildings.

The district round the ancient cathedral city of Canterbury contains numerous examples, but Canterbury itself has nothing much of early date to show. A house at the corner of St. Peter's and The Friars has a boarded gable with an apparently original leaded window with diamond glazing. There is an enormous boarded building, the City Mills, which is the largest mill-building encountered in the course of my researches, but which is obviously of eighteenth-century date. It has a gambrel or mansard roof covered with slates, a brick plinth one story high, and a remarkable tower. The vast height and bulk of this structure gives some idea of the great strength of the timber framework, for such a building is required to carry heavy loads on each of its numerous floors.

Two other mills, in and adjoining the charming little village of Wickhambreux, east of Canterbury, are of a very different type (Fig. 50). At Sturry, not far away, are two more boarded

[1] *Royal Commission on Historical Monuments, East London*, pp. 107-8 (London, 1930).

mills, one small and rather dilapidated: the other very large but apparently of the nineteenth century. It appears to me that a timber-framed structure with boarded walls was probably adopted for these water-mills because it lent itself to the purpose, being light and easily carried on stout timber beams across a river. All these mills are painted white or a light colour, a refreshing change from tarred woodwork elsewhere.

Another interesting little town in this district is Fordwich, formerly of considerable importance, where there is a beautiful old half-timbered Town Hall of the fifteenth century with a boarded annex. From the latter a primitive crane can be swung out across the little river, and here, it is alleged, was swung the 'ducking-school' or 'cucking-stool' in which 'scolds' were immersed in the water. A group of boarded cottages with boarded sides and an 'overhang' is illustrated in Fig. 47. The boarding and the windows are modern, but the hipped roof of tiles and the chimney suggest a seventeenth-century date. Brackets can be seen beneath the overhang.

My visit to Sandwich proved disappointing, for in an old town of such celebrity I had hoped to find some boarded buildings surviving from the time when William Bassett, builder, crossed over to New England in the *Fortune* in 1621. But my quest produced nothing more than the picturesque photograph reproduced here as Fig. 48. The Congregational Church, founded in 1644, now possesses a more modern building of little architectural merit. The famous Barbican or Watergate of Sandwich is a unique Tudor structure beloved of artists, and is partly boarded. Sandwich is a sketcher's paradise, and ranks with such old seaports as Rye, Ipswich, Lynn, and Boston as an early centre of foreign architectural influence.

Faversham, Dover, Deal, and Ramsgate were all favourable to 'Dissent' in the seventeenth century, but I have no records of boarded houses of that early period. Down by the harbour at Folkestone is a group of picturesque fishermen's cottages, as attractive to painters as they are shocking to housing-reformers, and these must be of considerable age. They may be compared with the example at Hastings already mentioned.

The Weald of Kent, or that part of it lying between Tonbridge, Headcorn, Tenterden, and the Sussex border, contains a number of particularly attractive houses with boarded walls, tiled roofs, and warm red brick chimney-stacks. There is a fine example in Tonbridge itself, on the left of the road as one descends into the town from London, and others in nearly all the surrounding villages, including Lamberhurst, Cranbrook, and Staplehurst. Mr. Basil Oliver, in his book, *The Old Cottages of England*, illustrates charming cottages at Groombridge near Tunbridge Wells, and at Hawkhurst near Cranbrook. But of all these beautiful villages, in undulating country covered with hop-fields, the most interesting for our purpose is Smarden, a mile or so from the main railway-line from Folkestone to London. Here are whole rows of boarded cottages with hipped gables, roofs covered with mellow tiles, and dormer windows. As already noted, buildings of the same type occur in adjoining villages just over the Sussex border, such as Robertsbridge, Northiam, and Hartfield.

Hertfordshire possesses a good many boarded houses, and still more boarded barns and mills, although the tide of suburbia is now beginning to reach its borders. It is not a large county, but contains a great variety of landscape for its size, and displays a similar variety in its architecture. In its chief towns—Hertford, Ware, St. Albans, Watford, and Hatfield—such boarded houses as survive are not of early date. On its east side, nearest to Essex, a few thatched examples are found, such as the cottages at Much Hadham illustrated in Fig. 54, with dormer windows and diamond glazing. Elsewhere, the roofs are generally tiled.

In the main street of Barnet, where the traffic from London to the Midlands and the North roars past the old church through a roadway not many yards wide, stands an old boarded house

46. ELTHAM, KENT

45. ELTHAM, KENT

Photo: Author

Photo: Author

IN SOUTH-EAST ENGLAND

with a tiled gambrel roof and a shop beneath (Fig. 43). Even since my photograph was taken in 1930, this interesting example, No. 88 High Street, has suffered further change. Inquiry of the local wiseacres failed to reveal its age.

Some few miles south of St. Albans, at Colney Street, on the river Colne near its source and close to the old Roman road known as Watling Street, is the fine boarded building, Moor Mills (Figs. 51, 52), with a tiled roof and brick substructure. The owner is unable to furnish any exact information as to the date, nor can I trace it elsewhere.

Cambridgeshire is a small county noted chiefly for the famous University which it contains. It would have been interesting for our purpose to have located within the town some examples of boarded houses to associate with the Pilgrims who, as we have seen, derived so much inspiration and learning from its various colleges. But a fairly exhaustive inquiry and a reference to architects practising there have failed to reveal a single instance of a seventeenth-century boarded building in the town itself. Most of the surrounding villages contain thatched cottages with plastered walls composed of clay lump or chalk or framed in timber. But at Denny Gate, some eight miles north of Cambridge, I came across a cottage (Fig. 32) with a thatched roof and walls of boarding with a gauge of about 8 in. The boards have a thickness of $\frac{3}{4}$ to 1 in. and are not feather-edged. The oak fillets at the angles are $3\frac{1}{2}$ by $1\frac{1}{2}$ in. Slightly nearer to Cambridge is the fine riverside barn at Clayhithe (Fig. 49), with a brick plinth, thatched roof, and feather-edged and tarred boarding laid to an 8-in. gauge. The age of this barn and many similar ones, at Landbeach and elsewhere round Cambridge, is uncertain.[1]

[1] As this book goes to press, the news is published that Cambridgeshire can now claim to have the oldest windmill of known date in England: the beautiful old post-mill at Bourn, about five miles west of Cambridge. It was working up to some seven years ago and has been recently restored. There is a working model of it at the Science Museum, South Kensington. The mill stands on an open

TIMBER HOUSES

We now come to Essex, the county which, as I have tried to establish in previous chapters, may be considered as the hub of the Pilgrim movement, in spite of rival claims advanced for the Scrooby area. Essex is a large county, but exhibits less variety of landscape than most of those described hitherto. In no part are there any notable hills, and slight eminences like Danbury (317 ft.), Billericay (319 ft.), or Laindon Hills (378 ft.) afford a ridiculously extensive view. Nevertheless, it is undulating everywhere except in a few flat districts near the sea, and at one time it must have been thickly wooded. The formerly isolated tongues of land and islands near the sea, between Clacton and Southend, have recently been opened up by motor-bus services; and now the sound of the klaxon is regularly heard in places where once there was nothing to break the windy silence except sheep-bells and the cry of gulls. Southend, Clacton, Walton, and Maldon have become noisy resorts of the proletariat on pleasure bent; and the north bank of the Thames from London to Tilbury is lined with docks and factories; while suburbia is now creeping all round Epping Forest and along the Brentwood road.

But within the fringe where this rapid development has occurred there remains a thinly populated and surprisingly quiet part of England, traversed only by one important highway (from London via Chelmsford and Colchester to Ipswich) and only altered from its older aspect where new centres of industry have sprung up, as at Braintree and Witham.

Boarded houses are to be found in nearly all parts of the county where the march of civilization has not swept them completely away. Beginning with the district north-east of London, there are examples at Loughton, Theydon Bois, High Beach, and Epping. Of the latter Fig. 16 gives an illustration,

---

trestle supporting the central post and the 'tail-beam' projects from the steps. The mill was in existence *before 1636*; and it is interesting to know that this earliest English windmill is to be found in East Anglia. (See vignette on p. 192.)

IN SOUTH-EAST ENGLAND

the building being of pleasant proportions with a tiled roof and massive brick stack, but the boarding and the windows are certainly modern. There is a beautiful boarded mill at Passingford, near Epping.

53. THE WINDMILL AT BILLERICAY, ESSEX

Proceeding along the main road from Epping to Stortford, one passes an interesting boarded cottage (Fig. 29) in the hamlet of Potter Street. It has a hipped gable covered with pantiles. Two miles farther on, the road to Roydon turns to the left, and along this road, close to the river Stort which forms the boundary with Hertfordshire, is a cluster of houses known as Netteswell Cross. Among these is a barn (Fig. 23) already mentioned on p. 79 as one of only two old examples known to me where vertical boarding is used. Returning to the main road, we find nothing of much use for our purpose in either Harlow or Bishop's Stortford. North of the latter, however, are some old boarded houses in Stansted; and there are said to be others at Rickling, farther north again. Newport and Saffron

Walden are full of beautiful houses of various periods, but here we are passing into the country of plastered timber-framing, and in neither place have I seen boarded houses of early date.

However, there are many such in the district between Harlow, Stortford, and Dunmow. One particularly attractive group is to be seen at Sheering (Fig. 55), three miles east of Harlow. Here the main roof is of thatch, but an addition to the main block is covered with pantiles. Passing through Hatfield Heath, and following the road to Takeley, one comes across the barn already mentioned (p. 61, and Fig. 24) as typical of Essex timber-framing and boarding methods.

Takeley, or 'Takeley Street' to give it its full name, is so called because it lies on Stane Street (=stone street), one of the two Roman roads in Essex (just as Colney Street in Hertfordshire lies on Watling Street). This road runs almost without a bend from Stortford through Braintree and Coggeshall to Marks Tey, where it joins the equally straight road coming from London through Romford and Chelmsford to Colchester. Mr. Basil Oliver[1] mentions Takeley as the only place he knows in Essex where an old tile-hung cottage is to be seen.

Between Takeley and Dunmow there are some pleasant boarded cottages with thatched roofs at Smith's Green and Bamber's Green (Fig. 60), and at Sheering Hall, close to the latter, are some old boarded barns. Mr. Oliver illustrates[2] some beautiful cottages at Little Dunmow with thatched roofs, overhung gables, and partly boarded fronts. In Stebbing, north of Little Dunmow, the boarded houses are of little interest; and Braintree, already cited in this as a stronghold of Congregationalism and a place after which more than one New England township has been named, has little to show. Here, again, traffic widenings have led to the recent demolition of an old boarded malt-house mentioned in the Inventory of Historical

---

[1] B. Oliver, *Cottages of England*, p. 55 (London, 1929).
[2] B. Oliver, *Old Houses of East Anglia*, Plate 40 (London, 1912).

51, 52. MOOR MILLS, HERTFORDSHIRE

Photos by Author

49. CLAYHITHE, CAMBRIDGESHIRE

50. MILL NEAR WICKHAMBREUX, KENT

Photo: Author

Monuments for Essex. A group of houses with gambrel roofs (Fig. 17), near the centre of the town, is the only outstanding example left. But at Bocking, which is practically part of Braintree nowadays, and has been previously mentioned as the home of the first Separatist congregation in 1550, there remains a wooden mill (Fig. 57) which must be of considerable age. It may be compared with another fine boarded mill at Stisted (Fig. 56), a few miles farther down the river Blackwater. Both these mills have tiled roofs, and that at Stisted is in particularly good condition.

In Bocking there is also a fine weather-boarded windmill (Fig. 58) in excellent preservation, of the type and shape traditional in Essex. The date is uncertain, but is before 1700.[1] The central post is of solid oak 25 in. square in section, and some of the beams in the superstructure measure 16 by 8 in. and 12 in. square respectively. The angle posts are 7 in. square, the braces 6 by 4 in., the intermediate studs 4 by 3 in. (15 in. apart), and the feather-edged boarding shows 5 in. on the face.

About seven miles north of Braintree lies Wethersfield, a small village which attracted my attention because its name is identical with that of a place in Connecticut where old boarded houses are still to be seen. But it provided me with no pleasant surprises. It is a typically English village with the church and the inns and a blacksmith's forge at its heart, narrow winding streets, and in them a sprinkling of boarded houses of no great interest (Figs. 22 and 36 B). On the road to Braintree are some old thatched and boarded barns.

A few miles north of Wethersfield is Toppesfield, a tiny village difficult to find, but bearing a name which recalls one of the most beautiful wooden houses in New England, Parson Capen's home at Topsfield, Mass. (1683, see p. 190 and Figs 86, 93, 94). Near to Toppesfield I came upon a sight unusual in modern England, two men thatching an old boarded house

[1] See R. T. Hopkins, *Old Watermills and Windmills* (London, 1930).

(p. 83 and Fig. 33). Adjoining it stood a small cottage, thatched and partly boarded, which must resemble very closely the type of dwelling erected by the Pilgrims after their first landing (Fig. 28).

In the quaint old town of Coggeshall I found nothing; and in Colchester only a wooden *gazebo* or garden-house adjoining the County School. This feature came into fashion in Jacobean days as part of the equipment of the formal garden, and fine examples are to be seen at Holland House in London and elsewhere. But the Colchester *gazebo* may be later in date than the seventeenth century.

The villages east of Colchester, in the peninsula between that town and the coast, contain many examples of boarded houses. Some of these, e.g. at Great Clacton and at Horseley Cross, have tiled gambrel roofs. Others, e.g. at Great Bentley, Great Oakley (Fig. 61), and Tendring Heath, have thatched roofs. Others again, such as those illustrated from St. Osyth (Fig. 18), have simple pitched roofs of plain tiles. Dormers are freely used, both with thatched and tiled roofs, and chimneys are generally massive with very simple caps. The general effect of these houses is long and low. Besides those mentioned, I noticed and photographed other cottages at Kirby Cross, Thorrington, and Thorpe-le-Soken, the last an interesting example of an overhang. At St. Osyth there is also a fine old boarded mill with a tiled gambrel roof (Fig. 31).

Brightlingsea contains a beautiful old timbered house called Jacobes Hall, and there is another fine example at Barn Cottage, East Bergholt; but in neither place are old boarded houses to be seen. The house named 'Southfields' at Dedham, on the Suffolk border, suggests associations with Dedham, Mass., where the Fairbanks House (see Fig. 91) is one of the oldest wooden houses surviving in America. But the building at the English Dedham is only partly boarded, and is chiefly interesting for its fine brick chimney-stacks (quite in the Essex tradition), its overhanging gable, and its mullioned windows (see Frontispiece). The house is a large timber-built block grouped round an inner quadrangle and is said to have been originally a 'bay and say factory'. It was erected in the late fifteenth or early sixteenth century. The illustration shows the south-west wing, known as the 'Master Weaver's House'.

Turning towards the south-eastern part of Essex from Colchester, one arrives at the interesting old town of Maldon on the estuary of the Blackwater. Here there are several boarded houses, the best being that which stands in an alley known as 'The Friary'. It has a gambrel roof, hipped at the end gables, and tiled. East of Maldon is a somewhat lonely area extending to the sea, and in this district, at Tillingham and elsewhere, are a number of boarded cottages and barns. Between Maldon and Chelmsford lies an old boarded house, Brook Farm, with gambrel roof, and a noteworthy barn. At Woodham Walter is a brick church, built in 1563-4, of which I shall have more to say later, as it closely resembles the oldest brick church in America, erected at St. Luke's in Virginia in 1632 (see p. 195 and Figs. 95 and 96). Danbury, a beautifully situated village on the Maldon-Chelmsford road, has some connexion with Captain John Smith (see p. 116), but has no boarded houses of importance.

The same applies more or less to Chelmsford and the neighbouring township of Springfield (a famous name in New England), but Barnes' Mill at Chelmsford has a boarded upper story and a great gambrel roof. On the main road between Chelmsford and London one sees few boarded houses of interest. At Ingatestone and at Mountnessing there are old wooden windmills, at Brentwood the courtyard of the 'White Hart' Inn has an overhanging boarded upper story, and Putwell Farm (between Brentwood and Romford) is an interesting boarded building (Fig. 59) with an overhang, a tiled roof, and a massive brick chimney-stack.

We have still to consider the area of south Essex, between the London-Chelmsford road, the river Crouch, and the estuary of the Thames. In spite of the rapid urbanization and industrialization of a large part of this district, it still contains a great number of examples of boarded houses and barns, though many are falling into decay as agriculture is superseded by other forms of employment. Beginning at the east boundary of this area, the North Sea, we find a very thinly populated farming district which includes Foulness Island and extends to Rochford. Rochford Hall, a Separatist place of meeting, has been mentioned more than once in this book (pp. 3, 74 and Fig. 27). The little town which adjoins it contains many boarded houses, many of them with gambrel roofs and all originally tiled. At Stambridge, a mile or so outside the town, is a tall wooden mill with a gambrel roof. South-east of Rochford is the charming village of Great Wakering, where the main street, with the old church at its end, affords the most picturesque sequence of boarded houses that I have seen in Essex (Fig. 20). Between this village and the great sprawling borough of Southend-on-Sea there is an attractive farm-house at Bourne's Green near Southchurch, with a tiled roof and overhanging boarded gables. In Southend itself there are a few examples, in the main street of Prittlewell, and in the fishermen's quarter at Leigh.

West of Leigh lies the growing village of Benfleet, where bungalows and villas are rapidly ousting the works of the past. Here there are a number of boarded houses of various dates, some with gambrel roofs, and all tiled.

From Benfleet one crosses over to Canvey Island—a perfectly flat area inhabited twenty years ago almost exclusively by a handful of farmers, but now crowded with bungalow-dwellers in search of seclusion—where one may see at least one enormous boarded barn with a thatched roof (Fig. 21) and a neighbouring farmstead with its attendant outbuildings.

54. MUCH HADHAM, HERTFORDSHIRE

55. SHEERING, ESSEX

56. MILL AT STISTED, ESSEX

57. MILL AT BOCKING, ESSEX

IN SOUTH-EAST ENGLAND

Canvey Island is a curious spot, lying so low that the sea-wall bounding the Thames estuary completely blocks the view over the water, yet when the speculative builders and the bungalow-dwellers have achieved their ambitions, it will look just like any other place, only rather more so.

Inland, however, there remain a few villages where arterial roads, motor-coaches, docks, cement-works, and oil dumps have not entirely eliminated the countryside; and in such places as Wickford, Horndon-on-the-Hill, and Runwell, scraps of old England may still be seen, or at any rate imagined! Some boarded cottages from Wickford are illustrated on Fig. 62, and another interesting group was noticed at Slicer's Gate near Billericay. Billericay itself, a noted centre of dissent, contributed various religious martyrs to our roll of honour (see p. 46) and inspired some early Pilgrim settlers to name a new town in Massachusetts in its memory.

There is a local legend, which I have not been able to substantiate, that Christopher Martin—one of several natives of Billericay who crossed in the *Mayflower*—once inhabited 'Chantry House' in the High Street. Two of my drawings of woodwork details in that house have therefore been included in this book (Figs. 34 and 35). But at any rate the little town contains many boarded houses (Fig. 15), and formerly possessed a typical Essex windmill (Fig. 53) which fell into disrepair and collapsed in a high wind some three years ago. Billericay also possesses, as an adjunct to its Congregational Church, a newly erected 'Mayflower Hall', to the building of which the 'General Society of Mayflower Descendants' contributed. Unfortunately, Billericay is being 'developed' out of all recognition, but its old High Street is still picturesque.

'Progress' is most evident in the line of villages extending along the banks of the Thames from Canvey Island to London, a matter of less than thirty miles. Practically the whole of the river-frontage is now occupied by docks (including the huge area of Tilbury), factories, oil-depots, and refuse-dumps, the latest comer being Mr. Henry Ford with works which are to employ 20,000 men. Here and there one encounters an unexpected little oasis like the hamlet of Fobbing, which stands among cornfields just out of sight of all the activity on the river-bank a mile beyond. Here there are two boarded houses of great interest: Fisher's Farm with its thatched roof and leaning walls, originally erected in the fifteenth century, with tarred elm boarding; and Wheeler's Farm, equally old, with an overhanging upper story, a tiled roof, painted modern boarding, and a diagonally-placed chimney-stack in the centre of the ridge. Vange lies on a main road near Fobbing, and contains a group of boarded cottages with hipped tiled roofs (Fig. 63), but the days of Vange as a rural village are numbered, as the bungalows creep up to it. There are still a few boarded houses in the ten miles or so of country that lie between Vange and the approaching outskirts of London, but it cannot be expected that many of them will remain for another twenty years, and the fate of the barns is even more certain. This part of Essex contains few windmills or watermills, the scarcity of the latter being accounted for by the lack of streams.

As one enters London from south Essex, one passes through the town of Barking, formerly a quiet country place with a considerable sea-going trade and a famous abbey, but now a manufacturing town where London's sewage enters the river and where London's gas is made and stored in vast works. To all intents and purposes it is part of London, though administratively it lies in the county of Essex. Among its rows of modern brick villas and its great factories there are still to be seen a few relics of its past: the beautiful brick Eastbury Manor House built in Queen Elizabeth's reign; the old parish-church with the ruins of the Abbey adjoining; and a few boarded houses of the seventeenth and eighteenth centuries.

One group of these, Nos. 107 and 109 in the Broadway, has

beaded and painted boarding, sliding windows, and an unusual cornice.

More interesting is the Old Rectory in Church Path, where the painted boarding has an ovolo moulding on its lower edge, a feature not met with before in the course of this quest. This building which, like the others in Barking just mentioned, has a tiled roof, has evidently been much altered. It does not compare in interest with most of the rural examples.

Formerly, one of the finest windmills in Essex stood at Barking: it is illustrated in Mr. Basil Oliver's *Old Houses in East Anglia*, but has recently disappeared.

We have now returned to London, having completed our rapid circuit of Essex; and having shed a few useless tears over the disappearance of so many links with English history, we may turn our attention to the first ventures in building of the Pilgrim settlers in New England.

VI. THE PILGRIMS IN NEW ENGLAND
1620–c. 1635

THE famous landing of the Pilgrim Fathers in the *Mayflower* in November 1620 was the first English settlement in New England, but by no means the first venture of Englishmen into North America. The Pilgrims, as we have seen (p. 27), had ample time, during their long exile in Holland, to ponder on the most suitable location for their colony, and a considerable amount of information was already available, even in book form. It was not entirely a leap in the dark. For several years settlers had been pouring into Virginia, which is estimated to have had a population of over 4,000 people before 1622, and their experiences were certainly known to the gatherings of merchants and refugees who, in England and in Holland, planned the daring *Mayflower* expedition. The Pilgrims had every opportunity of knowing something of the hardships and dangers which would inevitably attend the venture, and some guidance as to the equipment which they would need for their fourfold task of planting, housing, trade, and defence against the native 'Indians'. Their principal source of information was that redoubtable explorer and sailor, Captain John Smith, who for a time was Governor of Virginia, and whose enthralling books of travel are still regarded as classics in England and America. He was born in Lincolnshire in 1579, went to sea about fifteen years later, and made his first voyage to Virginia in 1605. In 1616 he published his book, *A Description of New England: or the Observations and discoueries, of Captain John Smith (Admirall of that Country) in the North of America, in the year of our Lord 1614: with the successe of sixe Ships that went the next year 1615*, &c. It appears that he himself suggested the name of the new country, which was 'called *New England, An.* 1616, at my humble suite, by our most gracious Prince *Charles*'. It is also revealed, in

Photo: Author

59. PUTWELL FARM, BRENTWOOD, ESSEX

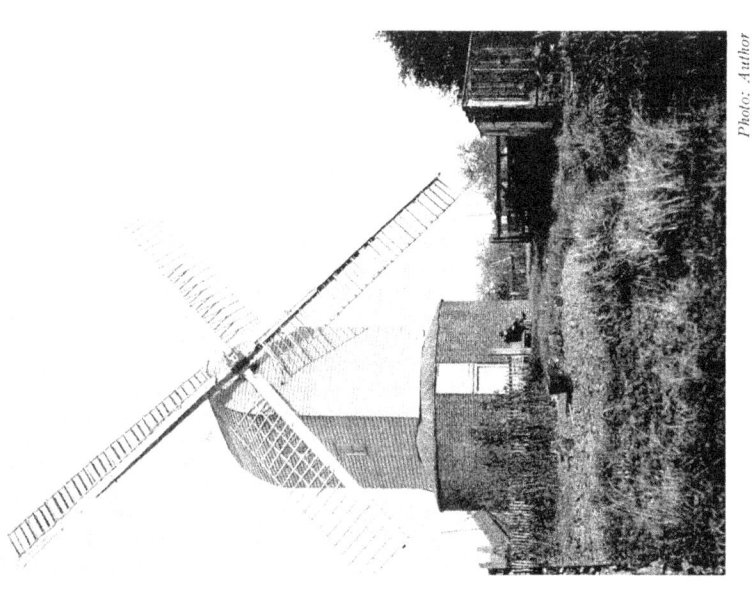

Photo: Author

58. WINDMILL AT BOCKING, ESSEX

60. BAMBERS GREEN, TAKELEY, ESSEX

61. GREAT OAKLEY, ESSEX

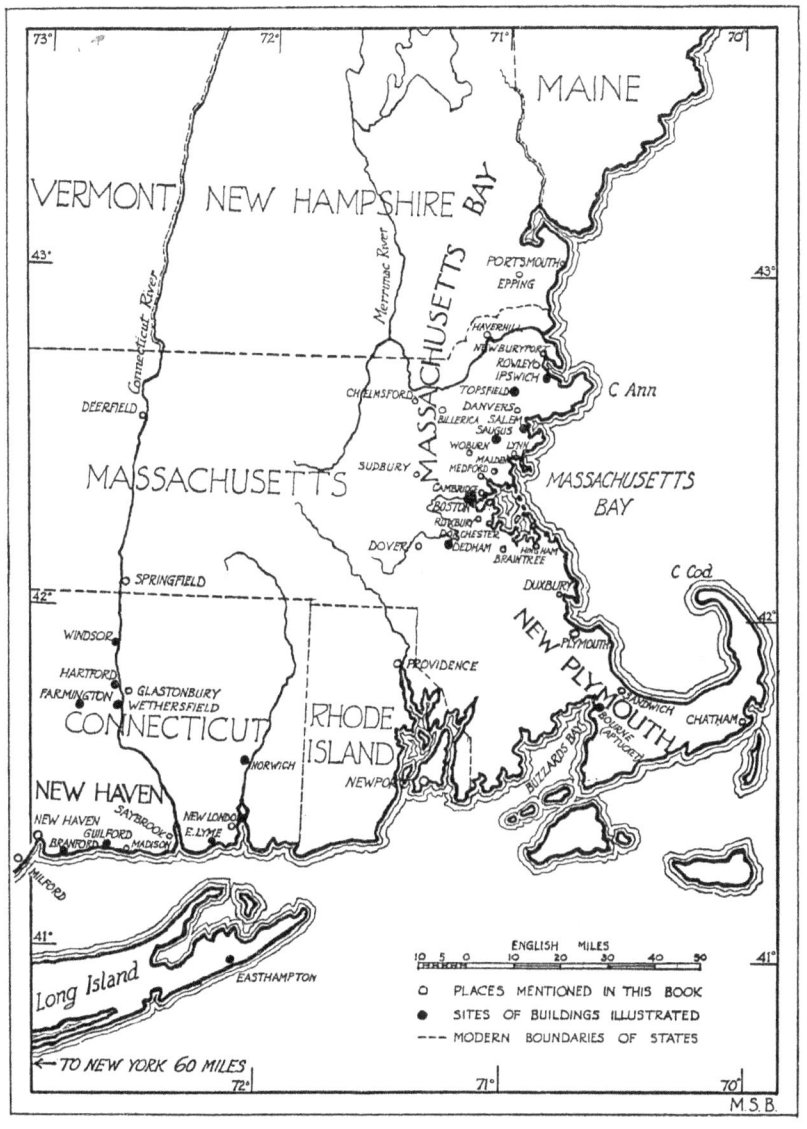

64. MAP OF NEW ENGLAND
(To the same scale as the map of S.E. England on p. 5)

one of Smith's later works, that he offered to conduct the Pilgrims' expedition personally, but that they declined his services 'to save charges' and 'would try their owne conclusions, though with great losse and much miserie till time had taught them to see their owne error; for such humorists [i.e. fanatics] will never beleeve well, till they bee beaten with their owne rod'. In refusing, he says that they added that 'my books and maps were much better cheape to teach them, than my selfe'. His map, which bears his own portrait in one corner and the date 1614, shows the whole coast of New England as he defined it, that is, from Penobscot Bay in the north to Cape Cod in the south.

The unwillingness of the Pilgrims or their English financiers to employ Smith may be partly due to the slenderness of their resources, as he suggests; but it is evident that he had little sympathy with their religious convictions or aspirations, and that he was a man of decided views and had a sailor's freedom of speech. Assuming that the Pilgrims relied mainly on his printed writings, let us see to what extent they must have been forewarned as to the risks to be encountered, and the precautions to be taken to meet them.

In the first place, Smith was responsible for painting a very rosy picture of the country as a whole, for he writes: 'Of all the foure parts of the world that I haue yet seene not inhabited, could I haue but meanes to transport a Colonie, I would rather liue here then [=than] any where: and if it did not maintaine it selfe, were wee but once indifferently well fitted, let vs starue.' He describes the rocky northern coast as a 'spectacle of desolation', the 'Countrie of the Massachusets' as 'the Paradise of all those parts', and the district farther south, where the Pilgrims eventually settled, as 'good land'. Here, among other places, his party encountered the Indians: 'Upon a small occasion, wee fought also with fortie or fiftie of those: though some were hurt, and some slaine; yet within an hour after, they became friendes.'

IN NEW ENGLAND (1620–c. 1635)

He makes much of the excellent climate, the vast possibilities of fisheries, and the abundant resources of the coastal lands in timber and other natural products. Among these are: 'Free stone for building, Slate for tiling, smooth stone to make Fornaces and Forges for glasse or iron, and iron ore sufficient, conueniently to melt in them. But the most part so resembleth the Coast of Deuonshire, I think most of the cliffes would make such lime stone.' He suggests that England might organize the apprenticeship and emigration of orphans, provided that the colonists included 'sufficient masters (as Carpenters, Masons, Fishers, Fowlers, Gardiners, Husbandmen, Sawyers, Smiths, Spinsters, Taylors, Weauers, and such like) to take ten, twelue, or twentie, or as ther is occasion, for Apprentises'. Elsewhere he indicates the possibilities of spare-time employment of craftsmen, in the gentle art of fishing. 'If a man worke but three daies in seuen [=seven], he may get more than hee can spend, vnlesse he will be excessiue. Now that Carpenter, Mason, Gardiner, Tailer, Smith, Sailer, Forger, or what other, may they not make this a pretty recreation though they fish but an houre in a day, to take more than they eat in a weeke? or if they will not eat it, because there is so much better choise; yet sell it, or change it, with the Fisher-men, or Merchants, for any thing they want. And what sport doth yeeld a more pleasing content, and lesse hurt or charge than angling with a hooke; and crossing the sweete ayre from Ile to Ile, ouer the silent streames of a calme Sea; wherein the most curious may finde profit, pleasure, and content.'

Such was the lure which tempted the exiled Pilgrims from Leyden to brave the terrors of the unknown, and encouraged merchants in London to finance their venture.

The party which, in November 1620, set foot on the shore of New England, where the town of Plymouth now stands, was not by any means an ideal unit for purposes of colonization; and it is one of the miracles of history that so small a company was able to determine the ultimate destiny of a great nation. Of the little band of 102 persons, there were 80 who had voluntarily sailed as refugees from England or Holland, and 22 who had enlisted as hired craftsmen or servants. The former section included 34 adult males, 18 of their wives, and 28 children (20 boys and 8 girls). The second category comprised 19 men and 3 women.

In spite of all the research that has been devoted to the question by modern scholars, it is not yet known, and probably never will be known, what were the occupations of this small company, or how many of them had any experience of the various crafts of building. There were only 53 adult men in the party, plus a few youths under 21 who may have partially mastered a craft. As has been pointed out in Chapter III, many of them were originally professional men or farmers who had learned some trade while sojourning in Holland. So far I can ascertain the occupations of only 16 of the 53 have been discovered, and none of these were building craftsmen. Moreover, at least 22 of the 53 died within a year.[1] Of all the company, only John Alden (the hero of Longfellow's poem, *The Courtship of Miles Standish*) is known to have had any connexion with one of the crafts, for he was taken on—probably at Southampton—as a cooper, being then 21 years of age. It has been stated, though perhaps on inadequate evidence, that he was responsible for most of the early wooden building. Of the Alden House at Duxbury, Mass., Wallace Nutting[2] writes as follows: 'The construction of the house-frame, with its great posts and beams, is clearly shown, and no doubt follows the plan, and may even be the handiwork of John Alden, who was the most skilled in tools of any man of the original settlers.'

Between 1621 and 1623, at least five more adult males appear

[1] Dr. Brown, *Chronicles of the Pilgrim Fathers*, p. 210, says: 'After the sickness had done its work, there were only 21 men and 6 growing lads left to do the work of the colony.'
[2] In *Furniture of the Pilgrim Century*, p. 334 (Boston, 1921).

IN NEW ENGLAND (1620–c. 1635)

to have landed at New Plymouth in the *Fortune*, the *Anne*, and the *Little James*. All their occupations are recorded, and among them is one whose name and trade are of importance to us here: William Bassett, described as a 'master-mason' of Sandwich in Kent. Here at last we have a definite record of a man who was competent to undertake building work in the new colony. It may be repeated here (see p. 44) that two-thirds of the immigrants in 1620 and 1621 came from the south-east of England —the indigenous home of the boarded house—and it is significant that William Bassett himself came from that region.

Having finally selected by ballot a site for their settlement at 'New Plymouth', some seven weeks after their arrival, they began building at once, parties of men going ashore daily to fell and carry timber, and returning each evening to sleep on the boat. This structure was 'the firste house for common use to receive them and their goods'.[1] It was about 20 ft. square, and its site is marked by a bronze tablet placed there in 1898. But only three weeks later (on 14 January 1621), Bradford records that—'The house which they had made for a generall randevoze by casulty fell afire, and some were faine to retire abord for shilter.'[2] Captain John Smith adds that the company was divided 'into 19 families, alotting to every person a poule in bredth and three in length', the sites being then chosen by lot.[3]

Nine months later 'they begane now to gather in the small harvest they had, and to fitte up their houses and dwellings against winter, being all well recovered in health and strenght'[4] (except, of course, the large number who had died in the meantime). The buildings completed up to this date consisted of seven dwellings on the main street, together with one meeting house used for both religious and civil gatherings, and three storehouses for their provisions, trading stock, and stores

---

[1] Bradford, *History of Plimoth Plantation, 1606–1646*, reprint of original MS. published in New York, 1908, p. 105.   [2] *Ibid.*, p. 115.
[3] Smith, *Description of New-England*, p. 232.   [4] Bradford, p. 121.

generally.[1] As there is no mention of framed buildings until 1624, and as none of the primitive dwellings now survives, we have no means of knowing the constructional methods employed. But assuming that the Pilgrims had profited by the example of Virginia, we may imagine that their dwellings were of more permanent character than the pitifully inadequate shelters described by Edward Johnson, in his *History of New-England from the English planting in the Yeere 1628, untill the Yeere 1652*,[2] which refers to the later colonization of Massachusetts Bay, and is a tiresome book written in Old Testament language, and mainly concerned with church progress and theological disputation.

'After they have thus found out a place of aboad, they burrow themselves in the Earth for their first shelter under some Hill-side, casting the earth aloft upon Timber; they make a smoaky fire against the Earth on the highest side, and thus these poore servants of Christ provide shelters for themselves, their Wives and little ones, keeping off the short showers from their Lodgings, but the long raines penetrate through, to their great disturbance in the night season; yet in these poore Wigwames they sing Psalmes, pray and praise their God till they can provide them houses, which ordinarily was wont to be with many till the Earth, by the Lords blessing, brought forth Bread to feed them.'

Writing his recollections of early life in Virginia, Capt. John Smith says: 'When I first went to Virginia, I well remember wee did hang an awning (which is an old saile) to three or foure trees to shadow us from the sunne, our walls were rales of wood, our seats unhewed trees till we cut plankes, our Pulpit a bar of wood nailed to two neighbouring trees. In foule weather we shifted into an old rotten tent; for we had few better, and this came by the way of adventure for new. This was our Church, till we built a homely thing like a barne, set upon Cratchets, covered with rafts, sedge, and earth; so was also the walls: the

---

[1] Brown, *op. cit.*, p. 214.   [2] Published 1653.

best of our houses [were] of the like curiosity; but for the most part farre much worse workmanship, that could neither well defend [from] wind nor raine.'[1]

It appears from the following extracts that the first buildings in New England were thatched, and that wattle was used in the construction of sheds. A reprint by Smith of an earlier chronicle, probably by Winslow, has this entry for 1621: 'That night the house they [the Pilgrim Fathers] had built and thatched, where lay their armes, bedding, powder, &c. tooke fire and was burnt.' A few pages later, the same writer describes the personnel of the colony, which in 1624 included 'some Gentlemen, some Merchants, some handy-crafts men', adding that 'These dwell most about London'. In 1624 there were in Plymouth about 180 persons and 32 dwelling-houses, 'whereof 7 were burnt the last winter', occupying a palisaded site about half a mile in circumference.

In his *New England's Memorial*, published in 1669, Nathaniel Morton describes another fire which took place at New Plymouth on 5 November 1624, or in 1623 according to Bradford,[2] whose account is as follows: 'This fire was occasioned by some of the sea-men that were roystering in a house wher it first begane, making a great fire in very could weather, which broke out of the chimney into the thatch, and burnte downe 3 or 4 houses, and consumed all the goods and provisions in them. . . . And shortly after, when the vemencie of the fire was over, smoke was seen to arise within a shed that was joyned to the end of the store-house, which was watled up with bowes, in the withered leaves whereof the fire was kindled.'

Of 1622 Bradford writes: 'This summer they builte a fort with good timber, both strong and comly, which was of good defence, made with a flate rofe and batelments, on which their ordnance were mounted, and wher they kepte constante watch,

---

[1] J. Smith, *Advertisements for the unexperienced Planters of New England, or anywhere* (London, 1631).   [2] Bradford, *op. cit.*

espetially in times of danger. It served them allso for a meeting house and was fitted accordingly for that use.'

By that time, the whole town had been enclosed within a stout palisade, owing to repeated threats from the Indians: 'They agreed [in 1621] to inclose their dwellings with a good strong pale, and make flankers in convenient places, with gates to shute, which were every night locked, and a watch kept and when neede required ther was also warding in the day time. ... This was accomplished very cherfully, and the towne impayled round by the beginning of March [1622], in which evry family had a prety garden plote secured.'

Thatched houses built of wood, whatever may have been the precise construction, were very liable to catch fire; and Nathaniel Morton notes the precautions taken in 1621: 'If ther should be any cry of fire, a company was appointed for a guard with muskets, while others quenched the fire; the same to prevent Indian treachery.'

From this date up to 1624, when the first mention of framed houses occurs, contemporary writers record little that throws any light on building methods in Plymouth Plantation. It does not seem likely that the Pilgrims learned much from the flimsy dwellings of the Indians which they often saw in their expeditions. About the Indian houses we have first-hand information from one Christopher Levett, 'His Maiesties Woodward of Somerset-shire, and one of the Councell of New-England', whose book, *A Voyage into New England, begun in 1623 and ended in 1624*, was published in 1628. He describes himself as 'but a young Scholler, though an ancient traviler by sea', and says of the Indians that 'their houses are built in halfe an houres space, being onely a few powles or boughes stucke in the ground and couered with the barkes of trees'. This supports Prof. Fiske Kimball's theory[1] that the first houses were not log cabins

[1] Fiske Kimball, *Domestic Architecture of the American Colonies*, p. 7 (New York, 1922).

copied from the Indians' dwellings, because, in this part of America at any rate, the Indians did not live in log cabins.

It was in November 1621 that the second instalment of Pilgrims arrived in the *Fortune* with thirty-five colonists on board, 'most of them lusty yonge men', according to Bradford,[1] though only a few of them appear to have stayed at Plymouth (cf. p. 120). Robert Cushman, who accompanied the party, delivered a *Discourse* at Plymouth during his short time there, in which he said: 'The country is yet raw; the land untilled; the cities not builded; the cattle not settled.' He returned to England in the *Fortune*, which, says Bradford, 'was speedily dispatcht away, being laden with good clapbord as full as she could stowe, and 2 hoggshedds of beaver and other skins. . . . The fraight was estimated to be worth near 500 li'. Another ship, the *Little James*, arrived with seven more colonists in May 1622. Its owner asked the colonists at Plymouth to 'goe in hand to fell trees and cleave them, to the end lading may be ready and our ship stay not'. In the next summer, 1623, came the *Anne* with about sixty recruits, 'some of them being very usefull persons', and some otherwise, according to Bradford.

'This ship was in a shorte time laden with clapbord, by the help of many hands', also with beaver and other furs, and Winslow was sent back in her 'to procure such things as were thought needfull for their present condition'.

The mention of timber being exported in the form of 'clapboards' (= very narrow boards such as are used in cooperage) is interesting; for it shows that, even in these very early days, the handful of settlers had organized some means of converting log-timber into marketable form, in order to sell it in England to pay for their many needs in manufactured goods. It seems probable that some of the party were (or had become) sawyers, perhaps under the direction of John Alden; and one wonders when the first saw-mill was established.

[1] *Op. cit.*, p. 121.

The only definite reference to their early equipment that I have been able to find occurs in William Wood's book: *New Englands Prospect: a true, lively, and experimentall description of that part of America commonly called New England, discovering the state of that Countrie, both as it stands to our new-come English Planters; and to the old Native Inhabitants. Laying down that which may both enrich the knowledge of the mind-travelling Reader, or benefit the future Voyager.* On p. 5 of that useful little work, published in 1634, he speaks of 'the English comming over so rawly and uncomfortably provided, wanting all utensils and provisions which belonged to the well being of Planters'. So he offers future colonists some hints as to the equipment needed, and in his list occur the following tools and materials needed at the time when he was writing (1634): 'All manner of Iron-wares, as all manner of nailes for houses . . . with Axes both broad and pitching axes. All manner of Augers, piercing bits, Whip-saws, Two-handed saws, Froes, both for the riving of Pailes and Laths, rings for Beetles heads, and Iron-wedges; though all these be made in the Countrey: (there being divers blacksmiths) yet being a heavy commodity, and taking but a little stoage, it is cheaper to carry such commodities out of England. Glasse ought not to be forgotten of any that desire to benefit themselves, or the Countrey: if it be well leaded, and carefully pack't up, I know of no commodity better for portage or sayle.'

Written so late as 1634, this passage would hardly apply to, say, 1623, when it seems unlikely that so many iron products could have been obtained locally. The list just quoted may be compared with another published by the Rev. Francis Higginson, M.A. Cantab., who came out to Salem as its first minister in 1629, and died there in the following year. The list appears as an appendix to his book *Notes from New-Englands Plantation*, published in 1630, and includes the following tools, *inter alia*, as essential to the equipment of each colonist: '1 Broad Axe, 1 Felling

Axe, 1 Steele Handsawe, 1 Whipsawe, 1 Hammer, 2 Augres, 4 Chissels, 2 Percers stocked, 1 Gimblet, 1 Hatchet, 2 Frowes, 1 Grindstone, 1 Pickaxe, Nayles of all sorts.' The list was prepared by one 'Master Graves, Engynere now there resident'.

The early writers make constant reference to the abundant natural resources of the colony in building materials. Capt. John Smith has already been quoted (p. 119) on this topic, and in his *General History of New England* (1624) he notes that the clapboards exported to England in 1621 were of 'Wainscot [i.e. oak] and Wallnut'. In another work he indicates that the Indians had some knowledge of timber felling, for he mentions 'how they make all their Instruments and Engines to cut downe Trees'.[1] In a later passage he compares the timber of Virginia with that of New England, and says that 'in New-England the trees are commonly lower, but much thicker and firmer wood, and more proper for shipping'.[2]

Higginson, writing in 1630, observes that: 'For Wood there is no better in the World I thinke, here being foure sorts of Oke differing both in the Leafe, Timber, and Colour, all excellent good. There is also good Ash, Elme, Willow, Birch, Beech, Saxafras, Juniper, Cipres, Cedar, Spruce, Pines and Firre that will yield abundance of Turpentine, Pitch, Tarre, Masts and other materials for building both of Ships and Houses.' As regards other materials, 'for Stone, here is plentie of Slates at the Ile of Slate Masachusets Bay, and Lime-stone, Free-stone, and Smooth-stone, and Iron-stone, and Marble-stone also in such store, that we have great Rockes of it, and a Harbour hard by'.

William Wood, writing in 1634, is more practical and precise in describing the timber resources of New England: 'Trees be not very thicke, though there be many that will serve for Mill posts, some being three foote and a halfe o're. . . . The chiefe and common Timber for ordinary use is Oake, and

---

[1] Capt. J. Smith, *Advertisements for the unexperienced Planters*, p. 15 (London, 1630). [2] *Ibid.*, p. 25.

Walnut: of Oakes there be three kindes, the red Oake, white, and blacke; as these are different in kinde, so are they chosen for such uses as they are most fit for, one kind being more fit for clappboard, others for sawne board, some fitter for shipping, others for houses.' He says that the local walnut is far more tough and durable than English walnut is. Cedar 'is commonly used for seeling of houses, and making of Chests, boxes and staves. The Firre and Pine be trees that grow in many places, shooting up exceeding high, especially the Pine: they doe afford good masts, good board, Rozin and Turpentine'.[1]

The mention of 'Mill posts' of timber in this extract is interesting, and will be referred to again in a later paragraph.

Prof. Fiske Kimball states[2] that 'in spite of the optimistic reports of John Smith, Higginson, and Morton, limestone was not abundant in the eastern part of Massachusetts'. (The first two of these authors have already been quoted in these pages.) William Wood, however, is more accurately informed: 'Some say there is Lime, but I must confesse I never saw any Limestone, but I have tried the Shels of Fish, and I find them to be good Lime.'

In default of specific documentary evidence and of surviving buildings, one must try to imagine the actual conditions of life in New England from 1620 to 1624, before coming to any conclusion as to the type of structure erected. The settlers at New Plymouth numbered only 102 on landing, and even in 1630 only about 400 or 500.[3] Of these only a small proportion were adult males, and the sickness of the first winter reduced the number of able-bodied men to six or seven towards its close.[4] For the first few years, there can never have been more than a handful of men available for house-building at any time, and there is reason to believe that skilled craftsmen were scarce.

---

[1] W. Wood, *New Englands Prospect*, pp. 17–18 (London, 1634).
[2] Fiske Kimball, *op. cit.*, pp. 35–6.
[3] J. Smith, *Advertisements,* &c., p. 29 (1630).
[4] N. Morton, *op. cit.*, p. 35.

62. WICKFORD, ESSEX

63. VANGE, ESSEX

Even a picked company of expert pioneers would have been hard put to it to carry out the necessary work of agriculture, fishing, and hunting in order to provide themselves with food. But when one remembers that there were numerous women and children to feed, that equipment was scanty, and that from the outset it was necessary also to create a substantial surplus of produce for trading purposes, then the survival and success of this hardy little band becomes phenomenal. It is known that the young and fit were originally selected for the venture; but even that fact hardly lessens their achievement, which becomes almost a miracle when one realizes that from the first landing, for fifty years at least, the Indians were a constant menace. This colony of a hundred persons had to form a standing army from its own number. Any one who is ignorant enough to regard the Pilgrims as a company of psalm-singing milksops has only to read the account of their early struggles to correct his ideas. For in spite of their Biblical language and their meeting-houses (at first serving also as forts), their record proves them to have been as tough as anything that England ever produced. Even John Smith, who had no love for them—as we have seen—admits that 'it is a wonder how they could subsist, fortifie themselves, resist their enemies, and plant their plants'.[1]

Arrangements for defence were at first improvised by Captain Miles Standish, who acted as Commander-in-Chief for many years, but soon compulsory military service was instituted, and in 1634 William Wood was able to write: 'No man must neglect to provide for himselfe, or those belonging to him, his munition for the defence of himselfe and the Countrey. For there is no man there that beares a head, but that beares military Armes: even Boyes of fourteene yeares of age, are practised with men in militarie discipline, every three weeks.'[2]

What sort of dwellings, then, are likely to have been erected

---

[1] J. Smith, *Advertisements*, &c., p. 17.
[2] W. Wood, *New Englands Prospect*, pp. 58–9.

by the men of Plymouth plantation during these early years of continual hardship and constant fighting, when their equipment was scanty and their financial resources most straitened? They were almost certainly constructed entirely of wood and they were quite certainly covered with thatch at first; that we know from documents. They appear to have had chimneys of wood,[1] with or without a lining of clay or mortar, at this period; they must have had doors, presumably 'batten' doors and not panelled doors, and it is extremely unlikely that any of them had glass windows. We may further assume that, at first, the floors were of beaten earth; and that no houses were more than one story high, though there may have been an attic in the roof. All this surmise is fairly plain sailing.

What we do not know is the method of construction of the wooden 'walls'. We may eliminate the 'log cabin' (p. 124), and assume that neither temporary dug-outs as built by the Massachusetts settlers (p. 122) nor the wigwams of the Indians (p. 124) were the kind of houses which stood in gardens within a palisade at New Plymouth. It is most unlikely that they were plastered externally, for we have already seen that lime was scarce, and though they may conceivably have been covered with 'wattle-and-daub', it seems to me far more likely that they were covered with the light 'clap-boards' which were being exported to England as early as 1621. As for the substructure, it seems reasonable to assume that it consisted of roughly-hewn timbers, perhaps braced diagonally as necessary, and formed of vertical trunks or studs let into stout sole-pieces and heads. My photograph of the English barn near Takeley in Essex (Fig. 24) gives a hint of a type of construction that might be adopted under even primitive conditions.

Prof. Fiske Kimball, however, makes a very good case against this supposition. 'In Plymouth Colony, Bradford and Winslow report that in 1621 a storm "caused much daubing of our

---

[1] Fiske Kimball, *op. cit.*, pp. 25–6.

houses to fall downe"', and they also mention the fire of 1623 (see p. 123 in this book). 'Since, as we shall see, framed houses were not in use in Plymouth even several years later, we must conclude that this wattle did not form the filling of a frame, but was on stakes or posts driven into the ground, as in the ordinary houses of the medieval period in England, which lingered in remote districts. The first buildings of timber in the colonies seem to have been of trunks or planks stood vertically, like palisades.... In 1629, when Ralph Sprague and his companions came to Charlestown, "they found there but one English palisadoed and thatched house". Of similar type would seem to have been the houses at Plymouth, seven years after its settlement, described by Isaack de Rasières as "constructed of hewn planks, with gardens also enclosed behind and at the sides with hewn planks". The phrase "*hewn* planks" excludes the possibility that the planks formed the covering of a frame, for in that case they would certainly have been sawn, like the "thick sawn plank" which formed the roof of the meeting-house.'[1]

In 1624 we begin to get some more light on the development of Pilgrim architecture. In that year Bradford mentions some disputes about wages, and refers to 'some of these [men] which came last, as the ship carpenter and sawiers, the salte man and others that were to follow constant imployments'. The arrival of sawyers obviously makes the construction of framed houses more feasible, but Bradford gives us a definite landmark when he adds that this recently arrived salt-man 'caused them to send carpenters to rear a great frame for a large house, to receive the salte and such other uses'. Two years later, Bradford records that the colonists 'had no ship-carpenter amongst them, neither know how to get one at presente; but they having an ingenious man that was a house-carpenter' he helped them to build a ship. Is this, one wonders, a reference to that John Alden who was immortalized by Longfellow, and does it not seem

[1] Fiske Kimball, *American Domestic Architecture*, p. 6.

probable that he was at that time a builder of framed and boarded houses?

There is another interesting entry in Bradford's *History* in this year, 1626: 'They gave the Governor, and 4 or 5 of the spetiall men amongst them, the houses they lived in; the rest were valued and equalised at an indifferent rate, and so every man kept his owne, and he that had a better alowed something to him that had a worse, as the valuation went.'

From the time of the *Mayflower* landing in 1620 until the settlement in Massachusetts Bay in 1628, there appear to have been few new arrivals beyond those already mentioned. Christopher Levett, on returning to England from New Plymouth in 1624, recommended emigration from the old country as a solution of the unemployment problem (a very modern touch) and thereby a reduction of parish relief at home, but his book was not published until 1628.[1] He makes the sage observation that—'It is a Countrey, where none can live except he either labour himselfe, or be able to keepe others to labour for him', and adds that it is no place for a man with a large family of small children.

Captain John Smith, writing of this period, says that 'those [i.e. the Pilgrim Fathers] in time doing well, divers others have in small handfulls undertaken to goe there, to be severall Lords and Kings of themselves; but most vanished to nothing'.[2]

All the early histories of this period show that great efforts were being continually made by the few colonists at Plymouth to create a trade to pay for their venture and maintain them in reasonable comfort. Captain Smith makes the surprising statement that up to the year 1624, 'New-England hath yeelded already by generall computation one hundred thousand pounds at the least' (and of course that represents a far larger sum to-day).[3]

---

[1] C. Levett, *A Voyage into New England*, pp. 28–35.
[2] J. Smith, *Travells & Observations*, p. 47 (1629).
[3] J. Smith, *General Historie*, p. 248 (1624).

It seems certain that the 'handfull' of Pilgrim Fathers cannot have handled all that trade, and presumably the estimate includes other enterprises in which merchant venturers were engaged.

The men of Plymouth Plantation traded largely with the Indians, almost from the outset, at first wholly by barter, until wampum came into use as a means of exchange. This useful commodity is believed to have been introduced by the Dutch, and it was the Dutch who were responsible for the next architectural venture on the part of the Pilgrim Fathers. In 1626 they bought Manhattan Island for the extravagant sum of 60 guilders (equivalent to about 24 dollars), and by the close of that year had erected thirty bark-covered houses there. 'New Amsterdam', as it was then called, was the predecessor of New York; but even in the middle of the eighteenth century its quayside looked far more like European Amsterdam, according to old prints, than any city I know, with its steep roofs and stepped gables. On 9 March 1627 letters[1] arrived at Plymouth from the Governor of Manhattan, Isaack de Rasières, 'written both in Dutch and French. The sum of the letters forementioned were, to congratulate the English here, taking notice of much that might engage them to a friendly correspondency and good neighbourhood, as the propinquity of their native country, their long continued friendship, etc., and desires to fall into a way of some commerce and trade with them'.[2] The Pilgrims were quick to take the hint. They had already resolved to build a small pinnace at Aptucxet (='little trap in the river'), a spot adjoining the Manamet river near its mouth in Buzzard's Bay, where the town of Bourne now stands. This site was only about twenty miles overland from New Plymouth, and as three-quarters of that distance could be travelled by boat up

---

[1] Translated in full in Bradford's *History*, p. 222.
[2] N. Morton, *New England's Memorial*, p. 88 in 1920 edition (in 'Everyman's Library').

creeks, goods had to be man-handled for only four or five miles between New Plymouth and Aptucxet. This avoided the long sail round Cape Cod and greatly reduced the journey to the Dutch settlements.

'Also for the saftie of their vessell and goods, they builte a house their, and kept some servants, who also planted corne, and reared some swine, and were allwayes ready to go out with the barke when ther was occasion. All whiche took good effecte, and turned to their profite.'[1]

A little later, De Rasières wrote home to Holland a description of a visit paid by him to Manamet (Aptucxet) and Plymouth. Of the former he writes that there is 'a house made of *hewn oak planks*, called Aptucxet, where they keep two men, winter and summer, in order to maintain their trade and possession. . . . From Aptucxet the English can come in six hours, through the woods, passing several little rivulets of fresh water, to New Plymouth'. His description of the houses of New Plymouth itself has already been quoted here (see p. 131).

The words italicized above (*gecloofde eyken plancken* in the original Dutch) may have referred either to the wooden frame of which the little building was constructed, or to the boarding with which it was covered. Mr. P. H. Lombard examined this question with great care in a very interesting article on the Aptucxet Trading Post,[2] and came to the conclusion that the reference is to the frame. He assumed that the exterior would be boarded, and that sawn boards would be used at that date, for De Rasières himself mentions the use of 'thick sawn planks' (*dicht gesaoged plancken*) in the roof of the fort at New Plymouth. Moreover, we have already seen that as early as 1624 there were sawyers among the colonists in New England.

On this assumption, the Trading Post at Aptucxet, built in

---

[1] Bradford, *op. cit.*, p. 222.
[2] P. H. Lombard, 'The First Trading Post of the Plymouth Colony', in *Old Time New England*, vol. xviii, no. 2, pp. 70–86 (Boston, 1927).

1627, has been rebuilt on its old foundations by the Bourne Historical Society, supported by the General Society of Mayflower Descendants. It was opened with considerable ceremony on 3 September 1930, when prayers were offered, the fire was rekindled on the ancient hearth, and the keys were handed over to the late Mr. P. H. Lombard (the President of the Bourne Historical Society) to whose long and patient researches[1] the accuracy of the restoration is due.

Of the original building nothing remains above the plinth, but the present reconstruction is interesting and even valuable to us in this study because it represents what modern American scholarship believes to be the type of building erected in the early days of the Pilgrims, some eight years before the assumed date of the oldest surviving houses described in the next chapter. The foundations, first excavated in 1852,[2] were of 'small flat stones, with natural faces, neatly laid in shell-lime cement, which still preserves considerable cohesion'. The later excavations by Mr. Lombard in 1926 revealed an L-shaped building, measuring 46 ft. by 27 ft. 6 in. over all, with two small cellars measuring 18 ft. by 8 ft. and 8 ft. by 8 ft. respectively, both about 6 ft. below ground-level. Between the two cellars was a huge chimney-stack containing two fire-places, back to back. The hearth of one fire-place was of flat field stones laid on white sand; the other hearth had no stones. The sides and backs of the fire-places were of bricks, 8 in. by 4 in. by $2\frac{1}{2}$ in. thick. Nearly in the centre of the long (south) wall a semi-circular platform of stones projected externally—obviously the door-step of the main entrance. As there was no sign of steps leading down into the cellars, it was assumed that they were approached by trap-doors in the wooden floor above. It was also assumed that the building was one story high, with an attic approached from the ground-floor rooms by means of a ladder. (In this respect it

---

[1] My own modest share in the work is explained in the Preface. M. S. B.
[2] See the *Proceedings of the Mass. Hist. Soc.*, vol. iii, pp. 252–6.

closely resembles 'Czar Peter's Hut' at Zaandam in Holland, built in 1632. See pp. 37–41, and Figs. 13–14 in this book.) The chimney was assumed to be massively built of brickwork with a simple capping, the 'walls' were of timber framing covered with boarding, and the roofs of oak shingles.

In regard to the windows, something beyond hypothetical evidence was available, for fragments of 'quarrels' (diamond-shaped panes) of glass set in lead were found in the excavations, together with part of a narrow iron hinge. Careful restoration of the glass, which was very thin, reveals the fact that the panes must have measured $5\frac{1}{2}$ in. in height and $4\frac{1}{2}$ in. in width. These dimensions may be compared with those of the English examples described and illustrated near the end of the previous chapter (Fig. 36).

We have already seen (p. 126) that William Wood, writing in 1634, mentions glass as a commodity which may profitably be shipped from England to America; so that Capt. John Smith's forecast of 1614, that 'Forges for glasse or iron' might be set up, had evidently not been fulfilled. Higginson, writing of the Massachusetts district in 1629, says: 'It is thought here is good Clay to make Bricke and Tyles and Earthen-Pots as needs to be. At this instant we are setting a Bricke-Kill on worke to make Brickes and Tyles for the building of our Houses.' But bricks were certainly being made in Virginia as early as 1611,[1] and though there seems to be no documentary evidence of their use in New Plymouth before 1643, it may be assumed that they were being made in that district by 1627. On the other hand, ten thousand bricks were shipped to Massachusetts Bay in 1628, but they may have been sent as ballast. The statement often made (e.g. in the *Encyclopaedia Britannica*, s.v. 'Brick') that the bricks used in New England up to 1650 were imported from England and Holland is not accepted by most modern scholars.[2]

---

[1] Bruce, *Economic History of Virginia*, vol. ii, pp. 134–43.
[2] See Fiske Kimball, *Domestic Architecture*, pp. 37–8.

65. RECONSTRUCTION (1930) OF THE TRADING-HOUSE AT APTUCXET (originally built 1627)

66. RECONSTRUCTION (1930) AT SALEM, MASS., OF THE HOUSES BUILT BY THE FIRST SETTLERS IN 1630. ('Lady Arbella's House' on right)

In the neighbouring Dutch colony of New Amsterdam brick-making began in 1628.

Higginson has something to say of the heating and lighting of the first houses in New England. 'Here is good living for those that love good Fires. And although New England have no Tallow to make Candles of, yet by the aboundance of the Fish thereof, it can afforde Oyle for Lampes. Yea our Pine-Trees that are the most plentifull of all wood, doth allow us plentie of Candles, which are verie usefull in a House; and they are such Candles as the Indians commonly use, having no other, and they are nothing else but the wood of the Pine-Tree cloven in two little slices something thin, which are so full of the moysture of Turpentine and Pitch, that they burne as cleere as a Torch. I have sent you some of them that you may see the experience of them.'[1]

In 1628 the Plymouth colonists founded a second trading-post, at Kennebec or Cushenoc, on the modern site of Augusta, the capital of Maine. Its position is marked by a tablet. In 1633 they built a third, called Matianuck, or Mettaneug, on the banks of the Connecticut River, where the town of Windsor now stands. Of this venture Bradford writes as follows: 'They having made a small frame of a house ready, and haveing a great new-barke, they stowed their frame in her hold, and bords to cover and finishe it, having nayles and all other provisions fitting for their use. . . . Comming to their place, they clapt up their house quickly, and landed their provissions, and left the companie appoynted, and sent the barke home, and afterwards palisadoed their house aboute, and fortified them selves better.'[2] Morton describes the same incident in very similar words, adding that it 'was done with great difficulty, not only of the Dutch, but also of the Indians'.[3] On the night of the 14th or 15th of August, 1635, Bradford records that 'a mighty storm of wind

[1] Higginson, *New Englands Plantation* (1630).
[2] Bradford, *op. cit.*, p. 301.   [3] N. Morton, *op. cit.*, p. 117.

and raine ... blew done sundry houses and uncovered others; diverce vessells were lost at sea.... It tooke of the borded roofe of a house which belonged to the plantation at Manamet and floted it to another place, the posts still standing in the ground'. Mr. Lombard is convinced that this statement does not refer to the trading post at Aptucxet, because in that building the posts would not stand in the ground, but would be let into a heavy timber sill or solepiece, resting on the stone plinth.

In 1638 Bradford notes that the Plymouth men were fortunate in their trading, 'with the first fruits of which they builte a house for a prison', clearly showing that the godly flock now contained a sprinkling of black sheep. At any rate, the prison marked a step forward towards civilization.

Meanwhile there had been an important settlement on Massachusetts Bay, destined to outnumber and eventually to absorb the older colony at Plymouth. Here the colonists came in several instalments, but the settlement had formed a definite organization by the year 1630. According to Capt. John Smith, the 1629 contingent consisted of 350 persons 'of good ranke, zeale, means and quality', admirably equipped for founding a plantation. On landing at Salem, 'they found some reasonable good provision and houses built by some few of Dorchester'. The party under John Winthrop which followed in the next summer included six or seven hundred people. The total number of English settlers in New England at the end of 1630, wrote John Smith, was more than 1,600, of whom 400 or 500 were the 'Brownists' [='Congregationalists'] of Plymouth Plantation, who 'lived well without want'. A patent of January 1630 states that there were 'near 300 people' in Plymouth at that time, but the number was swollen during the autumn by secessionists from Winthrop's colony.

According to Dr. John Brown,[1] who bases his statements on original authorities, the English population of New England

---

[1] Brown, *Pilgrim Fathers of New England*, pp. 293, 311.

had grown to nearly 4,000 in 1634, and to 26,000 in 1640; after which the rush of Separatist and Puritan refugees ceased for political reasons. The figures have some bearing upon the subject of our study, for the standard of building naturally developed with the growth of population, and with the consequent provision of sawmills, brick-kilns, glassworks, and iron-foundries—all of which followed in due course.

There were building craftsmen among the 1628–30 emigrants, but in 1634 William Wood could still write that among men 'most fit for these plantations' were 'an ingenious Carpenter, a cunning Ioyner, a handie Cooper, and a good Bricklayer, a Tyler and a Smith'. Evidently tiles were now replacing thatch and shingles as roofing materials. But some of the newcomers were not very expert builders judging by the sad case of the first Congregational church at Salem, as related by that frothy chronicler Edward Johnson. For when the Pilgrims commenced 'building the Temple for Gods worship there', only two men, 'Mr. Bright and Mr. Blaxton', could be found to hew stones for it 'in the Mountaines', and 'when they saw all sorts of stones would not fit in the building, as they supposed', they abandoned it as a bad job, one returning to sea and the other to farming. In spite of this temporary hitch, 'This Church of Christ, being thus begun, the Lord with the Water-spouts of his tender Mercy, caused to increase and fructify', and all's well that ends well. This expedition, Johnson notes, spent on 'Nayles, Glasse and other Ironworke for their meeting-houses, and other dwelling-houses before they could raise any meanes in the Country to purchase them, Eighteene thousand pounds'.

Soon after arriving in New England in 1630, Governor Winthrop 'ordered his house to be cut and framed' in Charlestown, and shortly afterwards he moved to Boston 'whither also the frame of the Governor's house was carried'. Only two years later he built another timber house at Cambridge, for it is recorded that in 1632 'the governour had removed the frame of his house, which he had set up at Newtown' [i.e. Cambridge].[1] But even before Winthrop's party arrived at Salem, a meeting-house had been erected, to serve also as a temporary hostel.

Apart from dwelling-houses, meeting-houses or churches, and trading-posts, water-mills and windmills must have been erected in New England at an early date. Writing about Boston in 1634, William Wood says that 'On the North-side is another Hill..., whereon stands a Winde-mill',[2] and in a later passage, discussing the ways of the Indians, he remarks that 'They doe much extoll and wonder at the English for their strange Inventions, especially for a Wind-mill, which in their esteeme was little less than the worlds wonder, for the strangenesse of his whisking motion, and the sharpe teeth biting the corne (as they terme it) into such small peeces; they were loath at the first to come neere to his long armes, or to abide in so tottering a tabernacle, though now they dare goe any where so farre as they have an English guide'.[3] He also mentioned Stony River, near Boston, 'upon which is built a water-milne', and he has already been quoted (p. 128) in reference to the availability of large timbers for mill-posts. The first windmill in New England was erected at Watertown and moved to Boston in 1632. Others followed at Salem and Plymouth in 1637, Lynn in 1664, and Ipswich in 1667.

There are still a number of old windmills standing in New England, admirably described and illustrated in a recent article by Mr. Rex Wailes, in *Old-Time New England* (vol. xxi, pp. 99–128, Boston, 1931). He names over twenty in varying states of repair. Many have perished by fire during the present century, including three out of four which stood in line along a hill at Nantucket. There were several more near Cape Cod, moved to Cataumet many years ago (Fig. 67). The ruined stone base of the Stone Mill at Newport, R.I., is the oldest known example.

---

[1] See Fiske Kimball, *op. cit.*, p. 10.
[2] *New-Englands Prospect*, p. 41.   [3] *Ibid.*, p. 87.

The remainder are of the eighteenth or early nineteenth century. There are also some examples in Long Island, of which the one illustrated (Fig. 68) from Easthampton is said to date from 1660. It resembles closely the Essex examples described in the previous chapter. The 'post-mill' is rare in America, the 'smock-mill' much more common. The conical roof found on many examples in Massachusetts is French rather than English, the pent-roof is English, and the round top distinctively East Anglian.

And now we may proceed to examine in some detail the oldest remaining buildings of New England, dating from about 1635.

VII. TIMBER HOUSES IN NEW ENGLAND
c. 1635–c. 1685

THE dates above represent approximately a definite epoch in the history of architecture in New England: the former indicating the age of the oldest surviving houses to which any date can be attributed, the latter the time at which the quasi-medieval forms introduced from East Anglia by the Pilgrim Fathers began to give way to the more academic forms of the Renaissance. But this second point of division is by no means arbitrary: as Prof. Fiske Kimball has stated, 'In many instances the medieval methods of the seventeenth century were continued long after 1700.... The wooden chimney and the leaded casement, as we have seen, long persisted in country districts, as did the lean-to and the overhang.'[1] Nevertheless it may be said, generally speaking, that about 1685 the Gothic type of design with steep roofs, gables, and casement windows gave place to the hipped roofs, formal classical features, and sash-windows favoured by Wren in England. It is with the earlier work that this book is concerned. Both in America and in England ample study has been devoted to the 'Colonial Period' of the eighteenth century; it is my object here to limit myself to the primitive buildings of the first settlers and to show their indebtedness to contemporary architecture in the districts of the Old Country from which they came. But it cannot now be claimed that America is indifferent, as she once was, to her oldest 'Ancient Monuments'. Every year the list of them is being increased, and many humble timber dwellings have been recently saved from destruction, and adequately recorded, by the devotion of New England antiquaries.

From 1635 to 1685 the various settlements in New England were steadily consolidating their position. If we are to trust the

---

[1] Fiske Kimball, *op. cit.*, p. 50.

figures quoted on p. 139, the comparatively small population (about 4,000) inhabiting the country in 1634 multiplied itself sixfold in six years. No records seem to be forthcoming as to the growth of population during the next half century, but it must have been large. We may assume that the later settlers came out better prepared for building and for colonization generally than the first Pilgrims, but even in the second half of the century life was not yet easy or secure. There was fierce fighting with the Indians in Massachusetts even so late as 1675, when the 'army' of the settlers was led by Governor Bradford's son, who had succeeded Miles Standish as 'commander-in-chief' of the military forces. Compulsory military service continued, and in 1643 the various 'plantations' (Massachusetts Bay, New Plymouth, Connecticut, New Haven, &c.) combined for mutual defence against the Indians, who had themselves formed a sort of federation. Two years later the force was composed of the following quotas of men: Massachusetts 190,[1] Plymouth 40, Connecticut 40, New Haven 30; total 300. Then there were occasional skirmishes with the French from Canada. It is therefore not surprising that Edward Johnson, writing in 1653, remarks that Boston is a strongly fortified town; and that many of the first governors' houses had a semi-fortified appearance. It is more remarkable that most of the surviving houses have so domestic and peaceful a character, considering the conditions under which their first occupants must have lived.

Perhaps the outstanding feature of the settlements was the intense importance which was attached to religion of one sort and other, but always of the ultra-Protestant variety throughout New England. The form of government seems to have been

[1] Johnson says that all except a few 'timerous' persons served 8 days in the year. There were twenty-six 'bands' in Massachusetts, of which most came from towns, but there were five county detachments, from Essex, Kent, Middlesex, Suffolk, and 'Northfolk'. It is noteworthy that these names recall the south-eastern counties of England, and thus provide one more link in the argument of this book.

in fact an extreme example of a theocracy. The parson was the central figure of each community, and in each plantation his home was generally the largest house after that of the governor himself, 'it being as unnaturall for a right New England man to live without an able Ministery, as for a Smith to work his iron without a fire'. It was for the training of ministers that Harvard College was originally founded in 1639, as is attested by the famous inscription over the gates: 'After God had carried us safe to New England, and wee had builded our houses, provided necessaries for our liveli-hood, and settled the Civill Government; One of the next things we longed for, and looked after was to advance Learning, and perpetuate it to Posterity; dreading to leave an illiterate Ministry to the Churches, when our present Ministers shall lie in the Dust.' The foundation of Yale College in 1700–1 as a 'school of the prophets' was another religious or sectarian movement. But Harvard retains no buildings older than 1720, and the earliest churches still remaining do not come either within the period covered by this chapter or the domestic architecture with which this book is concerned. Yet Johnson makes it clear that while 'The Lord with the Water-spouts of his tender Mercy' reduced the number of the Indians from 30,000 to 300—by means of warfare and disease—'this poore Church of Christ' grew to comprise 43 'Congregationall' churches with 7,750 members; and his *Historie of New England* treats each community as a unit round its church. He confines his account to Massachusetts, which at that period did not include Plymouth Plantation; and his account of the various towns gives us some idea of their state of development and their appearance about 1652.

Thus Charles Town, near Boston, 'hath a large Marketplace neer the water side built round with Houses, comly and faire, forth of which there issues two streetes orderly built with some very faire Houses, beautified with pleasant Gardens and Orchards, the whole Towne consists in its extent of about 150

Photo: Mr. Fred C. Small

67. WINDMILLS AT CATAUMET, MASS.

Photo: Mr. Kenneth Clark (Courtesy of the 'Monograph Series')

68. PAINE HOUSE AND WINDMILL, EASTHAMPTON, LONG ISLAND

IN NEW ENGLAND (c. 1635–c. 1685)   145

dwelling Houses. Their meeting house for Sabbath assembly stands in the Market-place, very comly built and large'.

Dorchester is 'almost like a serpent in shape ... her body and wings being chiefly built on, are filled somewhat thick of houses', numbering about 140. As for Boston, 'the chief Edifice of this City-like Towne is crowded on the Sea-bankes, and wharfed out with great industry and cost, the buildings beautifull and large, some fairely set forth with Brick, Tile, Stone, and Slate, and orderly placed with comly streets, whose continuall inlargement presages some sumptuous City'.

At Roxbury are about 120 'faire Houses', wide streets, and a church. Lynn has some 100 dwelling-houses, a meeting-house partly underground as it is on an exposed site, and 'an Iron Mill in constant use'. Watertown has 160 families, but 'their Sabbath-Assemblies prove very thin'. At Ipswich there are 140 families, and 'their meeting-house is a very good prospect to a great part of the town and beautifully built'. The inhabitants of 'Rouly', numbering about three-score families, 'were the first people that set upon making of cloth in this Western World; for which end they built a fulling-mill'. Elsewhere he observes that 'The Lord hath been pleased to turn all the wigwams, huts and hovels the English dwelt in at their first coming, into orderly, fair, and well-built houses, well-furnished many of them'. More specific are the statements that both at Reading and at Wenham there were a saw-mill and a corn-mill, and that there were ironworks at Braintree, where ironstone abounded. He tells us that among the staple commodities of New England are 'plank-board frames of houses', and that 'Carpenters, Joyners, Glaziers, Painters, Masons, Lime, Brick and Tilemakers' can find plenty of work to do.

But perhaps the most useful passage in an extremely wearisome book is the following description (referring to 'Wooburn') of the beginnings of a new settlement: 'This Town, as all others, had its bounds fixed by the General Court, to the contenese of four miles square . . . the grant is to seven men or [? of] good and honest report, upon condition, that within two year they erect houses for habitation thereon, and so go to make a Town thereof . . .; these seven men have power to give and grant out lands unto any persons who are willing to take up their dwellings within the said precinct. . . .

'These seven men ordered and disposed of the streets of the Town, as might be best for improvement of the Land . . . and' were helpful to the poorest sort, in building their houses. Thus was this Town populated, to the number of sixty families, or thereabout, and after this manner are the Towns of New England peopled.'

It would be pleasant to be able to say that this idyllic picture of early town-planning and communal solicitude represented New England in all its aspects. Unfortunately the greater part of Johnson's book is devoted to violent abuse of those fellow-colonists (and they were many) whose religious opinions happened to differ from his own. He cheerfully describes any opponent's faith as 'Hell's vomit', and is particularly bitter about a lady who had received a call to preach. It was in this spirit that certain of these refugees from intolerance in England received 'many of the pernicious sect, called Quakers' in 1657 in Massachusetts, where they were persecuted for 'their corrupt and damnable doctrines'; and it was because of this bigoted attitude that sundry offshoots from New Plymouth and Massachusetts were planted at Rhode Island and elsewhere. The treatment meted out to Baptists and Quakers included 'scourging, boring of tongues, cutting of ears, and in rare cases capital punishment'. Salem at one period specialized in the hanging of 'witches'—young girls convicted of dabbling in palmistry. Any man detected in the act of kissing his wife, or vice versa, on the Sabbath was punished by the magistrates; while fines or corporal punishment, the usual penalty for work or sport on Sunday, could be replaced by the death penalty if the sin was committed 'proudly, presumptuously and with a high hand'. Such was New England up to the end of our period: a colony containing a high proportion of educated, earnest, and well-meaning people who unfortunately chose sometimes to combine, with their many virtues and their tenacious character, an appalling lack of common tolerance. Yet these 'jarring sects' and discordant communities hung together in a loose federation for purposes of defence, Plymouth was absorbed by Massachusetts, and towards the end of the century there was for a short time a 'Dominion of New England'. Thus there is every reason for considering the domestic architecture of that region as a definite group.

It might hardly be expected that these dour settlers, prepared at any moment to torture a heretic or fight the Indians, would devote much attention to the gentler arts of life, and one is not surprised that a stark and uncompromising simplicity marks their earliest surviving buildings. But we must remember that their religious leaders were not mere uneducated fanatics with no background of culture. They were without exception graduates of Cambridge or Oxford, they were born into the splendid age of Shakespeare, and they had all vacated their livings in the Church of England for the sake of their convictions. Their occasionally rigid and uncharitable outlook was the result of the hard treatment which drove them across the Atlantic, and it is reasonable to assume that the simplicity of their dwellings in New England was the outcome of circumstances rather than of choice. Yet this very simplicity has its own charm, and its 'Gothic' directness makes an appeal quite as strong as the more academic and sophisticated refinement of American 'Colonial' architecture of the eighteenth century.

But one must not exaggerate the austerity of life as it was lived in New England. There were many people of rank among the colonists, jealous of their privileges in spite of the prevailing democratic atmosphere. It was necessary, even so early as 1651, to prohibit the lower classes from wearing gold or silver lace, 'great boots', 'silk or tiffany hoods or scarves' and so on; and this not because such vanities were unpleasing in the sight of the Lord, for they were judged to be 'allowable to persons of greater estates or more liberal education'! Armorial bearings were freely used in Boston from about 1660 onwards, and a visit to any of the great American museums shows that the larger houses of New England, from the middle of the seventeenth century at any rate, were well provided with every comfort and refinement known at that time.

Although an attempt has been made in this book (pp. 181–2) to provide a chronology of the surviving wooden houses of the seventeenth century (more precisely from 1635 to 1685) in New England, the reader will realize that exact dating of these humble dwellings is almost as difficult as in Old England itself (cf. p. 58). But whereas in England no special attention has ever been devoted to this rather obscure architectural byway, in America there has lately been a concentration of scholarly research on the buildings of the Pilgrim Fathers and their successors.[1] As a result, most of the outstanding examples have been restored, and recorded for students in excellent photographs and measured drawings; while the admirable books of Prof. Fiske Kimball[2] and Mr. Kelly[3]—to name only two out of a much larger number—contain descriptions and illustrations which are very valuable to an English student. Indeed, Mr. Kelly's volume is the most careful and complete study, known to the present writer, of vernacular architecture in any country. It is a model of its kind, and one could wish that the wooden houses of East Anglia could have found so patient an admirer to record their vanishing charms for posterity. At any rate, all

[1] The latest work, published very recently, is J. M. Howells' *Lost Examples of Colonial Architecture* (New York, 1931). It illustrates many fine houses of the Pilgrim Period which have been demolished or altered in modern times.
[2] Fiske Kimball, *Domestic Architecture of the American Colonies* (New York, 1922).
[3] J. F. Kelly, *Early Domestic Architecture of Connecticut* (Yale Univ. Press, 1924).

this research has produced far more documentary and other (inferential) evidence for dating the American examples than we can show for contemporary English houses of the kind. In the table on pp. 181-2 a distinction is drawn between authenticated and assumed dates.

It is very improbable that professional architects were employed on these comparatively small houses before the date 1685, selected as a suitable limit for the present study. In fact, Prof. Fiske Kimball states categorically that it was not until nearly the end of the eighteenth century that 'men of professional training in architecture first appeared in America'.[1] Perhaps the best explanation of the successive sources of inspiration prior to modern times is given by Mr. Tallmadge.[2] 'Information', he writes, 'came from three sources: memory, architectural books, architects themselves.' During the period 1635-85 men built mainly from their memory of the homes they had left behind in England or even perhaps in Holland. But certainly before the end of the century, and possibly in its middle third, they must have begun to use some of the little manuals of architecture and building which were then being widely published in England and other European countries. Elsewhere I have described more fully these often amusing manuals,[3] and there is some reference to them in an earlier chapter of the present work. Such books came to be widely used by scholarly patrons or by intelligent craftsmen, so that it may even be true, allowing for some exaggeration, that 'the carpenter of those days would have been as helpless without his handbook as without his ripsaw'.[4] There is no doubt of the existence of numbers of skilled craftsmen by the middle of the century. 'Among the trades mentioned in the early Court Records of the New Haven Colony we find the following:

[1] Fiske Kimball, *op. cit.*, p. 146.
[2] T. E. Tallmadge, *Story of Architecture in America*, p. 34.
[3] M. S. Briggs, *The Architect in History*, pp. 240-1, 296-7, &c.
[4] Tallmadge, *op. cit.*, p. 35.

sawyers, carpenters, "joyners", thatchers, brickmakers, plasterers, "ryvers of clapboards, shingles, and lathes", "naylers", and "massons". Owing to the system in vogue at the time, nearly every man who did not till the soil had a trade, and the artisans of various sorts were highly specialized and skillfully trained, thanks largely to the prevalent custom of serving out long apprenticeships.'[1]

If much of the surviving work is simple to the point of crudity, the explanation must be sought rather in the lack of tools, the rigours of the time, and the severity of Puritan taste rather than in any deficiencies on the part of the craftsman, whose capabilities are evident enough in many surviving buildings, and in fragments of many others now destroyed which obviously were carefully and even elaborately finished.

Prof. Fiske Kimball[2] quotes from the *Collections of the Massachusetts Historical Society* (1865, vol. vii, pp. 118–20) an interesting 'prescription', as he calls it, for a new house, written by its prospective owner, Deputy-Governor Samuel Symonds of Ipswich, in 1638. This indicates the kind of instructions which would be supplied to a builder at that time:

'Concerning the frame of the house . . . I am indifferent whether it be 30 foote or 35 foote longe; 16 or 18 foote broade. I would have wood chimnyes at each end, the frames of the chimnyes to be stronger than ordinary, to beare good heavy load of clay for security against fire. You may let the chimnyes by [? be] all the breadth of the howse if you thinke good; the 2 lower dores to be in the middle of the howse, one opposite the other. Be sure that all the dorewaies in every place be soe high that any man may goe vpright vnder. The staiers I think had best be placed close by the dore. It makes noe great matter though there be no particion vpon the first flore; if there be, make one biger than the other. For windowes let them not be over large in any roome, & as few as conveniently may be; let

[1] Kelly, *op. cit.*, p. 3.   [2] Fiske Kimball, *op. cit.*, pp. 11–12.

all have current shutting draw-windowes, having respect both to present & future use. I thinke to make it a girt howse will make it more chargeable than neede; however the side bearers for the second story, being to be loaden with corne &c. must not be pinned on, but rather eyther lett in to the studds or borne vp with false studds, & soe tenented in at the ends. I leave it to you & the carpenters. In this story over the first, I would have a particion, whether in the middest or over the particion vnder, I leave it. In the garrett noe particion, but let there be one or two lucome windowes, if two, both on one side. I desire to have the sparrs reach downe pretty deep at the eves to preserve the walls the better from the wether, I would have it sellered all over and soe the frame of the howse accordengly from the bottom. I would have the howse stronge in timber, though plaine & well brased. I would have it covered with very good oake-hart inch board, for the present, to be tacked on onely for the present, as you tould me. Let the frame begin from the bottom of the cellar & soe in the ordinary way vpright, for I can hereafter (to save the timber within grounde) run vp a thin brick worke without. I think it best to have the walls without to be all clapboarded besides the clay walls.'

A much more summary contract dated 1640,[1] for a small house to be built by John Davys, joiner, for William Rix, weaver, reads as follows: 'One framed house 16 foot long & 14 foot wyde, wth a chamber floare finisht, summer & ioysts, a cellar floare wth ioysts finisht, the roofe and walles Clapboarded on the outsyde, the Chimney framed without dawbing to be done with hewen timber.' The contract price for this building was £21.

The various constructional details mentioned in these two descriptions will be explained later in the chapter, but at this point attention may be drawn to the unusual familiarity with such things displayed by Symonds, who was no craftsman, but an official. It may also be noted that his house was one of the

[1] From *Trans. of the American Antiquarian Soc.* (1885, vii, p. 302).

larger kind built in these early years, consisting as it did of two stories besides attic and cellars, with two rooms on each floor. Rix's house, on the other hand, was a mere cottage of one room with an attic or loft above.

These two examples represent the commonest types of dwelling erected in New England during the middle years of the seventeenth century. The house erected in 1643 by Winthrop, one of the leading men in Massachusetts and the founder of ironworks at Braintree and Lynn, belonged to the former type; while most of the less important colonists probably occupied cottages resembling Rix the Weaver's. As noted in the previous chapter, the homes of the parsons were usually of the larger kind: thus two ministers' dwellings mentioned by Waters[1] measured respectively 38 ft. by 17 ft. and 36 ft. by 25 ft., each being two stories high.

The planning of these houses was very simple and hardly varied even in the different localities. The one-room type, assuming that it had a staircase at all, usually resembled in plan the Thomas Lee House (1664) at East Lyme, Conn., which is illustrated in its original form, before extension, on Fig. 71 A, or the Hathaway House at Salem (late 17th cent.). These two plans are almost identical. On the ground floor (='first floor' in U.S.A.) an entrance porch, containing a staircase leading to the upper floor, fills the angle between the enormous mass of the chimney-stack and the single living-room or 'fire-room', which also served as a kitchen in these primitive homes. This porch diverts the force of the wind from the actual door into the living-room, which opens out of it.

In the Older Williams House at Wethersfield, Conn. (c. 1680), there are two rooms of equal size on each floor, with the staircase-porch and the great chimney-stack in the centre of the house. This produces a symmetrical building and a more satisfactory grouping externally (see Figs. 71 B, 72, and 79).

[1] In *Homes of the Puritans* (Essex Inst. Hist. Collections, 1897, xxxiii, 50–1).

Courtesy of Mr. J. F. Kelly and Yale University Press

69. STONE HOUSE, GUILFORD, CONN.

Courtesy of Mr. J. F. Kelly and Yale University Press

70. STARR HOUSE, GUILFORD, CONN.

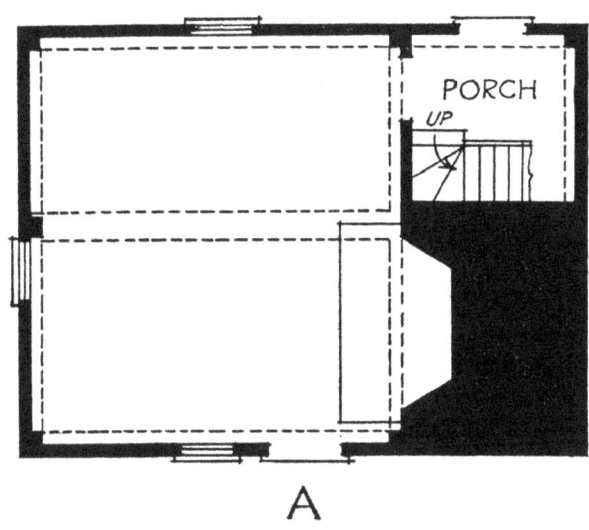

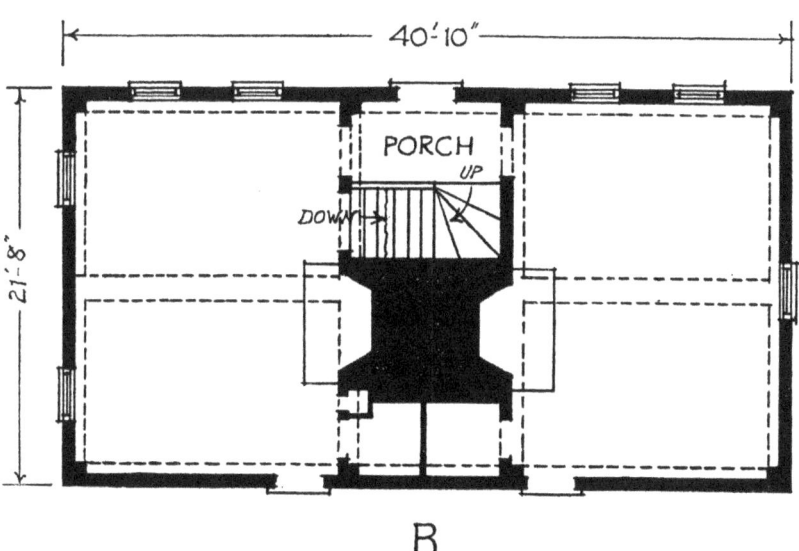

71. Plans of (A) Thos. Lee House, E. Lyme, Conn., before alteration, and (B) Older Williams House, Wethersfield, Conn. (Adapted by permission from J. F. Kelly's 'Early Domestic Architecture of Connecticut')

The Capen House at Topsfield, Mass. (1683), closely resembles the last-mentioned example in plan, but the two rooms are not precisely equal in size (see Figs. 93, 94).

It was apparently in the last quarter of the seventeenth century that the desire for increased comfort, seclusion, and refinement led to the addition of a 'lean-to' or 'ell' to the original plan. This room served generally as a working kitchen or scullery and was very low, the steep main roof being carried over it at a slightly easier pitch. This feature soon became characteristic of the period (see Figs. 69, 70, &c.).

A comparison of these simple dwellings with the English examples illustrated in Chapter V can leave no doubts in the reader's mind of their ancestry, for the resemblance to the old houses of Essex and the neighbouring counties is too obvious to be ignored. The plan of the New England cottage, as well as the structural methods by which it was erected, was borrowed direct from the small area of England already described.

It may be added that, though plans were practically uniform, there was a good deal of variation in other respects between the different localities and settlements. Such variations were due partly to the nature of building materials available, partly according to the district of England from which the colonists (and especially the craftsmen) had come, and partly owing to the relative accessibility of the different sites from the chief centres of trade and population. Thus 'dug-outs' in earth banks, roofed with branches and sods, were in use among the founders of Wethersfield in 1635, long after framed houses had become common farther east; and in the same way, architectural refinements and improvements crept slowly up the rivers and into the forests, some little distance behind the settler with his axe and his gun. Framing methods were also borrowed direct from England, but American scholars have explored this avenue of research so thoroughly that data from New England in this respect are more plentiful than in the old country.

IN NEW ENGLAND (c. 1635–c. 1685) 155

The substructure of the house consisted of a plinth of stone, usually local field-stone. Mr. Kelly[1] says that in Connecticut stone was 'invariably' used for this purpose and also for the cellar walls. Sometimes clay was used as a matrix in building these walls and plinths; sometimes they were built dry. Occasionally lime made from pounded oyster-shells was used for the purpose. The earliest known example of a brick plinth in Connecticut occurs at Wethersfield in 1730.[2] Cellars were very seldom used in English houses at this date, but in America they seem to have been built almost from the outset. They were always very low, being utilized for storage and not for habitation. Access to them was generally provided by means of outside steps; but at the Older Bushnell House, Saybrook, Conn. (1678–79), the Older Williams House at Wethersfield, Conn. (c. 1680), and many others, internal stairs were used. At Aptucxet, as we have seen, there was probably a hatchway (p. 135).

On the stone plinth rested the main sill of the framing, which we may now proceed to consider. The size of the timbers used was enormous, and must have entailed great difficulty in handling at a time when labour was certainly scarce, and lifting tackle probably not available. Oak seems to have been invariably employed throughout the seventeenth century, in America as in England. Kelly mentions one rare exception where hard pine was used. Sawing and hewing was entirely carried out by hand at first, but saw-mills at Reading and Wenham, Mass., are mentioned in Johnson's book already quoted (see p. 145), published in 1652, and a mention of another occurs in the Connecticut records of 1653. Prior to that date or thereabouts, the conversion of timber was done by means of whip-saw in saw-pits. The broad axe was used to finish timber where we nowadays should use a plane, and a wonderfully smooth surface was produced. Chamfering was done with the same tool. In the New Haven records for 1640 occurs this passage:[3] 'Price

[1] Kelly, op. cit., p. 69.   [2] Ibid., p. 206.   [3] Quoted by Kelly, op. cit., p. 24.

for hewing sills, beames, plates, and such like timber, square hewen to build with, not above a penny a foote running

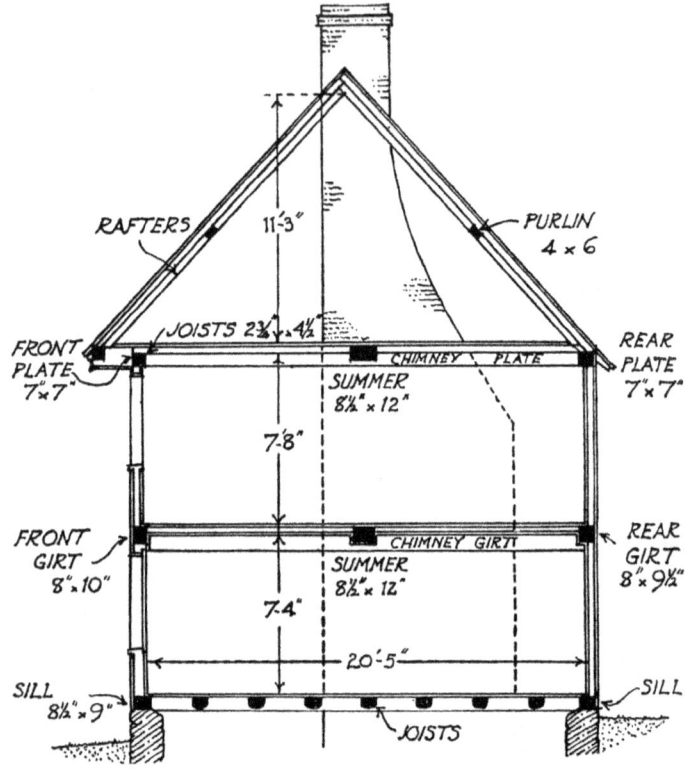

72. SECTION OF OLDER WILLIAMS HOUSE, WETHERSFIELD, CONN.
(Adapted, by permission, from J. F. Kelly's 'Early Domestic Architecture of Connecticut')

measure. Sawing by the hundred not above 4s. 6d. for boards, 5s. for plancks, 5s. 6d. for slitworke and to be paid for no more than they cutt full and true measure.'

The following description of the various parts of a house-frame and their functions may be more clearly understood by a reference to Fig. 72, which is based upon Kelly's Fig. 36. This

IN NEW ENGLAND (c. 1635–c. 1685) 157

is a transverse section of the Older Williams House at Wethersfield, Conn. (c. 1680), also illustrated in Figs. 71 B and 79.

As in contemporary English practice, the sill was a heavy oak

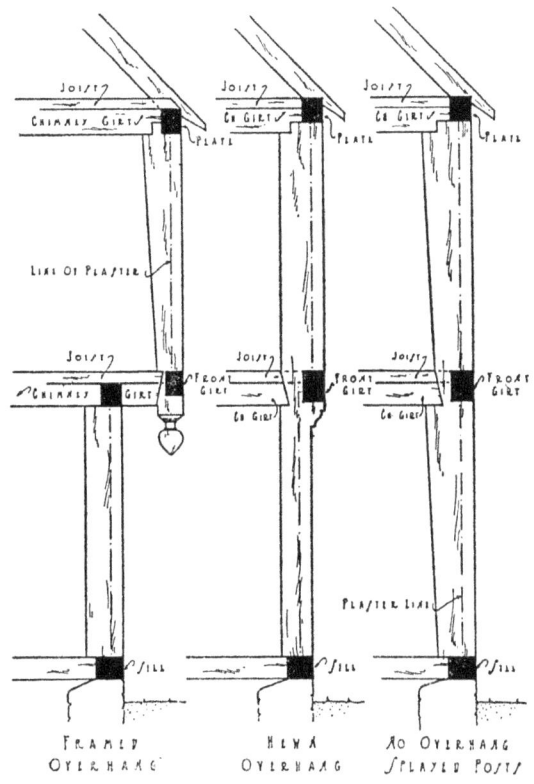

73. DETAILS OF POSTS AND FRAMING
(Courtesy of Mr. J. F. Kelly and the Yale University Press)

member, oblong in section, bedded on its broader side, the smaller measurement usually being 5 in. or more. At the angles it was generally mortised, tenoned, and pinned; but Kelly[1] illustrates a rare and ingenious angle joint found in a few examples.

[1] Kelly, *op. cit.*, fig. 25.

Into the sill were framed horizontally the ends of the ground-floor (='first floor' in U.S.A.) joists. Occasionally, however, these joists were built into the stone foundation-walls, and the sills laid on the top of them. These joists were usually rough logs, 6 in. to 10 in. in diameter, with the upper surface levelled to receive the floor-boards, while the lower side was rough, with the bark left on, showing in the cellar (if any). Sometimes a beam, known as a 'cellar-summer', is used in larger houses, to bridge the cellar and thus to reduce the span and consequently the size of the floor-joists.

At each angle of the house there was a corner-post, tenoned into the sill by means of a tusk-tenon and mortise joint pinned with a wooden peg. Unless there was a framed 'overhang', as described hereafter, the corner post ran up to the base of the roof in one piece.

In the 'two-room' type of house (see Fig. 71, B) there were two intermediate posts on each of the longer sides of the house, making eight posts in all. The latter were known as 'front and rear chimney posts' according to their position. In the earliest houses all these posts 'flare' or increase in size at each floor-level, so that in a two-story house each post would have a double 'flare'. This detail was a direct survival of the old English half-timber tradition and was used to provide a better bearing for the ends of the various beams. Some posts are shouldered, not flared. Fig. 73, reproduced from Kelly's Fig. 27, illustrates various types of posts, the one on the right having a double 'flare'. The size of these posts was usually 8 in. by 10 in. up to 12 in. by 10 in., but might be increased in the greater dimension to produce a single or double flare. Thus a post measuring 8 in. by 14 in. at sill level might be 8 in. by 14 in. or more at roof level.

At the level of the upper floor or first floor (='second floor' in U.S.A.) of houses more than one story high, occur the 'girts', a name of obvious significance. The girts correspond to the sills at the lower level, and the ends of the upper-floor joists are similarly framed into them; but are more massive, as a rule, than the sills. They are known respectively as 'front girt', 'rear girt', and 'end girts' according to their position.

In the two-room houses there are also 'chimney girts' on each side of the central stack. The end girts and chimney girts in such houses are stronger than the front and rear girts, because they have to carry the ends of the heavy beams known as 'summers' which traverse each room parallel with the long front of the house. A comparison of a number of girts shows a range of size from $3\frac{1}{2}$ in. by 5 in. up to $11\frac{3}{4}$ in. by 8 in. Similarly, a series of summers shows a range from about 11 in. by 8 in. upwards.

The ends of the upper floor joists were notched into the summers, but the summer is often connected to the girt by the ingenious joint illustrated in Kelly's book. These joists were much smaller than those in the cellar (except where a cellar-summer is found) and were carefully planed on all sides, as they showed in the living-rooms beneath. Usually their lower edges were chamfered or beaded. They were spaced about 20 in. centre to centre, and averaged about 10 sq. in. in section; common sizes ranging from $2\frac{3}{4}$ in. by $3\frac{1}{2}$ in. up to $2\frac{1}{2}$ in. by $4\frac{1}{2}$ in.

At the level of the first story (='second story' in U.S.A.) ceiling in two-story houses, or the ground story (='first story' in U.S.A.) ceiling in one-storey houses, there was a horizontal framing of timbers known as 'plates'. They corresponded to the girts below, so that in a two-room house we have 'chimney-plates' as well as 'front plate', 'rear plate', and 'end plates'. Sometimes they were called 'second girts', and occasionally they were made very wide so that they overhung the vertical face of the framed 'walls' and gave a protective eaves or cornice.

Between these various posts, sills, girts, and plates—occasionally stiffened with stout curved or diagonal braces—there was a system of vertical studs, usually about $2\frac{1}{2}$ in. by 3 in., spaced about 20 in. apart and framed flush with the main members. In

Connecticut there are a few rare examples (e.g. Norton House, Guilford) where, instead of studs, planks, from 10 in. to 12 in.

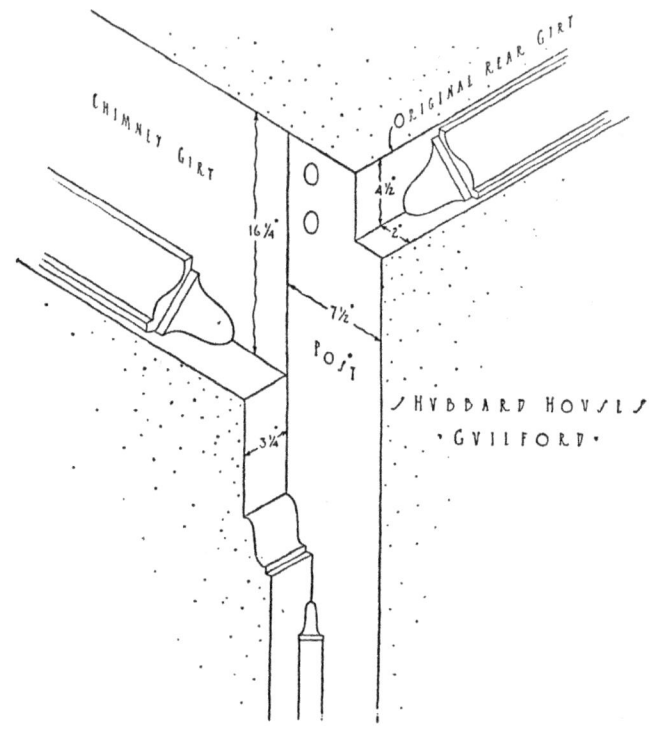

74. DETAIL OF CHIMNEY GIRT, ETC., HUBBARD HOUSE, GUILFORD, CONN.
(Courtesy of Mr. J. F. Kelly and the Yale University Press)

wide and from $1\frac{1}{4}$ in. to 2 in. thick, are used, let into rebates in the main framing and pinned to it with stout oak pegs.[1]

Before proceeding to study the roof-framing, mention must be made of the so-called 'overhang' or jetty, another characteristic feature derived direct from England. In this book, overhangs from England are illustrated in Figs. 19, 26, 46, 47, 59, and from America in Figs. 70, 80, 81, 89, 90, 92, 93 (see also

[1] Kelly, *op. cit.*, pp. 40–1 and Fig. 46.

Courtesy of Mr. J. F. Kelly and Yale University Press

75. OLDER COWLES HOUSE, FARMINGTON, CONN.,
showing framed overhang and drop

Courtesy of Mr. J. F. Kelly and Yale University Press

76. HYLAND-WILDMAN HOUSE, GUILFORD, CONN.,
showing hewn overhang

the section in Fig. 72). Kelly attributes its introduction into Connecticut to the Yorkshire carpenters who settled there,[1] but as a matter of fact this feature is far more common in southeastern England than in Yorkshire. Its use, however, is not confined to any one part of England, and it is found in most parts of Europe where timber-framed houses occur, e.g. in France, Germany, and elsewhere. In Chapter V (pp. 63–6) I have suggested various possible explanations of this curious feature; and there seems to be no need to devise others for New England. If indeed it was evolved as a means of obtaining larger rooms upstairs in the narrow streets of crowded towns, it is conceivable that town-bred craftsmen introduced this urban and perhaps unsuitable fashion into remote country farmhouses just as some of the colonists' wives offended against common-sense with their high heels and other vanities in the midst of these half-civilized regions.

In New England we find the same type of framed overhang as in the mother-country, occurring generally on the front, though the gables were at the *ends* of the house, whereas in our old towns the gables usually face the street. Chandler[2] repeats a legend that the overhang was introduced as a defensive feature from which approaching Indians could be fired upon; but slyly adds that the Indians must have displayed a singular courtesy in always approaching the house from the front, not from the end or rear. But several houses have an end-overhang and others again have overhanging end gables (Fig. 79, 90, 92, 93). New England possesses some interesting examples of turned and carved drops, pendants, or pendills, as used under the corner posts of these framed overhangs. The Capen House at Topsfield has drops under the front overhang and the end gables (Fig. 93).

But America also produced a type of overhang not found in England, the 'hewn overhang', where wide girts and flared or

[1] *Ibid.*, p. 62.   [2] Chandler, *The Colonial House*, p. 83.

shouldered posts were used to make the outer face of an upper story project from 3 to 6 in. in front of the story beneath (Fig. 76). So small a projection has little aesthetic value, and compares unfavourably with the bold effect of the framed overhang from which it was presumably imitated. Some of the English examples illustrated in this book (e.g. Figs. 19, 26) have only a slight overhang, but the structural system in these cases is more evident than in the case of the American hewn overhang.

We now come to the framing of the roof, which in New England as in the mother-country is an integral part of the house-frame. A reference back to Fig. 72 will make the following paragraph clear. For many years after the Pilgrims landed in 1620, roofs assumed the simplest possible form, known as the span roof or pitched roof, and consisting of two steep slopes rising from the front and rear plates to a central ridge, with a plain gable at each end. The single chimney-stack pierced this roof, near one end in the one-room type of house; at or near the centre in the two-room type.

The length of the rafters between plate and ridge being considerable (usually from 12 to 20 ft.), they were supported by one or more purlins, beams running parallel with the front and rear walls of the house and themselves carried by principal rafters spaced 8 or 9 ft. apart (see also Fig. 25). In the Harrison-Linsley House (1690) at Branford, Conn., the principal rafters measure $4\frac{1}{2}$ in. by $6\frac{3}{4}$ in., the purlins 3 in. by 4 in. In the Older Williams House at Wethersfield, Conn. (1680, see Fig. 72), the principals are 4 in. by 8 in., the purlins 4 in. by 6 in., and the common rafters 4 in. in diameter.

In another type, stout common rafters were used with collars, the rafters measuring 5 in. or 6 in. square and being spaced at 3 ft. or 4 ft. centres. These rafters were hewn to a smooth face in the larger houses, and left rough with the bark showing in the small houses, where the attics were frequently used as bedrooms. The feet of the rafters were secured to the plates by means of an ingenious double notch and then pegged. Where collars were used, they were joined to the rafters by means of a mortise and tenon or by dovetail halving, and secured with oak pegs about $\frac{3}{4}$ in. in diameter. The roof of the Moulthrop House (now demolished) at East Haven had small purlins $1\frac{3}{4}$ in. by $2\frac{1}{2}$ in., spaced only a foot apart, which served as thatch-poles.

The pitch or slope of the early span roofs was steep, on an average about 50°, as in England at the same date. Kelly[1] states that the pitch of the roof of Whitfield House, Guilford, Conn. (1639), was originally 60°, but this is unusually steep. At Hempstead House, New London, Conn. (1643), and at the Capen House, Topsfield, Mass. (1683), the slope is about 50°. As time progressed, the pitch was gradually reduced to about 45°. Before long, gables were introduced at right angles to the main ridge, as at the Capen House and the famous 'House of the Seven Gables' at Salem.

Another early type of roof, commonly called the 'rainbow' roof, is found near Cape Cod and the south shore of Massachusetts Bay; it has slightly convex surfaces which suggest the curving lines of a ship's hull, and presumably has curved rafters on purlins. It may be true that such roofs were designed and built by ship's carpenters; but something approaching the same type is to be found among thatched cottages in East Anglia.

From this form it is an easy transition to the type of roof which is always known in New England as the 'gambrel', that is, a roof with two slopes, steep in the lower portion above the eaves, much less steep in the upper portion between the change of slope and the ridge. The utilitarian advantage of such a type is obvious: it provides a spacious attic with adequate headroom, so there is no doubt as to its purpose. Its origin is much more obscure. A roof of this form, commonly associated with the name of the architect François Mansart, is found in France in the sixteenth century; and a very early but isolated example occurs

[1] Kelly, *op. cit.*, p. 58.

in the Tudor roof over the Great Hall of Hampton Court Palace. It appeared in America some time in the second half of the seventeenth century, but it is impossible to date its arrival more precisely. As already remarked in Chapter V, it is quite inaccurate to state, as Chandler does,[1] that 'the gambrel roof is

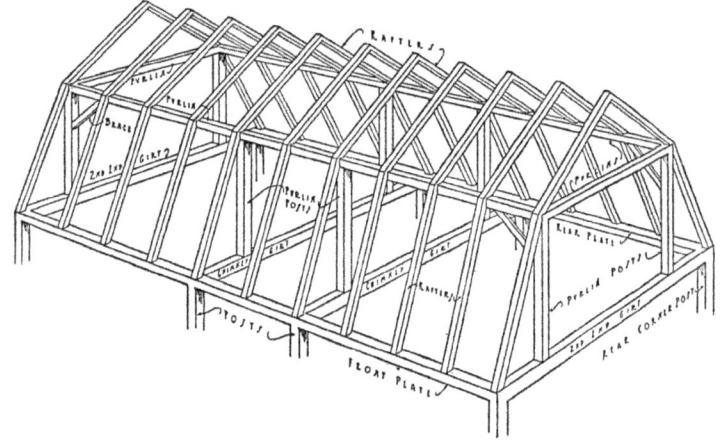

77. TYPICAL GAMBREL ROOF FRAMING
(Courtesy of Mr. J. F. Kelly and the Yale University Press)

almost unknown in England'. Even among the comparatively few East Anglian examples illustrated in Chapter V, quite a number have gambrel roofs. But their dates are doubtful, and one cannot trace a clear line of influence here on the New England buildings.

The word gambrel probably has a derivation from Old Norman-French.[2] It appears as early as 1715 in the *London Gazette*, an official publication, referring to the joint in the upper part of a horse's hind leg. By analogy, the double slope of the gambrel roof obtained its name, and the word appears in American books in that sense from the middle of the nineteenth century.

[1] Chandler, *The Colonial House*, p. 47.
[2] *New English Dictionary*, s.v. 'Gambrel'.

IN NEW ENGLAND (c. 1635–c. 1685)

The classical example occurs in Wendell Holmes's *Autocrat of the Breakfast Table* (Chapter XII):

> Know Old Cambridge? Hope you do.—
> Born there? Don't say so! I was, too.
> (Born in a house with a gambrel roof,—
> Standing still, if you must have proof.—
> 'Gambrel'?—'Gambrel'?—Let me beg
> You'll look at a horse's hinder leg,—
> First great angle above the hoof,—
> That's the gambrel; hence gambrel-roof.)

It is equally uncertain when the hipped roof was introduced into New England. Fiske Kimball considers that it appeared late in the seventeenth century,[1] that is, a little later than the first English examples; but Kelly states that in Connecticut it is characteristic of a much later date, 1800 or even later.[2] Examples of the 'hipped gambrel' are also found in America, as in England, but these are probably later than 1685.

The steep pitch of the early roofs is accounted for partly by the covering materials employed. There is no doubt that the first buildings were mainly roofed with thatch, boards, or shingles. Thatch was certainly used during the first fifty years of New England's history, as records of the various plantations clearly prove. There is one reference, for example, to 'a skilfull thatcher' (1640), another to the tools employed (1662), and many to the burnings of thatched houses. Even the meetinghouses, the most important and honoured buildings among the early settlers, were roofed with the same material. But whereas in parts of England, notably the south-eastern counties, the use of thatch continues right up to the present time (as several illustrations in this book prove, especially Fig. 33), it appears that it was rare in America after *c.* 1670 and that no examples now survive (see Fig. 66).

---

[1] Fiske Kimball, *op. cit.*, p. 46.   [2] Kelly, *op. cit.*, p. 61.

It passed into disuse partly because of the rigours of the climate, but still more because of its liability to fire. Hence came into being the curious office of 'chimney viewer'. This functionary was appointed in many townships to examine the chimneys of all houses every six weeks in winter, and every quarter during the summer. The primitive construction of the early chimneys, described hereafter, affords an additional reason for the post of 'chimney-viewer', who was elected in Hartford, Conn., up to 1706.[1] This date probably indicates the limit of the use of thatch in New England.

But shingles had come into use long before that time, and are frequently mentioned in records and letters from 1640 onwards. Such shingles were generally from one to three feet long and were nailed to wide oak boarding covering the whole roof. If rafters were used, the boarding was fixed horizontally to them; if not, it was nailed vertically to them. In some examples (e.g. the 'borded roof' of the house at Manamet, blown off in 1635, see p. 138), narrow 'clapboards' were used, nailed to the wider under-boarding.

Slate was used for roofing in Boston at least as early as 1654 (see p. 145); and there are references to tilers and tilemakers in the early writers previously quoted. Pan-tiles were in use in England before 1678 (see p. 83), both home-made and imported: and were certainly employed in America before 1685.[2]

The external clothing of the 'walls' of these old wooden houses in New England was usually, and after a time almost invariably, of boarding, known in England as 'weather-boarding'. In the previous chapter it has been explained that 'clap-boards' were among the earliest exports from New England to the mother-country, and that almost certainly clap-boards were used for covering the homes of the first settlers. Of course there was a still more primitive stage during the

[1] Kelly, *op. cit.*, p. 58.
[2] S. Smith, *History of New Jersey* (1765), p. 184.

IN NEW ENGLAND (c. 1635–c. 1685)

temporary period before the building of framed houses began. During that stage the pioneers hastily constructed dug-outs or wigwams to shelter them.

Thus Winthrop records in his diary the following entries during the first year of the Massachusetts settlement:

Sept. 1630. 'Finche of waterton had his wigwam burnt and all his goodes.'

Nov. 1630. 'Firmin of waterton had his wigwam burnt.'

Yet two months earlier, in a letter to his wife, he had written to ask her to send forthwith '12 axes of severall sortes of the Braintree smithe, or some other prime workman, whatever they cost, and some Augurs great and small', which clearly suggests the construction of framed houses.[1]

The derivation and early meaning of the word 'clapboard' is somewhat doubtful. The *Dictionary of Architecture* suggests a derivation from the German *Klapholz* or *Klapperholz*, translated as 'barrel-staves, clapboards', in Ludwig's *Lexicon* of 1789. Wright's *Dialect Dictionary* describes it as an obsolete North-country term, denoting the board upon which 'clap-bread' was beaten out. It is not mentioned in Moxon's *Mechanick Exercises* (1678) or in *The Builder's Dictionary* (1724). It is used to describe barrel-staves in State papers of the sixteenth century, and in its architectural sense at Boroughbridge in Yorkshire in 1520, 'le wayne scott et clap bordes'.[2] One of the earliest references to clapboards in American building occurs in Winthrop's *Journal* for 1632: 'Mr. Oldham had a small house all made of clapboards.'

The American use of this type of boarding differed considerably from the English practice already described in Chapter V (pp. 77–80). In both countries the boards were fixed overlapping and nailed direct to the 'studding' of the frame. But whereas in England the old boarding is generally 8 or 9 in.

---

[1] From *Winthrop Papers*, vol. ii (Mass. Historical Society, 1931).
[2] *New English Dictionary*, s.v. 'Clapboard'.

wide in fairly long lengths, and oak or elm is the material most often used, in America the 'clapboards' are comparatively narrow and short boards, and are often sawn out of pine. Occasionally shingles were used, but strictly speaking a clap-board only differs from a shingle in being longer and narrower than the latter. Normally clapboards 'are "riven" or split from short oak logs, usually from 4 ft. to 6 ft. in length, by means of a special tool called a froe. This tool was very much like a knife, with a heavy broad blade about 15 inches long, except that the handle, which was of wood, was offset and turned up at right angles to the blade. In making clapboards a log was stood on end and split in half with this tool. Each half was again split into halves, and then into quarters, eighths and so on, until a number of thin pieces had been produced. Owing to the radial plan of splitting, each piece was wedge-shaped in section; that is, one edge of the clapboards came to a thin or "feather" edge, while the other, or butt side, was from $\frac{3}{8}$ in. to $\frac{1}{2}$ in. in thickness.'[1]

Thus the boards were far thinner than in English practice. They were also much narrower, about 5 in. wide as a rule, and as there was a 'lap' of about an inch, the exposed width was only 4 in. This is an average, and exceptional cases show a width of 8 in. or so, resembling English usage. Sawn pine boards appear to have been used very early, since they occur in the Thomas Tupper House, Sandwich, Mass. (1637, recently destroyed), the Stephen Wing House at Sandwich (? 1641),[2] and the Thomas Buckingham House, Milford, Conn. (? 1639),[3] where the boarding has a 'bead' on the lower edge. In the rare cases where shingles were used for external covering of walls, they also were sometimes made of pine or cedar. American authorities differ as to the use of 'sheathing' or underboarding behind the clapboards, some saying that it was never used; others that it was so

[1] Kelly, *op. cit.*, p. 81.
[2] P. H. Lombard, 'The First Trading Post of the Plymouth Colony', in *Old-Time New England*, vol. xviii, p. 81.
[3] Kelly, *op. cit.*, p. 83.

Courtesy of Mr. J. F. Kelly and Yale University Press

78. HARRISON-LINSLEY HOUSE, BRANFORD, CONN.

Courtesy of Mr. J. F. Kelly and Yale University Press

79. OLDER WILLIAMS HOUSE, WETHERSFIELD, CONN.

IN NEW ENGLAND (c. 1635–c. 1685)

used, as on Doty House, Plymouth (1640, recently destroyed), where this inner boarding was vertically fixed.[1]

The following quotation from Christian Dankers' *Journey to the Delaware* (1679) is of interest in this connexion:

'Most of the English and many others, have their houses made of nothing but clapboards, as they call them there, in this manner: They first make a wooden frame, the same as they do in Westphalia, and at Altona, but not so strong; they then split the boards of clapwood so that they are like coopers' pipe staves, except they are not bent. These are made very thin, with a large knife, so that the thickest end is about a pinck [little finger] thick, and the other end is made sharp, like the edge of a knife. They are about 5 or 6 ft. long and are nailed on the outside of the frame with the ends lapped over each other. They are not usually laid so close together as to prevent you from sticking a finger between them, in consequence either of their not being well joined, or the boards being crooked. When it is cold and windy the best people plaster them with clay. Such are most all the English houses in the country, except those they have which were built of other nations.'[2]

Further information on the use of clapboarding may be found in Wallace Nutting's *Furniture of the Pilgrim Century*, p. 538.

There do not appear to be any surviving examples (at any rate earlier than 1685) of buildings where the timber framing is exposed externally, with panels of plaster between the members, as is so common in English work of the period; but it does not follow that this practice was never adopted in America, where in some cases boarding may have been added later.

It may be that the interior of the first Pilgrim homes had no internal linings, the studs of the framing and the inside of the external boards being left exposed as in my photograph of the Essex barn at Takeley (Fig. 24). But the rigor of the climate

---

[1] Chandler, *Colonial House*, p. 86.
[2] *Collections of the Long Island Historical Society*, i. p. 173.

demanded something more than this, and, in some houses at least, brick filling was used and may still be seen, e.g., in the Ward House at Salem, Mass. More frequently the outer boards were daubed internally with clay. Plastering does not appear to have been introduced generally until the second quarter of the eighteenth century.

But some form of wooden lining came into use very early. Thus, in Thomas Dudley's house at Cambridge, Mass. (1632), there was an interior lining of clapboards. More often the covering consisted of wide oak boards, commonly known as wainscot when used in this position, and fixed vertically (Fig. 82). This practice had two merits: the vertical lines of the boarding tended to increase the apparent height of the low rooms, and also served to conduct downwards any moisture which penetrated through the outer covering. The vertical joints were sometimes covered with moulded strips of great delicacy, as in the Caleb Dudley House at Milford, Conn. (*c.* 1690).

Internal partitions were few, as may be seen from the plans illustrated in Fig. 71. For the most part they were framed and lined with boarding; but probably, in some cases where they were of no great extent, wainscot would be used without framing. As previously remarked, the underside of the upper floor was usually left exposed in the room below, the edges of the summer and the joists being chamfered or moulded for ornamental effect. The main posts of the framing, as well as the massive sill, were also visible internally. Thus the appearance of these domestic interiors was simple in the extreme, but none the less attractive, as may be realized from the admirable reproductions in the Metropolitan Museum of Art (American Wing) in New York of the kitchen of the Capen House, Topsfield, Mass. (1683), and of the parlour of the Hart House at Ipswich, Mass. (*c.* 1640).

The floor of the lower story (='first floor' in U.S.A.) seems

IN NEW ENGLAND (c. 1635–c. 1685)   171

generally to have been of boards, not of earth or of stone flags as one might expect from English precedent. It often consisted of a double layer of boards 10 or 12 inches wide or even more, occasionally with a layer of fine white sand between the two

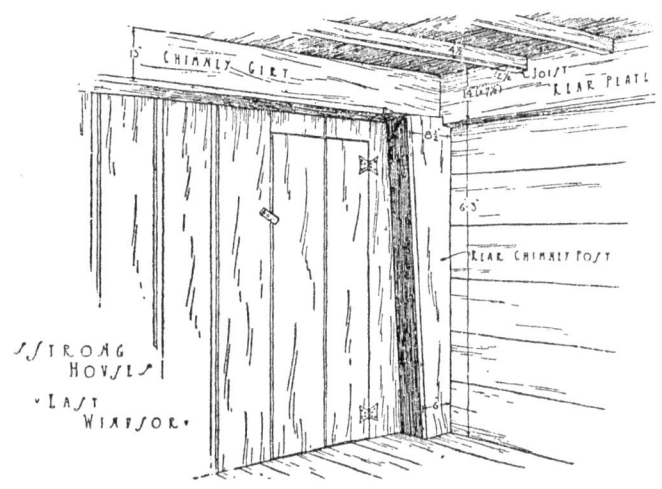

82. STRONG HOUSE, EAST WINDSOR, CONN., FRAMING AND PANELLING
(Courtesy of Mr. J. F. Kelly and the Yale University Press)

thicknesses. Chandler says[1] that the upper surface of the floors of some of the earliest houses was 'sand-covered with somewhat coarse, sharp, clean sand; the adept person who cleared the visible effects of use from the floors at the close of the strenuous work of Saturday, in preparation for the early beginning of the New England Sabbath, often tracing on the clean surface intricate patterns with the rough broom'.

For the upper floor (='second floor' in U.S.A.), single boarding was used, generally of considerable thickness and of oak, pine being introduced at a later date.

Doors, whether internal or external, were made of boards, the

[1] Chandler, op. cit., p. 91.

panelled door not appearing before *c.* 1700. External doors were strongly constructed, for the need of defence against the Indians was an ever-present possibility; and in the museum at Deerfield, Mass., is preserved a massive front door which bears the marks of tomahawks from an Indian attack as late as 1704. It consists of two thicknesses of boards, the outer layer vertical and the inner layer horizontal. It is studded with diagonal rows of stout iron nails with large rough heads, and is hung on massive iron strap-hinges. In all respects it resembles the late medieval type of door found in England, and this type continued to be used in New England right into the eighteenth century, long after men were experimenting with Renaissance forms derived from Italy. Internal doors were, naturally, of lighter construction and often of pine. A common form consists of two wide boards, the joint between them covered by a moulding or moulded strip; two or three battens hold them together. Very few examples survive, but it is curious that none of three Connecticut specimens illustrated by Kelly,[1] and ranging in date from 1675 to 1680, is more than 6 ft. in height, one being only 5 ft. 9½ in. Remembering that the Pilgrim Fathers are always depicted in rather high hats, and that they probably wore them as they entered a room, one wonders whether they were in fact much less in stature than their modern descendants who expect at least 6 in. more in the height of a door. The same applies to the English doors, of almost identical design, illustrated on Fig. 34.

Windows, again for reasons of defence, were few in number and small in size; moreover, glass was scarce, and difficult to replace in the event of breakage. It appears fairly certain that the double-hung sash-window with pulleys, weights, and cords did not appear in America until after 1685, the limit of time covered by this book. At that date it was being employed fairly widely in England for houses and buildings of the larger sort, but was

[1] Kelly, *op. cit.*, figs. 137, 139, 140.

Photo: Mr. F. Cousins: Courtesy of the Essex Institute

80. HATHAWAY HOUSE ('OLD BAKERY'), SALEM, MASS.

Courtesy of Society for Preservation of New England Antiquities

81. PAUL REVERE HOUSE, BOSTON, MASS.

Courtesy of the Metropolitan Museum of Art
83. HART HOUSE, IPSWICH, MASS. (*c.* 1640)
(*from the reproduction in the Metropolitan Museum of Art*)

Courtesy of the Essex Institute
84. PAUL REVERE HOUSE, BOSTON, MASS. (*c.* 1676)

even then decidedly a novelty, and for some time the older types persisted.

There is a considerable difference in American and English nomenclature in regard to windows. Thus an English architect

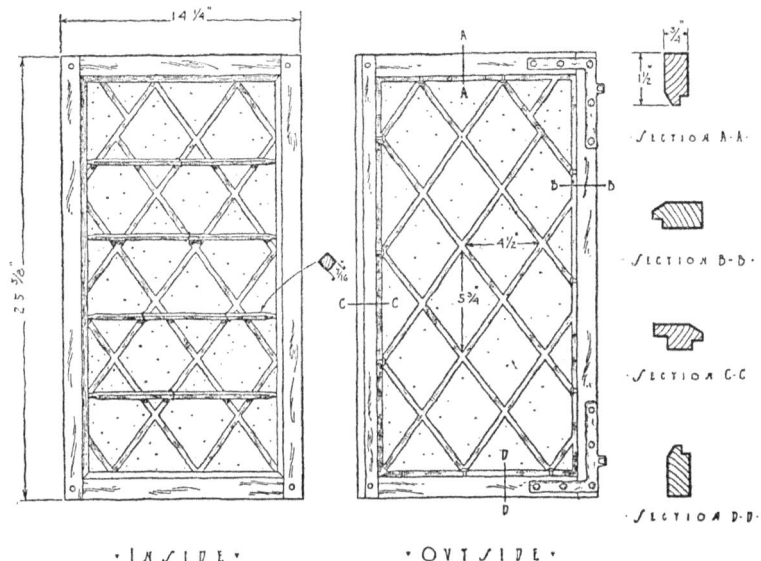

85. CASEMENT WINDOWS FROM CONNECTICUT
(Courtesy of Mr. J. F. Kelly and the Yale University Press)

speaks of 'a three-light casement-window', corresponding to 'a bank of three sash' in America; and he confines the use of the word 'sash' to a double-hung sash-window. To make the following paragraph clear to readers of either nationality, it may be said that the windows used in American homes of the seventeenth century were side-hung casements or 'sash', that is wooden frames hung at the side by hinges to an outer frame of wood, and secured by iron stays and fasteners at the other side and at the sill. These windows might consist of single units ('one-light' in England, 'single sash' in America), or of a row of units ('two or three lights' in England, 'a bank of two or three sash' in America). There may be surviving examples of one 'light' or 'sash' occurring above another in America, as frequently occurs in English examples of the seventeenth century; if so, the horizontal bar of the frame between them is called a 'transome'. But no such American examples are known to me. Nor is there any clear indication of the use of horizontally sliding windows, known in England as 'Yorkshire lights' (see p. 90). Fiske Kimball is of opinion that the 'current shutting draw windows', mentioned in the specification for Symonds's house at Ipswich in 1638 (cf. p. 151 in this book), were 'sliding panels of board, closing windows which were later to be provided with glass'.[1] This seems a probable and reasonable explanation; on the other hand, 'Yorkshire lights' were largely used, not only in Yorkshire but in all the south-eastern counties from which the Pilgrims came—as many illustrations in this book confirm, and they may well have been adopted occasionally in New England. Unfortunately, architectural history appears to be still silent as to the date of their first appearance in England itself. In America, as in England, many original casement windows have been replaced by double-hung sashes, for the latter are not only a more scientific form of window giving better light and ventilation, but they were also inserted freely into old houses as a mark of social superiority. Hence our present knowledge of early windows in America is largely derived from fragments, and where buildings have recently been restored to their primitive form, the architects for the restoration have had to rely mainly on such fragments and on inference.

The early 'sash' or casements were made of oak with mortise and tenon joints, and were often of very light construction. The width and height were seldom more than two feet, unless the window consisted of more than two 'lights' abreast, when the total width of the window would exceed that amount. Iron bars ('saddle-bars' in England) were often used at intervals

[1] Kimball, *op. cit.*, p. 27.

to strengthen the leaded glazing, which seems generally to have had diamond panes even in the seventeenth century, when rectangular or oblong panes, which were simpler and cheaper to construct, had already been introduced; but the Capen House at Topsfield, Mass. (1683), has oblong panes. Innocent[1] explains the primitive unglazed lattice of twigs from which these diamond panes were thoughtlessly copied in the oldest English examples. A common size for the American diamond panes was about 6 in. high by 4½ in. wide, which may be compared with the English example illustrated on Fig. 36, from the obscure Essex village of Toppesfield and elsewhere. (As explained in the preface, I have been at some pains to draw my examples from English villages with names corresponding to early settlements in New England.)

Probably oiled paper was used in the first small Pilgrim homes, but the quotations from Wood (p. 126) and Johnson (p. 139) mention the early export of glass to America from England; and in 1638 there is a record of an early and unsuccessful attempt to start glass-manufacture in New England. According to Kelly,[2] this industry was not established on a commercial basis until the end of the eighteenth century; and he describes the various qualities of English glass procurable before that time. He also quotes a New Haven Court Record of 1651: 'It is desired that the casements of the Meeting-house may have the glass taken out and boards fitted in, that in ye winter it may bee warm; and in the summer they may bee taken out to let in ye ayre; and Jeremiah (Whitnell) was desired speedily to doe it.'[3]

Staircases in the seventeenth century, as already explained, occupied an almost invariable position in an oblong space or porch between the entrance door and the great mass of the chimney-stack. This space was generally rather wider than its depth from door to chimney, the latter dimension ranging from

---

[1] C. F. Innocent, *The Development of English Building Construction* (1916), pp. 255-7.   [2] Kelly, *op. cit.*, p. 97.   [3] *Ibid.*, p. 87.

about 7 to 9 feet. Hence the stairs were narrow and steep with many winders. At first they were cased with plain vertical boarding and had no handrail or balusters (e.g. in the Older Bushnell House, Saybrook, Conn., 1678–9). Then came the successive introduction of square newels, and handrails, turned newels, turned balusters (rather heavy in section) and moulded handrails. Oak balusters are met with in such early examples as the Hyland-Wildman House at Guilford, Conn. (*c.* 1660), and the Graves House at Madison, Conn. (1675). The Stowe House, Milford, Conn. (1685–90), has a dog-legged stair with newel-posts. Other good examples occur at the Older Williams House, Wethersfield, Conn. (*c.* 1690); the Beniah Titcomb House, Newburyport, Mass. (*c.* 1680 or 1695); the Capen House at Topsfield, Mass. (1683); and the Corwin House at Salem, Mass. (finished 1675).

Where internal steps to the cellar were used, they were of rectangular oak logs, triangular oak logs, or stone. Access to the attic or loft was usually by means of a simple wooden ladder, through a trap-door.

Lastly we come to the central feature of all these Pilgrim homes, the chimney-stack, containing one or more fire-places. It was often of enormous size, on a foundation measuring 10 ft. or 12 ft. square; and in a few instances where the timber house itself has perished, the great brick stack stands gaunt and lonely in the fields. But at first, and for long afterwards, the chimneys of the smaller houses were of wood daubed with clay or even without daubing, as in the house of William Rix the weaver (1640), where the chimney was to be 'framed without dawbing, to be done with hewen timber'. This, in conjunction with the prevalent use of thatch for roofing, accounts for the importance of the office of 'chimney-viewer', already mentioned; and it is not to be wondered at that fires were frequent. Dudley[1] wrote in 1631, . . . 'in our new towne intended to be builded, we haue

---

[1] Quoted in Fiske Kimball, *op. cit.*, p. 25.

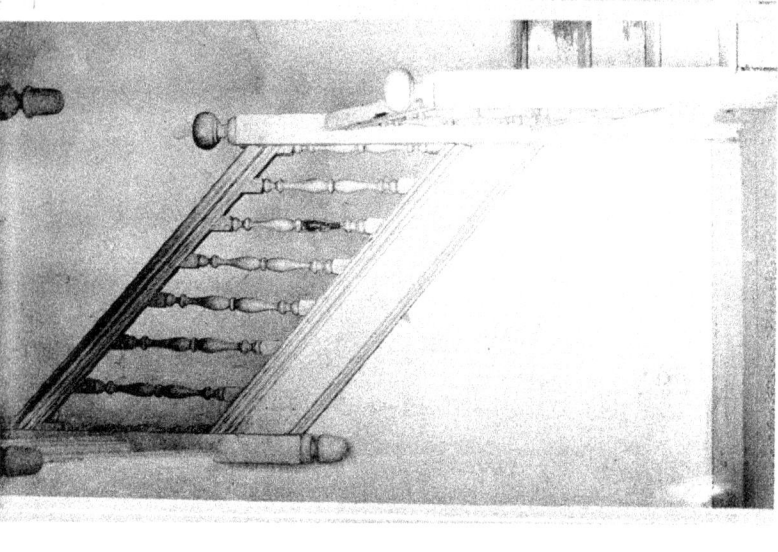

Courtesy of Society for Preservation of New England Antiquities

86. 'PARSON' CAPEN HOUSE, TOPSFIELD, MASS.

Courtesy of Mr. J. F. Kelly and Yale University Press

87. HYLAND-WILDMAN HOUSE, GUILFORD, CONN.

IN NEW ENGLAND (c. 1635–c. 1685)

ordered that noe man there shall build his chimney with wood'; but by the middle of the century chimney-stacks had come to be built of stone wherever possible. The introduction of brickwork came slowly, as the manufacture of bricks spread over New England. Often the cap of the chimney, above the roof-level, was made of brick even when the substructure was of stone; but many of the existing brick chimney-tops were added at a later date. The stone was usually bedded in clay, for lime was scarce in New England, and had often to be made from pounded oyster-shells. The caps of the chimneys, if of brick, were not often decorated with pilasters or blind arches as in the more elaborate English buildings of the period; and have seldom any other finish than one or two 'oversailing courses' of bricks. They are sturdy and simple, containing one immense flue into which the flues from the various fireplaces are carried. Flashings of lead or cement were not used, but sometimes an oversailing course of brick or a projecting strip of stone was employed to serve the same purpose. The bricks used varied from the standard size now employed down to very small thin bricks, those at Moulthrop House, East Lyme, Conn. (c. 1690), measuring $6\frac{1}{2}$ by $2\frac{7}{8}$ by $1\frac{5}{8}$ in.

Fire-places were generously planned, for oak logs formed the staple fuel. The following measurements are suggestive:

Buckingham House, Milford, Conn. (? 1639): 7 ft. 8 in. wide, 3 ft. 9 in. high.
Hyland-Wildman House, Guilford, Conn. (1660): 8 ft. 5 in. wide, 3 ft. 10 in. high.
Hart House, Ipswich, Mass.: 8 ft. 6 in. wide, 4 ft. 6 in. high 3 ft. 5 in. deep.
Whipple House, Ipswich, Mass. (1682): 7 ft. 4 in. wide, 4 ft. $1\frac{1}{2}$ in. high, 2 ft. 7 in. deep.

These measurements may be compared with those of the English example at Rochford Hall, described on p. 74. At the side of the fireplace there was often a small oval bake-oven constructed of brick, measuring internally about 2 ft. 6 in. by 1 ft. 6 in., with an iron door and a stone floor about 3 ft. above the floor of the house. This oven had no flue and was heated by hot embers from the adjoining fireplace, which were swept out before baking commenced (Fig. 83). The great open fireplace was lined with stone at first; then brick came into use, and (much later) Dutch tiles. The hearth was formed of large stone slabs.

The fireplace was spanned by a stone lintel. Oak was used for the very wide spans. The lintel of the Older Bushnell House, Saybrook, Conn. (1678-9), measures 15 by 12 in.; another example cited by Kelly measures $17\frac{1}{2}$ by 10 in. A wrought-iron bar was fixed across the fire-place to carry pots and kettles; later this gave place to a wrought-iron crane with pot-hooks and trammels.

American readers who wish to obtain some idea of the appearance of the fire-place and its surroundings in the early Pilgrim homes are fortunate, for several of the best surviving houses have been acquired by various historical societies and restored to their (presumed) original state, with appropriate furniture and utensils. Among these may be mentioned the Capen House, Topsfield (1683); the Abraham Browne House, Watertown (? 1663); the John Ward House, Salem (c. 1684); and Hathaway House (1682-93) at Salem. The Metropolitan Museum of Art (American Wing) contains a series of 'period rooms' reproduced from the originals (Fig. 83); also a magnificent collection of furniture and utensils of every kind, dating back to the first years of the Pilgrims. Indeed, some of the articles of furniture are reputed to have come over in the *Mayflower*, and a large number of the remainder were brought from England by the early settlers in succeeding years.

English readers who are unable to see these treasures at first hand are recommended to refer to the *Handbook of the American Wing* by Messrs. Halsey and Cornelius;[1] to Wallace Nutting's

---

[1] Published by the Museum (New York), third edition, 1926.

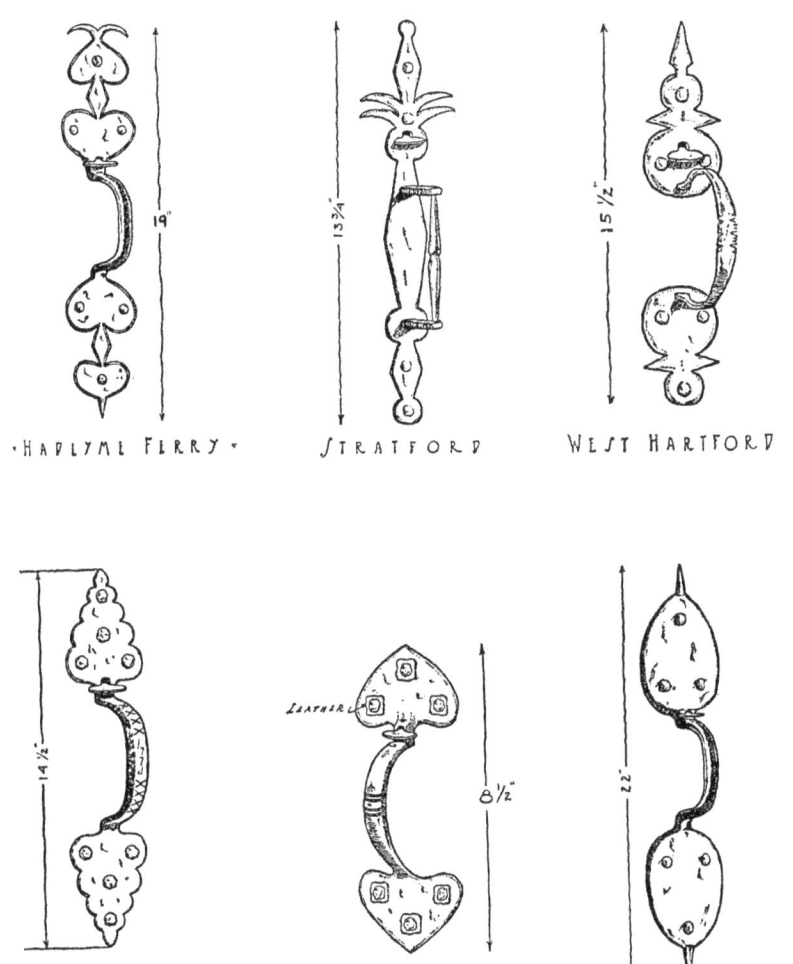

88. IRON LATCHES FROM CONNECTICUT HOUSES
(Courtesy of Mr. J. F. Kelly and the Yale University Press)

Furniture of the Pilgrim Century (Boston, 1921); and to L. V. Lockwood's *Colonial Furniture in America* (London and New York, 1902); also to the chapter on 'American and Colonial Implements' in J. S. Lindsay's *Iron and Brass Implements* (London and New York, 1927).

From these various sources, the indebtedness of America to English craftsmen in all the accessories of domestic life is abundantly evident: and not less remarkable is the care with which surviving examples have been brought together from all the scattered homes of New England into the great national museums, where they are preserved for posterity and recorded for students.

It is impossible in this book to describe the chairs, tables, chests, and other furniture of the Pilgrim settlers, their cutlery and silver, their lanterns and glassware and clocks, their porringers and plates.

But the simple ironwork required for their doors and windows may be taken as typical of much other craftsmanship. In the first fierce years of the settlement, all hinges and handles and locks had to be brought from home, as appears from early writers already quoted in this book. Thirty or forty years after the *Mayflower* landing, the first iron foundry was established in New England, but smiths were imported from the mother-country; so the English tradition continued to be followed closely, and the beautiful examples illustrated by Kelly[1] (Fig. 88 in this book) from the early homes of Connecticut resemble in every respect the fine contemporary specimens in the Victoria and Albert Museum (Fig. 37).

The following is a brief chronology of surviving timber houses in New England up to 1685, compiled by the writer mainly from the works of Fiske Kimball, J. F. Kelly, and J. E. Chandler. The dates given here are vouched for by the

[1] J. F. Kelly, *Early Domestic Architecture of Connecticut*, pp. 194–207.

IN NEW ENGLAND (c. 1635–c. 1685)

authority (denoted as 'F', 'K', or 'C', respectively) whose initial is appended to the date: and where uncertainty exists a question mark is added, or the prefix 'c.' (= *circa*).

Auth.	Date	Building	Town	State
Various	1635 (?)	'House of the Seven Gables' (Turner House)	Salem	Mass.
‡	1636	Rebecca Nourse House	Danvers	Mass.
C.	1636	Fairbanks House	Dedham	Mass.
*	1637	Abraham Hoxie House	Sandwich	Mass.
†	1639	Curtis House	Jamaica Plain	Mass.
‡	1639	Hartwell House	Lincoln	Mass.
K.	1639 (?)	Thomas Buckingham House	New London	Conn.
†	1640	Minot Homestead	Dorchester	Mass.
†	1643	Old House	Pigeon Cove	Mass.
K.	1643	Hempstead House	New London	Conn.
K.	1645 (?)	Starr House	Guilford	Conn.
‡	1648	Emerson House	Ipswich	Mass.
K.	1650	Baldwin House	Branford	Conn.
†	1650	Putnam House	Danvers	Mass.
K.	c. 1650–60	Gleason House	Farmington	Conn.
‡	Before 1650	Caldwell House	Ipswich	Mass.
F.	1651	Scotch (Boardman) House	Saugus	Mass.
K.	1650–60	Older Cowles House	Farmington	Conn.
F.	1651–60	Pickering House (Eastern part)	Salem	Mass.
**	1652	Loomis Homestead	Windsor	Conn.
†††	c. 1657	Cooper-Austin House	Cambridge	Mass.
‡‡‡	1658	Woods House	Nashua	N.H.
**	1659	Reynolds House	Norwich	Conn.
K.	1660	Avery House	Groton	Conn.
K.	c. 1660	Hyland-Wildman House	Guilford	Conn.
F.	1661–71	Narbonne (Willard) House	Salem	Mass.
†††	1663 (?)	Abraham Browne House	Watertown	Mass.
†††	c. 1664	Jackson House	Portsmouth	N.H.
K.	1664	Thomas Lee House	East Lyme	Conn.
K.	1664	Moore House	Windsor	Conn.
K.	1664	Whitman House	Farmington	Conn.
C.	1666 (?)	Standish House	Duxbury	Mass.
†	1667	Ely Tavern	Springfield	Mass.
K.	ante 1669	Whipple House, W. part (E. part before 1682)	Ipswich	Mass.
†††	ante 1670	Swett-Ilsley House	Newbury	Mass.
K.	1670	Acadian House	Guilford	Conn.
K.	1670	Morris House	New Haven	Conn.

TIMBER HOUSES

Auth.	Date	Building	Town	State
K.	c. 1670	Lyons House	Nr. Greenwich	Conn.
†	c. 1671	Chaplin-Clarke-Williams House	Rowley	Mass.
K.	1675	Graves House	Madison	Conn.
F.	1675	Jonathan Corwin House	Salem	Mass.
C.	c. 1676	Paul Revere House	Boston	Mass.
**	1676	Beckwith House	Old Lyme	Conn.
K.	1678–9	Bushnell House	Saybrook	Conn.
†††	1678	Rebecca Nourse House	Danvers	Mass.
†	1680	Red House Inn	Sudbury	Mass.
†	1680	Old Indian House	Deerfield	Mass.
K.	c. 1680	Older Williams House	Wethersfield	Conn.
K.	c. 1680	Hollister House	Glastonbury	Conn.
‡‡	1681	Adams House	Quincy	Mass.
F.	1682–93	Hooper (Hathaway) House	Salem	Mass.
F.	1683	Capen House	Topsfield	Mass.
†	1684	Waller House	Salem	Mass.
F.	after 1684	John Ward House	Salem	Mass.
‡‡‡	1685	Abbott House	Andover	Mass.
	?	Brown House	Hamilton	Mass.
	?	Old Bray House	Gloucester	Mass.

* See P. H. Lombard in *Old-Time New England*, xviii, p. 81.
† Date from *The Georgian Period* (Boston, 1899).
‡ Date from A. G. Robinson's *Old New England Houses* (New York, 1920).
** Date from Trowbridge's *Old Houses of Connecticut* (1923).
‡‡‡ Date from A. G. Robinson's *New England Houses* (New York, 1920).
‡‡ Date from D. Millar, *Measured Drawings of Colonial Houses* (New York, 1916).
††† Date from Society for Preservation of New England Antiquities.

The following additional dates are taken from the publications of the 'White Pine Bureau'.

Date	Building	Town	State
1638–70	Burnham House	Ipswich	Mass.
1646	James Noyes House	Newburyport	Mass.
c. 1660	Mulford House	Easthampton	Long Island
c. 1660	J. H. Payne House	Easthampton	Long Island
c. 1675	Old Ship Tavern	Essex	Conn.
c. 1676	Noah Webster House	W. Hartford	Conn.

Of the examples cited in the foregoing list, which does not pretend to be exhaustive and is confined to buildings which

IN NEW ENGLAND (c. 1635–c. 1685)

have been described in books, a few may be selected for mention here.

The 'House of the Seven Gables' (Fig. 90), 54 Turner St., at Salem,[1] has become famous because it supplied Nathaniel Hawthorne with the title for a book published in 1851. It has been restored recently by Mr. Chandler, but there still seems to be some doubt as to its precise date and original form. A series of alterations and additions have produced a picturesque group, very different in appearance from the long low old house of two stories which formed the nucleus and resembled the 'two-room plan' with a central chimney described at the beginning of this chapter. The later additions include an overhanging gable end, with 'drops' or pendants beneath.

The Fairbanks House at Dedham, Mass. (Fig. 91), has been credited with a date of 1636, but Fiske Kimball points out the rashness of such an assumption.[2] It consists of an original central block, extended at either end by a gambrel-roofed addition, and on one side by an 'ell', altogether a quaint and homely jumble. Chandler is of opinion that the group was completed by 1680. The windows include some leaded casements with rectangular panes. (It will be noticed that this book contains some reference to the English village of Dedham, see pp. 110–111.)

Connecticut homes of this very early period include the Hempstead House, New London (1643),[3] originally of one-room plan, two stories high, with a large chimney-stack, a stair-case-porch, and a stone cellar. It was afterwards enlarged by the addition of a second room on each story and then by an 'ell' running the whole length of the enlarged house. The pitch of the roof, since altered, was originally 50°.

The Starr House, Guilford[4] (? 1645), is a charming two-room building of two stories with an 'ell' at the back and a central

---

[1] See Kimball, op. cit., p. 296; Chandler, op. cit., p. 74, &c.
[2] See Kimball, p. 35; Chandler, p. 56, &c.
[3] See Kelly, op. cit., pp. 11, 59, &c.
[4] Ibid., Plate II.

chimney-stack of stone (Fig. 70). Sash-windows and shutters are evidently later additions.

The Gleason House, Farmington[1] (c. 1650–60), is a two-storied and two-roomed building covered with shingles. The front has a framed overhang with shaped brackets and drops. There are also overhanging gables at each end. Sash-windows have been inserted at some later date.

The Boardman House[2] at Saugus, Mass. (1651), was built to house Scotch prisoners who had been captured at the battle of Dunbar and were brought here to work in the neighbouring ironworks; hence it is commonly called the 'Scotch House' (Fig. 89). It is a two-room, two-story building with an overhanging front (now without 'drops'), an 'ell' at the back, and a central chimney with pilasters on the front and back, an unusual feature. Sash-windows have been inserted, but several original doors still remain. Undoubtedly this is one of the most attractive and perfect of the early examples.

The Cooper-Austin House, 21 Linnaean St., Cambridge, Mass., was built c. 1657, by John Cooper, deacon of the First Church in Cambridge; but it has been much restored, and the west end is a later addition. It is a two-room, two-story house, and the central chimney has pilasters, as at the 'Scotch House'. Sash-windows with shutters have been added; also a projecting porch.

The Abraham Browne House, 562 Main St., Watertown, Mass., was built c. 1663, has been restored, and is now used as a museum. It is said to contain the only surviving three-light casement in New England. The Jackson House, on 'Christian Shore', near Portsmouth, N. H., is a quaint little house of the one-story type, originally built c. 1664, and since enlarged by lean-to additions.

The Swett-Ilsley House, High St., Newbury, Mass., was a one-room, two-story house when it was originally erected,

[1] See Kelly, *op. cit.*, p. 63 and Plate VIII. [2] Kimball, pp. 297 and fig. 3.

Photo: *Halliday Historic Photo. Co., Boston*

89. BOARDMAN HOUSE, SAUGUS, MASS.

Photo: *Mr. F. Cousins: Courtesy of the Essex Institute*

90. HOUSE OF THE SEVEN GABLES, SALEM, MASS.

some time before 1670, but has been greatly extended and altered since. One room contains a fire-place over 10 ft. wide. All the last-named six examples belong to the Society for the Preservation of New England Antiquities, some being privately occupied but visible to visitors under certain conditions.

The Hyland-Wildman House[1] at Guilford, Conn. (c. 1660), is one of the principal examples of a house with a 'hewn overhang', which is boldly stop-chamfered and moulded (Figs. 76, 87). It is a two-room, two-story house with a stone plinth, chimney-stack, and hall fire-place. There is an 'ell' at the back.

The Older Cowles House at Farmington, Conn. (1650–60), and the Whitman House (1664) in the same township, both provide examples of an overhang (Fig. 75) with ornamental drops.[2]

The Thomas Lee House[3] at East Lyme, Conn. (1664), had originally a one-room plan of two stories (Fig. 71 A), afterwards extended by adding another room to the frontage and an 'ell' at the back of the house. It contains a seventeenth-century window-frame and some good moulded wainscot.

The Narbonne (or Simon Willard) House, 71 Essex St., Salem, Mass., is a one-room building, two stories high without overhang, and was built between 1661 and 1671.

The John Pickering House, 18 Broad St., Salem, was begun about 1651, and extended about 1671; an 'ell' was added next, then the roof was altered in 1751, and the building remodelled generally in 1841. Originally it was a one-room house of two stories, a second room being added in 1671.[4]

The John Whipple House at Ipswich, Mass., has been fully described in a monograph by Thos. F. Waters,[5] and is also described and illustrated by Fiske Kimball and by Chandler. The western part, which has no overhang, was built before 1669;

---

[1] Kelly, pp. 63–4: Plates VIII and X.   [2] *Ibid.*, Plates VIII and IX.
[3] *Ibid.*, pp. 7, 11, 87, 145: figs. 1, 10, 91, 157: Plates II, XIV.
[4] Kimball, *op. cit.*, p. 295, &c.
[5] *Publications of the Ipswich Historical Society*, No. XX (1915).

the east end before 1682. The hewn overhang occurs on the gable end and is double, one overhang to each story, as one finds on the gables of English and French medieval houses in the narrow streets of towns.[1] Like so many other examples mentioned, it began as a one-room house of two stories, and was afterwards extended. It has been thoroughly restored, and the present windows are casements with diagonal lead glazing. Its appearance is very English, except for the narrowness of the boarding and the rather aggressively spick-and-span effect of the new diamond glazing. It contains some of the finest moulded framing in New England and at least one noteworthy fire-place.

Connecticut also has a number of examples of the period 1660–70. Moore House, Windsor[2] (1664), is a framed house, partly of hard pine, with an overhang gable, and ornamental 'drops'. It consisted originally of two rooms, with an interesting system of summer beams. The Morris House, New Haven[3] (1670), differs in plan from any yet described, in having stone ends, each with a pair of fire-places. It originally had four rooms on each floor, with a central passage containing a straight flight of stairs. The masonry walls were built in lime mortar made from oyster-shells. Considerable alterations and additions have been made to the house since its erection. The Lyons House[4] on the Post Road near Greenwich (1670) has clay-filling between the studs of the framing and is covered with hand-made pine shingles. This gives the exterior a curious imbricated effect. It is a two-room house of two stories, with a sturdy central chimney of stone.

Several important houses have survived from the next decade. The Chaplin-Clarke-Williams House (*c.* 1671) in Bradford St., Rowley, Mass., is now the property of the Society for the

---

[1] See vignette on title-page in this book.
[2] Kelly, *op. cit.*, pp. 21, 34, 63, and 65; and Plate IX.
[3] *Ibid.*, pp. 20, 50, 70; fig. 20 and Plates IV and XVII.
[4] *Ibid.*, pp. 80 and 85; and Plate II.

Preservation of New England Antiquities. It is an attractive two-room house of two stories with a central chimney, an 'ell' or lean-to at the back, and two hewn overhangs at one end. It is partly embedded in a hill-side and has a cellar.

The Jonathan Corwin House (1675), sometimes known as the 'Witch House', 310 Essex St., Salem, Mass., which has been partly reconstructed in recent times, was originally a two-room house of two stories with (probably) three subsidiary gables besides those at each end, and a framed overhang along the front. The chimneys are of brick with pilaster strips. The rooms are plastered with clay.[1]

The Paul Revere House (c. 1676) in North Square, Boston (Figs. 81, 84), has recently been restored very skilfully by the architect J. E. Chandler, in whose book *The Colonial House*[2] it is also illustrated and described. It is a typical one-room house of two stories with an 'ell' in the rear. There is the usual great fire-place flanked by a baking-oven, and a porch containing stairs with winders. There is an overhang with drops on the front, and another curious overhang to the 'ell'. There is a cellar with stone walls. The external boarding has moulded edges. The roof is covered with large and thick shingles of split cedar. The casement-windows are mostly of two lights each, without an intervening mullion; and have leaded glazing in diamond panes.

The Graves House[3] at Madison, Conn. (1675), is a two-story building with two rooms of different sizes on each floor, a central chimney-stack with staircase-porch, and an 'ell' in the rear. It has an interesting original wooden latch in one of the upper rooms.

The Older Bushnell House[4] at Saybrook, Conn. (1678–9), is a two-room house of two stories with central chimney and

---

[1] Kimball, *op. cit.*, p. 293, &c. [2] Pp. 65–7, &c., plan, and Plates 46 and 47.
[3] Kelly, *op. cit.*, pp. 12, 65, 203; and fig. 11.
[4] *Ibid.*, pp. 7, 26, 30, 75; and figs. 3, 26, and 196.

staircase-porch. Under one of the rooms is a cellar approached from the porch by a flight of stone steps under the stairs. There is an 'ell' at the back, added later, when the pitch of the original steep roof was altered. The main sill is above the ground-floor (=first floor in U.S.A.) level, and the ends of the ground-floor joists are built into the stone walls of the plinth and cellar. The main posts of the frame are shouldered. The large fire-places have wood lintels 15 in. deep and 12 in. wide.

Another interesting Connecticut house is to be found at Wethersfield, the name of which recalls the little English village of Wethersfield in Essex, mentioned previously in this book. It is the Older Williams House[1] (c. 1680), almost identical in plan with the last-described example and with steps leading down to the cellar from the staircase-porch (Figs. 71 B, 72, 79). There is an unusual overhang at the eaves (see Fig. 72), which project nearly 2 ft. and are finished with a small ogee moulding to form a cornice. This is the first example we have yet encountered where the strongly-defined cornice used so largely in England at the period makes its appearance in America, and shows the tardy arrival of Renaissance fashions among the settlers of New England; but there are somewhat similar cornices, if they be original, in the Gleason House at Farmington and the Hyland-Wildman House at Guilford. The Older Williams House contains some noteworthy doors and fire-places, also a staircase with dwarf balusters and deep moulded strings. Externally it is plain but attractive, the strong horizontal line of the cornice being continued across the base of the end gable by means of an overhang.

The last Connecticut example to be mentioned here is the Hollister House[2] at South Glastonbury (c. 1680). It is a two-room house in two stories, following the usual type; but has a hewn overhang at the upper floor level and another at the foot

---

[1] Kelly, *op. cit.*, pp. 8, 37, 127, 135, 138; figs. 4, 36, 59, 81, 126, 140, 146; and Plates II and XLIII.   [2] Kelly, *op. cit.*, p. 64, and Plates VIII and X.

Photo: Mr. P. H. Lombard
91. FAIRBANKS HOUSE, DEDHAM, MASS.

Photo: Mr. F. Cousins: Courtesy of the Essex Institute
92. JOHN WARD HOUSE, SALEM, MASS.

Courtesy of the Topsfield Historical Society

93. 'PARSON' CAPEN HOUSE, TOPSFIELD, MASS. (1683)
EXTERIOR

Courtesy of the Topsfield Historical Society

94. 'PARSON' CAPEN HOUSE, TOPSFIELD, MASS. (1683)
INTERIOR

of the end gable, prolonging the boldly projecting front eaves, a further instance of approaching Renaissance fashions.

Massachusetts contains at least three important houses built in the last three or four years of the period covered by this book; and it is remarkable how faithfully they maintain the 'Gothic' tradition at a time when Wren was in full career in England and when all fashionable people were adopting Roman ideas from architectural copybooks. Nevertheless, in the parts of England where boarded cottages were then being built, as well as in the stone-using districts of Yorkshire and the Cotswolds, the old tradition of steep roofs and mullioned windows persisted among the rustic builders, just as it did among the settlers of New England.

The Hathaway House[1] (also known as the 'Benjamin Hooper House' and 'The Old Bakery') at Salem (Fig. 80) originally occupied a site at 23 Washington St., Salem, but was recently restored and rebuilt on a new site adjoining 'The House of the Seven Gables' at 54 Turner St., where it now stands. It was built some time between 1682 and 1693. In its rehabilitated condition it is a charming little house of the one-room type, two stories high with the usual attic and massive chimney. On the front is an overhang with an ornamental 'drop' or pendant at each end. The plinth is of stone, and above it occurs a most unusual feature, a board or plank some 2 ft. in width instead of the normal clapboarding which covers the rest of the exterior. Presumably this feature was considered to be more weatherproof than the ordinary method of construction. The curved head to the front door is rather unexpected: it is a hypothetical restoration, based upon old prints of contemporary houses in Salem, and the nail-studded door similarly follows Salem precedents. The leaded casements with diagonal panes are modern, but their size and disposition was indicated by the framing.

[1] See Chandler, *The Colonial House*, pp. 61–3 (with elevations); and Fiske Kimball, *op. cit.*, p. 294, &c.

Their curiously asymmetrical arrangement, together with the uncentral gable on the front and the other Gothic features mentioned, produces an extraordinarily medieval effect, and causes one to speculate whether this, the most medieval in character of all the American buildings described in this book, can really be of so late a date.

The John Ward House[1] at Salem (Fig. 92) was probably built immediately after 13 November 1684, on which date John Ward acquired the site at 38 St. Peter St., where it originally stood. About 1911 the house was taken down and rebuilt, with considerable restoration, in the grounds of the Essex Institute. At the outset it consisted of two rooms with the usual staircase-porch and chimney-stack. The remaining rooms on the other side of the chimney were added rather later, and the lean-to in the rear had been built some time before Ward's death in 1732. The restoration has been considerable, and includes the staircase, the chimney, the internal wainscot, the casement windows and the front gables—but for the last two items there were clear indications in the framing. There is a framed overhang along the front and on one end, at the level of the upper floor. The Ward House is a most satisfying building—simple, strong, expressive of its material and construction, very English, and surprisingly medieval in spite of its late date (apparently authentic).

The last house to be described, the Capen House[2] at Topsfield, Mass. (1683 (Figs. 86, 93, 94)), is perhaps the most beautiful of all the fifty odd houses mentioned in this book. Moreover, it is definitely dated, it contains many original interior features, it was acquired in 1913 by the Topsfield Historical Society and carefully restored, it is properly maintained, it is accessible to the public, and it has been admirably illustrated and described in print. What more could a lover of 'Old-Time New England'

[1] Kimball, *op. cit.*, p. 297, &c., and figs. 6 and 9.
[2] *Ibid.*, pp. 298, &c., and figs. 5, 8, 13 and 14.

want? The recording of the date upon the timber frame is an unusual occurrence, only too welcome to historians in the future. Documents show that this was one of those parsonage-houses which generally formed the chief dwellings of every New England township, excelled in importance only by the less numerous residences of the Governors. Parson Capen's House certainly affords some evidence of the status accorded to the ministry in those days. But apart from mere size, it is of singularly charming design. A restful effect is produced by the deep horizontal shadows cast by the bold eaves, the overhanging gable at the end, and the overhang on the front at the upper floor level. The severity of this horizontal line is relieved by graceful 'drops' or pendants, one opposite each main post of the framing. The plan follows the familiar two-room type with a central chimney-stack and a staircase porch. The rooms are large, the parlour measuring about 20 ft. by 17 ft. 6 in. and the 'hall' about 20 ft. by 16 ft. The staircase is original, with shaped newel-top, graceful turned balusters, and stout handrail. The fine parlour has the massive summers and joists of the ceiling exposed and retains the original fire-place with brick jambs. In the 'hall' or kitchen is a still larger brick fire-place with the usual bake-oven adjoining. The latter room, with the fire-place, the fine ceiling and all other accessories, has been reproduced in the American Wing of the Metropolitan Museum of Art in New York (cf. p. 170).

The Capen House, appropriately furnished, affords a perfect idea of the homes and surroundings of the Pilgrims and their descendants in New England in the latter half of the seventeenth century, when the hardships of the early years were over. It is evident that, in spite of their dour and tenacious character, their simplicity of life and their preoccupation with religion, they were men of culture and refined taste. And here, in the home of one of their honoured ministers we see not only the most attractive side of their life but also its essentially English origin.

For if Parson Capen's house could be transported overseas and planted somewhere in the little Essex hamlet of Toppesfield,[1] it would harmonize perfectly with the pleasant rolling country, the thatched cottages and the sturdy oak trees of the district of England which was the real cradle of the Pilgrim Fathers.

[1] See pp. 81, 83, and Figs. 28, 33 in this book.

Post-Mill at Bourn, near Cambridge (England)
(built before 1636)

APPENDIX

The Influence of Essex (England) on early Brickwork in America

THE purpose of this book, as explained in the Preface and subsequently, is to trace the connexion between the framed and boarded houses of New England and similar buildings in those districts of south-eastern England from which the bulk of the Pilgrims came. As a result of study, it has become clear that the architectural centre of gravity for our purpose lies in Essex. This fact naturally prompts a question, whether the other building-craft for which Essex is noted —the skilful use of moulded and decorated brickwork in Tudor and early Stuart times—had any similar effect on the other side of the Atlantic.

At first glance the inquiry would appear to be futile. For, as we have seen already, brickwork played a minor part in New England architecture during the seventeenth century. It was only used, in the framed houses with which this book is concerned, for the upper parts of chimneys, for the sides of fire-places, and occasionally for the main construction of chimneys in later works. Even the chimney caps are often subsequent additions, and the only form of decoration allowed to them is a few oversailing courses, except in a few instances where simple pilasters are worked on their faces or where the faces are worked into recessed planes. There is nothing to recall the fanciful and elaborate treatment of chimney-stacks common in many parts of Essex during the sixteenth and seventeenth centuries, though an acute observer may detect points of similarity, even in the simple arrangement of oversailing courses, between the Essex tradition and New England practice.

There are obvious and practical reasons why brickwork was so seldom used in New England. One reason was the shortage of lime, chiefly obtained in limited quantities by pounding oyster-shells. Stone was fairly plentiful; but even stone was employed with the minimum of dressing, generally in the form of rough field-stones, and was nearly always bedded dry or in clay. The second reason was the abundance of suitable timber, which was made to serve every possible purpose, including even the construction of chimneys in the early period. The third was the comparatively late and meagre establishment of brickworks, to which reference has already been made. Higginson certainly records the setting of a kiln in 1629, and brick-making is mentioned in the early records of Plymouth (1643), New Haven (1644, &c.), and Hartford. In the New Haven Court records for 1651 appears the following passage: 'John Benham informed the Court that when this plantation was first begun, he was by the Authority then settled here, sent forth for claye to make brickes, wherein he spent as much time as was worth twenty shillings, W^{ch} he thinkes the towne should allow him....'[1]

These scanty instances do not prove that brick was widely used, rather the contrary; but a few buildings in New England were erected with walls of masonry, and some of brick. Edward Johnson's reference in 1654 to Boston as a town of whose houses some were 'fairely set forth with Bricke, Tile, Stone, and Slate' has already been quoted; none of these, however, have survived. The 'Province House' at Boston (1676–9), an imposing building of four stories besides an attic, has perished.[2] In fact the only remaining example which can be dated with any certainty before 1685 is the Peter Tufts (or Cradock) House of Medford, Mass., erected between 1677 and 1680, which has a gambrel roof.

A recently published book, J. M. Howell's *Lost Examples of Colonial Architecture* (New York, 1931), which has come into my hands just as my volume is going to press, furnishes a most interesting example of Dutch or Flemish or East Anglian influence in America. In that work, Fig. 141 illustrates a brick gable, with the explanatory note: 'Probably before 1700. Brickwork same as in Amsterdam.' This gable formerly existed in Albany, N.Y., which was first settled permanently by 18 families of Dutch Walloons in 1624.[3] The gable is steep, and on each side it has a series of 'brick tumblings', such as may be seen not only in Amsterdam, in other Dutch towns, and in Flanders, but also in south-eastern England, and even as far north as Lincolnshire (see my Fig. 8). This characteristic treatment probably emanated originally from Holland or Flanders, but may conceivably have reached Albany by way of East Anglia.

But in Virginia, purposely excluded from this survey because it had no connexion with the Pilgrim Fathers and was indeed very little in touch with New England up to the end of the seventeenth century, brickwork was constantly used during the early history of

---

[1] Quoted by Kelly, *op. cit.*, p. 78.   [2] Illustrated in Kimball, *op. cit.*, Fig. 24.
[3] *Encyclopaedia Britannica*, s.v. 'Albany'.

APPENDIX

the colony. Brick-making had certainly begun there by 1611, and in Maryland not later than 1653. A house at Jamestown, Va., was built entirely of brick in 1638, 'the fairest that ever was known in this country for substance and importance'. Yet Fiske Kimball can only cite two surviving examples from Virginia which can be authentically dated before 1685, viz. Warren House,[1] Smith's Fort, in Surrey County (begun 1651 or 1652), and Bacon's Castle,[2] also in Surrey County (before 1676). The former is an aggressively plain little building with sash windows and dormers, and has nothing distinctive about it. Bacon's Castle, on the other hand, is a striking 'Jacobean' house, with tall detached chimney-stacks set diagonally, curved Dutch gables, and other features obviously derived from the south-eastern counties of England.

Research into the history of Virginia might establish some connexion between Bacon's Castle and Essex (England), but I am unable to trace anything useful. Messrs. Coffin and Holden[3] say that it was 'built about 1660 by Arthur Allen'.

But apart from dwelling-houses, Virginia possesses a building of first-class interest to students of architectural origins in America. It is St. Luke's Church in Isle of Wight County (not far from the two brick houses just mentioned), built in 1632 and restored in 1888. Under the photograph of its east end, reproduced in Tallmadge's *Story of Architecture in America*, is printed the legend: 'The oldest church in America and the last of the Gothic.' And a few pages later occurs the following passage:

'Here, in a clearing in the pine forest, is an astonishing building, the oldest church standing in the United States—and it is Gothic! Gothic not only in architecture, but in chronology! What does that mean? It means that it is the last legitimate descendant of that glorious race that arose in Chartres and Notre Dame, the last puny offspring from the stone loins of Salisbury and Durham. It means that its builders, who may have come over with Captain John Smith long before the productive days of Inigo Jones and Sir Christopher Wren, were ignorant of the Renaissance or oblivious to it.

'This ancient fane was begun about 1632. Until about thirty years ago it had stood roofless, windowless, and despoiled of its

---

[1] Kimball, *op. cit.*, Fig. 18.   [2] *Ibid.*, Figs. 20, 21.
[3] In *Brick Architecture of the Colonial Period in Maryland and Virginia* (New York, 1919).

interior woodwork since its abandonment in 1836. Up to that time it had been used continuously as a place of worship for two hundred years. Its restoration was done with zeal and skill, thanks to the energy and initiative of the Rev. Dr. David Burr of Washington. In fact, a few thousand of the bricks used in its repair were taken from the ruins of the ancient church at Jamestown, across the river. Some of the old bricks found in St. Luke's Church bear the date of 1632, but its architecture is the best evidence of its antiquity. The large east window and the nave windows have curious blunted pointed arches and brick tracery. Heavy buttresses uphold the walls, and a great square tower, almost Norman in its proportions, marks the portal. Its crown was probably battlemented, as the postern wall still is.'[1]

The resemblance of this building to the unique brick churches of S.E. Essex (England), themselves closely akin to Dutch and Flemish examples, led me to make an exhaustive search through hundreds of illustrations of similar buildings in that district. Of these, the most promising subject was the little brick church of Woodham Walter, a hamlet between Maldon and Colchester, near to the small and beautifully situated town of Danbury (see map, p. 5). In due course I achieved a pilgrimage there, and as a result am able to offer a parallel of two sketches, from photographs of St. Luke's Church, Va. (1632), and Woodham Walter church, Essex, Eng. (1563–4), respectively. This latter building has stone tracery in the windows, original in the small window of the north aisle, restored in the large window. Mr. Tallmadge suggests that St. Luke's Church may be the work of some craftsman who accompanied Captain John Smith. That famous voyager was born in Lincolnshire in 1597, apprenticed at King's Lynn some fifteen years later, learned to ride in the stables of Tattershall Castle (one of the great houses which sent some of its family to New England a few years afterwards), and was in Virginia from 1605 to 1609. After a long series of travels, he finally spent the remaining years of his life in authorship at home, and wrote his last book in 1630, a year before his death. In that work (*Advertisements for the unexperienced*) he compares the trees in Virginia to 'the high grove or tuft of trees upon the high hill by the house of that worthy Knight Sir Humphrey Mildmay, so remarkable in Essex in the Parish of Danbery, where I writ this discourse . . . '. It is certainly

[1] T. E. Tallmadge, *The Story of Architecture in America* (? 1928), pp. 42–3.

95. ST. LUKE'S CHURCH, VIRGINIA, 1632

96. WOODHAM WALTER CHURCH, ESSEX, 1563-4

a curious coincidence, though one cannot pretend it to be anything more, that the old explorer and 'President of Virginia' should be writing his last book at Danbury in Essex, only two miles away from the little church at Woodham Walter, a couple of years before America's oldest church was erected in a very similar style. But of this one can be sure: that the architect or designer of St. Luke's Church was either an Essex man or a man familiar with Essex brick churches, for nowhere else in England is such a style to be found. In Nathaniel Lloyd's monumental work, *A History of English Brickwork*, every detail of the little Virginian building may be matched from English examples occurring in Essex, and only in Essex. Thus the brick tracery of the large east window, with its two transoms, is somewhat similar to that existing in Sandon Church (1502); the design of the small two-light window is identical with other windows in Sandon Church; the curious and rather clumsy square finials perched at the foot of the gable resembles the slightly more finished examples at Eastbury Manor House, Barking (*c.* 1557); and the 'corbie steps' or 'crow steps' of the gable itself are found not only at Woodham Walter church, but in many other Essex churches and on a few isolated examples in East Kent. Essex ecclesiastical brickwork may be seen at its best in the churches of St. Osyth (late 15th cent.) and Chignal Smealey (early 16th cent.)

The corbie-step gables are a characteristically Flemish detail, and doubtless a further parallel with the design of the two churches described and illustrated here could be found by a patient study of contemporary work in Holland and Belgium, countries which were in constant touch with Essex and other counties of south-eastern England at the time, so that Dutch and Flemish features appear in the architecture of Boston, Lynn, Sandwich, and other seaport towns, where, as we have seen, Separatism and Puritanism flourished. It would be odd if the designer of St. Luke's Church in Royalist Virginia were discovered to be some Puritan refugee from Essex

BIBLIOGRAPHY

(A) CHAPTERS I–III

ADDISON, A. C. *Romantic Story of the Mayflower Pilgrims*. London, 1911.
ARBER, E. *The Story of the Pilgrim Fathers*. London and New York, 1897.
BARTLET, J. V. Article 'Congregationalism', in *Encyc. Britannica*. London, 1910–11.
BARTLETT, W. H. *The Pilgrim Fathers*. London, 1853.
BLAXLAND, G. C. *Mayflower Essays*. London, 1896.
BRADFORD, W. *History of Plimoth Plantation* (reprint). New York, 1908.
  History of the Plymouth Settlement (in modern English). London, 1909.
BROWN, DR. J. *The Pilgrim Fathers of New England*. London, 1895.
CAMPBELL, D. *The Puritan in England, Holland and America*. London, 1892.
CARPENTER, E. J. *The Mayflower Pilgrims*. New York, 1918.
COCKSHOTT, W. *The Pilgrim Fathers*. London, 1909.
DALE, DR. R. W. *History of English Congregationalism*. London, 1907.
DEXTER, DR. H. M. *The England and Holland of the Pilgrims*. Boston, Mass., 1905.
DEXTER, M. *The Story of the Pilgrims*. London, 1894.
GRIFFIS, W. J. *The Pilgrims in their three Homes*. London, 1914.
HORNE, C. S. *A Popular History of the Free Churches*. London, 1903.
HUISH, M. B. *The American Pilgrims' Way in England*. London, 1907.
HUNTER, DR. JOSEPH. *Collections concerning the Church at Scrooby*. London, 1854.
  Collections concerning the History of the Founders of New Plymouth. London, 1849.
LALLY, A. V. *Story of the Pilgrim Fathers*. Boston, Mass., 1926.
LEE, ROSALIND. *The Pilgrim Fathers*. London, 1911.
LODGE, H. C. *The Pilgrims of Plymouth*. Boston, Mass., 1921.
MACKENNAL, DR. A. *Homes and Haunts of the Pilgrim Fathers*. London, 1920.
MASEFIELD, J. (editor). *Chronicles of the Pilgrim Fathers* (in Everyman's Library). London, 1910.
MASON, T. W., AND NIGHTINGALE, B. *New Light on the Pilgrim Story*. London, 1920.
MATHEWS, B. J. *Adventures of the Mayflower Pilgrims*. Plymouth, Mass., n.d.
MELLORS, R. *Scrooby* [a guide-book]. Nottingham, 1920.
NELSON, L. A. *Our Pilgrim Forefathers*. Chicago, 1904.
PIKE, G. H. *Ancient Meeting-houses in London*. London, 1870.
SAWYER, J. D. *History of the Pilgrims and Puritans*. New York, 1922.
TUNNICLIFF, H. G. *Story of the Pilgrim Fathers*. New York, 1920.
USHER, R. G. *The Pilgrims and their History*. New York, 1918.
WHITEFIELD, E. *Homes of our Forefathers*. Boston, Mass., 1889.
YOUNG, A. *Chronicles of the Pilgrim Fathers*. Boston, Mass., 1841.

(B) CHAPTER IV

BROWNE, J. *History of Congregationalism in Norfolk and Suffolk*. London, 1877.
DAVIDS, T. W. *Annals of Evangelical Nonconformity in Essex*. London, 1863.
URWICK, W. *Nonconformity in Hertfordshire*. London, 1884.

[Also the works by J. V. Bartlet, C. S. Horne, R. W. Dale, and G. H. Pike cited in Section A.]

BIBLIOGRAPHY

(C) CHAPTER V

ADDY, S. O. *Evolution of the English House.* London, 1898.
BRIGGS, M. S. *A Short History of the Building Crafts.* Oxford, 1925.
GOTCH, J. A. *The Growth of the English House* (2nd edition). London, 1928.
INNOCENT, C. F. *Historical Development of English Building Construction.* Cambridge, 1916.
JONES, S. R. *The Village Homes of England.* London, 1912.
OLIVER, B. *Old Houses in East Anglia.* London, 1912.
The Cottages of England. London, 1929.

[Also the four volumes dealing with Essex, published by H. M. Stationery Office for the Royal Commission on Historical Monuments (England).]

(D) CHAPTER VI

DEXTER, H. M. *Library of New England History.* Boston, Mass., 1865.
DOYLE, J. A. *The English in America* (vols. i and ii). London, 1887.
ELLIOTT, C. W. *A General History of New England.* New York, 1857.
FISKE, J. *The Beginnings of New England.* London, 1889.
GOODWIN, J. A. *The Pilgrim Republic.* Boston, Mass., 1888.
HIGGINSON, F. *New England's Plantation* (reprint). Salem, Mass., 1908.
HUTCHINSON, T. *History of Massachusetts.* Boston, Mass., 1764, &c.
JOHNSON, EDW. *A History of New England* (1628-52). London, 1653.
LEVETT, C. *A Voyage into New England* (1623-4). London, 1628.
Mass. Hist. Soc. Publications (various). Boston, Mass., 1792 onwards.
The Towns in New England, 1630. Boston, Mass., 1902.
MORRELL, WM. *New-England.* London, 1623.
MORTON, N. *New England's Memorial.* Cambridge, Mass., 1669.
PRINCE, T. *Chronological History of New England.* Boston, Mass., 1736-55.
SMITH, CAPT. J. *Works* (1608-31) in The English Scholar's Library. Birmingham, 1884.
UNDERHILL, J. *Newes from America.* London, 1638.
WALKER, WILLISTON. *History of the Congregational Churches in the U.S.* New York, 1894.
WINTHROP, J. *Journal, History of New England.* Hartford, Conn., 1790.
WOOD, WM. *New England's Prospect.* London, 1634.

[See also various works on the Pilgrim Fathers in Section A.]

(E) CHAPTER VII

[*American Architect, The.*] 'The Georgian Period.' Boston, Mass., 1899.
CHANDLER, J. E. *The Colonial House.* New York, 1924.
COUSINS, F. *Colonial Architecture.* London, 1912.
EBERLEIN, H. D. *Architecture of Colonial America.* Boston, Mass., 1915.
Manor houses... of Long Island, &c. Philadelphia, 1928.
HALSEY AND CORNELIUS. Metropolitan Museum: *Guide to the American Wing.* New York, 1926.

BIBLIOGRAPHY

HALSEY AND TOWER. *Homes of our Ancestors.* New York, 1926.
HOWELLS, J. M. *Lost Examples of Colonial Architecture.* New York, 1931.
ISHAM, N. M. *Early American Houses.* Topsfield, Mass., ?
ISHAM AND BROWN. *Early Connecticut Houses.* Providence, R. J., 1900.
JACKSON, J. F. A. *American Colonial Architecture.* Philadelphia, 1924.
KELLY, J. F. *Early Domestic Architecture of Connecticut.* New Haven, Conn., 1924.
KIMBALL, FISKE. *Domestic Architecture of the American Colonies, &c.* New York, 1922.
LATHROP, E. L. *Historical Houses of Early America.* New York, 1927.
LINDSAY, J. S. *Iron and Brass Implements.* London and Boston, Mass., 1921.
LOCKWOOD, L. V. *Colonial Furniture in America.* London and New York, 1902.
MILLAR, D. *Measured Drawings of Colonial Houses.* New York, 1916.
MIXER, K. *Old Houses of New England.* New York, 1927.
NORTHEND, M. H. *Colonial Houses and their Furnishings.* Boston, Mass., 1912.
NUTTING, WALLACE. *Furniture of the Pilgrim Century.* Boston, Mass., 1921.
ROBINSON, A. S. *Old New England Houses.* New York, 1920.
TALLMADGE, T. E. *Story of Architecture in America.* London, [1928].
WATERS, J. F. *Early Homes of the Puritans* (in Essex Historical Collections). Salem, Mass., 1897.

[Also, all publications of the Society for the Preservation of New England Antiquities, including the journal *Old-time New England.*]

Also the following publications of the 'White Pine Bureau':

Vol.				
I (i)	Colonial Cottages.	St. Paul, Minn.	1915.
II (v)	Old Woodbury and Connecticut.	,,	1916.
III (iii)	Old Homes of Newburyport, Mass.	,,	1917.
V (i)	The Seventeenth-century Colonial House.	,,	1919.
– (ii)	Settlements on the E. end of Long Island	,,	1919.
VI (i)	The Boston Post Road.	,,	1920.
– (ii)	A New England Village.	,,	1920.
IX (v)	The Road from Hartford to Litchfield.	,,	1923.
XI (ii)	Interior Woodwork in New England.	,,	1925.
XII (ii)	Farmington, Connecticut.	,,	1926.

INDEX

Acton (England), 43.
— (U.S.A.), 43.
Albany (N.Y.), 194.
Alden, John, 30, 120, 125, 131.
Amersham, 46.
Amsterdam (Holland), 4, 6, 8, 18, 27, 28, 29, 35, 36, 133, 194.
— House in the Begijnen Hof, 36.
— Rijks Museum, 41.
Amsterdam, New, *see* 'New York.'
Andover (Mass.), Abbott House, 182.
Anne, The, 30, 121, 125.
Antwerp, 4, 7, 33, 41, 67.
Aptucxet (Mass.), Trading House at, 16, 22, 133–5, 138.
Architects in England, 66–8.
— in New England, 149.
Ashburnham (England), 43.
— (U.S.A.), 43.
Ashford, 49.
Ashstead, 98.
Attleborough (England), 43.
— (U.S.A.), 43.
Audley End, 68.
Augusta (Maine), 137.
Austerfield, Bradford House, 7, 12–13, 16, 80.

Bacon's Castle (Va.), 195.
Bamber's Green, Dunmow, 108.
Baptists, 47, 49.
Barking, 81, 114–15.
— Eastbury Manor House, 114, 198.
— Old Rectory, 115.
— Windmill at, 115.
Barnby Moor, 17.
Barnet, 81, 104.
Barrowe, Henry, 3, 4, 49.
Bassett, William, 31, 33, 35, 101, 103, 121.
Battle (Sussex), 99.
Bawtry, 6, 9, 11, 13, 16, 80.
Beccles, 49.
Bedford (England), 43.
— 'Bunyan Meeting,' 49.

Bedford (U.S.A.), 43.
Benfleet, 81, 112.
Billerica (U.S.A.), 43.
Billericay (England), 43, 46, 106, 113.
— 'Chantry House,' 85–8, 113.
Bishop's Stortford, 107, 108.
Blickling Hall, 68.
Blyth, 17.
Bocking, 46.
— Watermill, 109.
— Windmill, 109.
Books on building, 70–3.
Boroughbridge, 167.
Boston (England), 6, 8, 19–22, 43, 49, 50, 198.
— Guildhall, 20; Church House, 20.
— Shodfriars Hall, 20.
Boston (Mass.), 19, 43, 50, 140, 145, 148, 194.
— Paul Revere House, 182, 187.
— Province House, 194.
Bourn, Cambs. (England), 105 n.
Bourne, Lincs. (England), 21, 49.
— (Mass.), 133.
Box Lane (Herts.), 48.
Bradford, Governor, 6, 7, 9, 11, 12, 91.
— *quoted*, 121, 123–4, 125, 130, 131, 132, 137–8.
Braintree (England), 3, 43, 46, 49, 106, 108, 109, 167.
— (Mass.), 43, 145, 152.
Brandt, *quoted*, 28.
Branford (Conn.) Harrison-Linsley House, 162.
— Baldwin House, 181.
Brentwood (England), 3, 46.
— 'White Hart' Inn, 111.
— Putwell Farm, 111.
Brewster, William, 6, 7, 9, 10, 11, 12, 49, 91.
Brickwork, in England, 14, 15, 52–3, 72–7, 193–8.
— in Holland, 33–5.
— in America, 136–7, 177, 193–8.

INDEX

Brightlingsea, 110.
Broek-in-Waterland, 35.
Brown, Dr. J., *quoted*, 138.
Browne, Robert, 2, 49.
Brownists, 2, 4.
Buckinghamshire, 56.
Builder, the, 68.
Burnham, 46.
Burton Hall, near Boston (England), 20, 22.
Bury St. Edmunds, 2, 49, 57.
Butterwick, 21.
— Windmill, 22.
Buzzard's Bay, 133.

Caen stone, 52.
Cambridge (Mass.), 43, 50, 139, 170.
— Cooper-Austin House, 181, 184.
Cambridge, town of (England), 3, 67.
Cambridge University, 2, 3, 4, 6, 7, 49–50, 105.
Cambridgeshire, 42, 43, 45, 51, 56, 105.
Campen (Holland), 27.
Canterbury (England), 41, 43, 49, 82, 91, 100–1, 103.
— (U.S.A.), 43.
Canvey Island, 112–13.
Cape Cod, 118, 134, 140, 163.
Capel, 98.
Carpenter, the, 69.
Cataumet, Windmills at, 140.
Ceilings, in England, 13, 16.
— in Holland, 38, 40.
— in America, 170.
Cellars, in England, 72, 73.
— in America, 135, 155, 176.
Chandler, J. E., *quoted*, 81, 164, 180, 183, 185, 187.
Charlestown (Va.), 131.
— (Mass.), 139, 144–5.
Chatham (England), 43, 49.
— (Mass.), 43.
Chelmsford (England), 4, 43, 46, 81, 106, 111.
— Barnes' Mill, 111.
— (U.S.A.), 43.

Chelsea (England), 43.
— (U.S.A.), 43.
Cheshunt, 48.
Chesterton, 46.
Chignal Smealey, 198.
Chiltern Hills, 52.
Chimneys, in England, 13, 16, 73, 76–7.
— in America, 135–6, 166, 176–8.
'Chimney-viewer,' the, 166.
Clacton, 81, 106.
Clapboards, 125, 127, 130, 166–7.
Clapham, A.W., *quoted*, 56.
Clapton, 97.
Clare, 76.
Clayhithe, barn at, 105.
Clyfton, Richard, 7.
Coffin and Holden, *quoted*, 195.
Coggeshall, 4, 46, 108, 110.
Colchester (England), 4, 43, 46, 49, 106, 110, 111, 196.
— (U.S.A.), 43.
Colney Street, Moor Mills, 105.
Congregationalists, 2, 3, 4, 47, 138.
Connecticut, 137, 143, 155, 165, 180.
Corby, barn at, 19.
Corringham, 46 n.
Cotswolds, stone houses in, 24–5, 59, 92, 189.
Cotton, Rev. John, 19, 49.
Cranbrook, 104.
Crowle, 49.
Cushman, R., *quoted*, 125.

Dale, R.W., *quoted*, 47.
Danbury (England), 43, 106, 111, 196, 198.
— (U.S.A.), 43.
Dankers, C., *quoted*, 169.
Danvers (Mass.), R. Nourse House, 181.
— Putnam House, 181.
Davison, William, 4, 7.
Davys, John, 150.
Deal, 104.
Dedham (England), 43, 90.
— 'Master Weaver's House,' 110–11.

INDEX

Dedham (*cont.*)
— (U.S.A.), 43, 110.
— Fairbanks House, 181, 183.
Deerfield (Mass.), Indian House, 182.
Delaware (U.S.A.), 2.
Delft (Holland), 36.
Denny Gate, 105.
Deptford, 49.
Detroit, house at, 59.
Dexter, Dr. H. M., *quoted*, 9, 12, 43.
Doors, in England, 84–6.
— in America, 171–2.
Dorchester (Mass.), 138, 145.
— Minot Homestead, 181.
Dover (England), 41, 43, 49, 101, 104.
— (U.S.A.), 43.
Droitwich, 54.
Dudley, *quoted*, 176.
Dunmow, 108.
Dunstable (England), 43.
— (U.S.A.), 43.
Dutch in America, 1–2, 133–4.
Duxbury (England), 54.
— (Mass.), Alden House, 120.
— Standish House, 181.

East Bergholt, 110.
East Haven, Moulthrop House, 163.
East Lyme (Conn.), Lee House, 152, 181, 185.
East Retford, 17.
Easthampton (Long Island), Windmill, 141.
— Mulford House, 182.
— Payne House, 182.
Easton (England), 43.
— (U.S.A.), 43.
Edgware, barn at, 61.
Eliot, George, *quoted*, 17.
Eltham, 'The Courtyard,' 101–2.
— Other buildings, 102.
Enfield (England), 43.
— 'Fallow Buck' Inn, 97.
— (U.S.A.), 43.
Epping (England), 43, 48, 83, 106–7.
— Forest, 106.
— (U.S.A.), 43.

Epworth, 14, 18, 49.
Essex (England), a centre of Dissent, 43–5, 46.
— description of scenery, 51, 106.
— architecture described, 53, 56, 62, 65, 73, 82, 107–15.
— (Conn.), Old Ship Tavern, 182.
Eythorne, 49.

Farmington (Conn.), Gleason House, 181, 184, 188.
— Older Cowles House, 181, 185.
— Whitman House, 181, 185.
Faversham, 46, 103.
Finningley, 17.
Fire-places, in England, 73–6.
— in America, 177–8.
Flint work, 53.
Floors, in England, 16, 72–3.
— in Holland, 38, 40.
— in America, 158–9, 170–1.
Florence, 31.
Fobbing, 46 n., 114.
Folkestone, Fishermen's cottages, 103.
Fortune, The, 30, 43, 121, 125.
Fordwich, Town Hall, 103.
— Other buildings, 103–4.
Foulness Island, 112.
Friskney, Windmill, 22.
Furniture, in England, 91.
— in America, 179–80.

Gainsborough, 6, 7, 8, 17–18, 27.
— Old Hall, 18.
Gambrel roof, in England, 81–2.
— in America, 163–5.
Garner and Stratton, *quoted*, 18.
Gerbier, Sir B., *quoted*, 82.
Glass, use of, in America, 126, 136.
Glastonbury (Conn.) Hollister House, 182, 188.
Gloucester (Mass.), Old Bray House, 182.
Great Bentley, 110.
Great Clacton, 110.
Great Oakley, 110.
Great Wakering, 81, 112.
Greensted, church at, 56–7.

Greenwich (England), 43.
— Queen's House at, 67.
— (Conn.), 43.
— Lyons House, 182, 186.
Greenwood, John, 3, 49.
Grimsby, 8, 19.
Groombridge, 104.
Groton (England), 43.
— (Conn.), 43.
— Avery House, 181.
Grumbold, Robert, 67.
Guildford (England), 43.
Guilford (Conn.), 43.
— Whitfield House, 163.
— Hyland Wildman House, 176, 177, 181, 185, 188.
— Stowe House, 176.
— Acadian House, 181.
— Starr House, 181, 183.
Gutters, use of, 84.

Haarlem (Holland), 32, 33, 35, 36.
Hadley (England), 43.
— (U.S.A.), 43.
Hague, The (Holland), 36.
Halesworth, 49.
'Hall i' th' Wood,' 54.
Hamilton (Mass.), Brown House, 182.
Hampstead, 97.
Hampton Court Palace, 82, 164.
Harlow, 107.
Harmondsworth, 79, 98.
Harrison, 3, 49.
Hartfield, 105.
Hartford (Conn.), 43, 166, 194.
Harvard, John, 47, 50, 94.
Harvard College, 50, 144.
Harwich (England), 43.
— (U.S.A.), 43.
Hastings, 99, 104.
Hatfield (England), 43, 104.
— (U.S.A.), 43.
Hatfield House, 68.
Haverhill (England), 43.
— (U.S.A.), 43.
Hawkhurst, 104.
Hawthorne, Nathaniel, 183.

Haxey, 17.
Hayes (England), 98.
Headcorn, 104.
Henley, 46.
Henry VIII, King, 10.
Hertford (England), 43, 104.
Hertfordshire, 42, 43, 45, 51, 53, 56, 82, 92, 104.
Hickman, Thomas, 18.
Higginson, Rev. F., *quoted*, 126-7, 136, 137, 194.
High Beach, 106.
Hingham (England), 43.
— (U.S.A.), 43.
Hobby, Will, 69.
Holland, Pilgrims in, 4, 7, 26, 27-41, 47, 116.
Holmes, O. W., *quoted*, 165.
Horndon-on-the Hill, 4, 46, 113.
Horningsham, 48.
Horseley Cross, 81, 110.
Horsfield, Rosamond, 29.
Howells, J. M., *quoted*, 194.
Hull, 8, 25.
Hunstanton, 51.

Ickenham, 63-4.
Ilford, 49.
Indians in New England, 124-5, 129, 130, 133, 137, 143, 161.
Ingatestone, Windmill, 111.
Innocent, C. F., *quoted*, 57, 61, 69, 78, 83, 84.
Ipswich (England), 43, 106.
— Friar Street Chapel, 48.
— Old Neptune Inn, 84.
Ipswich (Mass.), 43, 140, 145, 150.
— Burnham House, 182.
— Caldwell House, 181.
— Emerson House, 181.
— Hart House, 170, 177.
— Whipple House, 177, 181, 185-6.
Ironwork, in England, 76, 91.
— in America, 180.

Jackson, Sir T. G., *quoted*, 32.
Jamaica Plain (Mass.), Curtis House, 181.

INDEX

Jamestown (Virginia), 1, 195, 196.
Jepson, William, 29, 33.
Johnson, Edward, *quoted*, 122, 139, 143, 144, 146, 155, 175, 194.
Johnson, Francis, 4, 6, 8, 27, 49.
Joiner, the, 69.
Jones, Inigo, 67, 195.

Kelly, J. F., *quoted*, 62, 148, 155, 156, 161, 163, 165, 172, 180.
Kennebec, 137.
Kent (England), 42, 43, 45, 46, 51, 53, 55, 56, 59, 62, 73, 79, 80, 81, 82, 92, 100–5.
Kimball, Fiske, *quoted*, 23–4, 26, 124–5, 128, 130–1, 142, 148, 149, 150, 165, 180, 183, 185, 195.
Kingsbury, 64, 97.
Kirby Cross, 110.
Kist, Gerret, 38.

Laindon Hills, 106.
Lamberhurst, 104.
Lancashire, huts in, 24.
Landbeach, 105.
Leigh (Essex), 81, 112.
Leland, *quoted*, 10.
Levett, C., *quoted*, 124–5, 132.
Lewes, 99.
Leyden, 6, 8, 27, 28, 29, 30, 31–4.
— Stads Timmerhuis, 33–4.
Lieven de Key, 33.
Lime in America, 128, 155, 193.
Lincoln (England), 19, 43.
— (Mass.), 43.
— Hartwell House, 181.
Lincoln, Lord, 19.
Lincolnshire, 17–22, 25, 43, 45, 51, 56.
Little Dunmow, 108.
Little James, The, 30, 121, 125.
Lloyd, N., *quoted*, 77, 79, 198.
Lombard, P. H., *quoted*, 134, 135, 138 (*see also* Preface).
London, 53, 92–6.
— early churches in, 4, 27, 47, 48.
— Banqueting House, Whitehall, 32, 67, 88.

London, Houses in Gt. Queen St., 88.
— Inner Temple Gatehouse, 94.
— Old London Bridge, 94.
— Staple Inn, 94.
— Victoria and Albert Museum, 90, 91.
[*See also* 'Clapton, Eltham, Hampstead, Southwark, Streatham, Woolwich.']
Longfellow, H. W., 30, 120, 131.
Long Island, windmills on, 141.
Loughton, 107.
Louth, 19.
Lynn, King's (England), 43, 196, 198.
Lynn (Mass.), 43, 140, 145, 152.

Mackennal, Dr., *quoted*, 13, 36.
Madison (Conn.), Graves House, 176, 182, 187.
Maidstone, 41.
Maine (U.S.A.), 42.
Malden (U.S.A.), 43.
Maldon (England), 4, 43, 46, 106, 196.
— The Friary, 111.
Manamet, 133, 138, 166.
Manhattan Island, 133.
'Mansard' roof, 82, 163–4.
Marken (Holland), 35–6.
Marks Tey, 108.
Martin, Christopher, 86, 88, 113.
Massachusetts, 50, 118, 122, 132, 136, 138, 143, 144, 146, 147, 152, 167.
Mayflower, The, 2, 27, 30, 43, 44, 49, 86, 91, 113, 116, 132, 178.
Matianuck, 137.
Medford (Mass.) Cradock House, 11, 194.
Merton, 98.
Middelburg (Holland), 3, 4.
Middlesex (England), 43, 45, 51, 53, 56, 82, 92, 96–8.
Mildmay, Sir H., 196.
Milford (Conn.), Buckingham House, 168.
— Caleb Dudley House, 170.
Mill Hill, 83, 97.
Mitcham, 98.

INDEX

Morton, Nathaniel, *quoted*, 123, 124, 137.
Mountnessing, Windmill, 111.
Moxon, Joseph, *quoted*, 70-2, 83, 88, 167.
Much Hadham, 104.

Naarden (Holland), 27, 36.
Nantucket (Mass.), 140.
Nashua (N.H.), Woods House, 181.
Netteswell Cross, 79, 107.
'New Amsterdam', *see* New York.
New England, 1, 2.
New Hampshire, 42.
New Haven colony, 143, 149, 155, 175, 194.
— Morris House, 181, 186.
New Jersey, 2.
New London (Conn.), Hempstead House, 163, 181, 183.
— Buckingham House, 181.
New Netherlands, 1.
New Plymouth, *see* 'Plymouth (Mass.)'.
New York, 1, 2, 133, 137.
— Metropolitan Museum, 91, 170, 178, 191.
Newark (England), 19.
Newbury (England), 46.
Newbury (Mass.), Swett-Ilsley House, 181, 184-5.
Newburyport (Mass.), Titcomb House, 176.
— Noyes House, 182.
Newmarket (England), 43.
— (U.S.A.), 43.
Newport, Essex (England), 43, 107.
— (R.I.), 43, 140.
North Downs, 51, 52, 101.
North Hykeham, Windmill at, 19.
Northiam, 99, 105.
Norfolk (England), 43, 45, 51, 53, 56, 59.
Norwich (England), 3, 7, 25, 41, 43.
— (Conn.), 43.
— Reynolds House, 181.
Nottinghamshire, 6-7, 9-11, 45.
Nutting, Wallace, *quoted*, 120, 169.

Old Lyme (Conn.), Beckwith House, 182.
Oliver, Basil, *quoted*, 91, 99, 100, 104, 108, 115.
Ongar, 56.
'Overhang,' the, in England, 63-6.
— in America, 160-2.
Oxfordshire, 56.
Oxford University, 50.

Panelling, in England, 86-8.
— in America, 170.
Parging or pargetting, 54, 77.
Passingford Mill, 107.
Peasants' Revolt, 46 n.
Penobscot Bay, 118.
Penry, John, 3, 49.
Pepys, Samuel, 78.
'Peter the Great,' Czar, 37.
Petersham (England), 43.
— (U.S.A.), 43.
Pigeon Cove (Mass.), 181.
Plans of New England houses, 152-4.
Plymouth Company, 1.
Plymouth (Mass.), 7, 119, 121-2, 123, 124, 125, 128, 130-1, 133-4, 137, 138, 143, 144, 146, 147, 194.
— Doty House, 169.
Ponders End, 97.
Portsmouth (N.H.), Jackson House, 181, 184.
Potter Street, near Epping, 107.
Powys, A. R., *quoted*, 81.
Primatt, S., *quoted*, 70.
Prittlewell, 112.

Quincy (Mass.), Adams House, 182.

Raleigh, Sir W., 1, 4.
Ramsgate, 103.
Rasières, Isaac de, *quoted*, 131, 133-4.
Rayleigh, 4, 46.
Raynham Park, 81, 88.
Reading (Mass.), 145, 155.
Renaissance in architecture, 31.
Rendham, 49.
Rhode Island, 42, 146.

INDEX

Rich, Lord R., 3.
Rickling, 107.
Ripley (Surrey), 81, 98.
Rix, William, 150, 176.
Robertsbridge, 104.
Robinson, John, 7.
Rochester (England), 43.
— (U.S.A.), 43.
Rochford, 81, 112.
Rochford Hall, 3, 74–6, 112, 177.
Romford (England), 43, 111.
— (U.S.A.), 43.
Roofs, in England, 16, 59, 80–4.
— in Holland, 36, 37, 40.
— in America, 162–6.
Rowley (Mass.), 145.
— Chaplin-Clarke-Williams House, 182, 186–7.
Roxbury (Mass.), 145.
Roydon, 107.
Runwell, 113.
Rye, 53, 80, 101.

Saffron Walden, 107.
St. Albans, 105.
St. Alban's Abbey, 52.
St. Luke's Church, Virginia, 1, 31, 32, 34, 195–8.
St. Osyth, 81, 110, 198.
Salem (Mass.), 138, 139, 140.
— Corwin House, 176, 182, 187.
— Hathaway House, 152, 178, 182, 183, 189–90.
— 'House of the Seven Gables', 163, 181, 189.
— Narbonne House, 181, 185.
— Pickering House, 181, 185.
— Waller House, 182.
— Ward House, 170, 178, 182, 190.
'Saltpetre man,' the, 73.
Sandon church, 198.
Sandwich (Kent), 31, 35, 41, 43, 49, 53, 91, 101, 103, 198.
— The Barbican, 103.
— (Mass.), 43.
— Tupper House, 168.
— Wing House, 168.

Sandwich (Mass.), Hoxie House, 181.
Saugus (Mass.), 'Scotch' House, 181, 184.
Saybrook (Conn.), Bushnell House, 155, 176, 178, 182, 187.
Scrooby, 6, 7, 8, 12, 16, 29.
— Manor House, 9–12.
— Old Vicarage, 12.
— 'Wolsey's Mill,' 12.
Separatists, 2, 3, 6, 8, 18, 27, 28, 29, 47.
Shakespeare, Wm., 94.
Sheering, 108.
Shingles, use of, in England, 83.
— in America, 166.
Shute, John, 66, 67.
Simons, Ralph, 67.
Slate roofs, in England, 82.
— in America, 119, 127, 145, 166.
Smarden, 49, 104.
Smith, Capt. John, *quoted*, 111, 116, 118, 121, 122, 123, 127, 129, 132, 136, 138, 195, 196, 198.
Smith's Fort (Va.), Warren House, 195.
Smith's Green, Dunmow, 108.
Smithson, Robert, 66.
Smyth, Rev. John, 6, 8, 27.
Southampton (England), 30, 120.
Southborough (England), 43.
— (U.S.A.), 43.
Southchurch, 112.
Southend, 106, 112.
Southwark, 47, 48, 94–5.
— 'Fishermen's Houses,' 47, 95.
— 'George' Inn, 94.
— 'Pilgrim Church,' 94.
Spalding, 49.
— Warehouse at, 22.
Sprague, R., 131.
Springfield (Essex), 111.
— (Mass.), Ely Tavern, 181.
Staircases, 175–6.
Standish, Capt. Miles, 30, 54, 129, 143.
Stanford-le-Hope, 46 n.
Stansted, 107.
Staplehurst, 49.
Stisted, 81, 109.

INDEX

Stebbing, 108.
Stone in England, 51–2.
— in New England, 119, 127, 128, 135, 155, 177.
Stony River (Mass.), 140.
Stratford (Essex), 4, 46.
Streatham, 98.
Strype, *quoted*, 46.
Sudbury (Suffolk), 48.
— (Mass.), Red House Inn., 182.
Suffolk (England), 45, 51, 53, 73, 92.
Surrey (England), 42, 45, 51, 55, 56, 62, 81, 98–9.
Sussex (England), 45, 53, 55, 79, 99–100, 101.
Symonds, Samuel, 150, 151.

Takeley, 108, 130, 169.
Tallmadge, T. E., *quoted*, 149, 195–6.
Tattershall Castle, 19, 20, 196.
Tendring Heath, 110.
Tenterden, 104.
Thanet, 101.
Thoroton, *quoted*, 11.
Thorpe, John, 66.
Thorpe-le-Soken, 110.
Thorrington, 110.
Thatched roofs, in England, 76, 82–4, 109–10.
— in America, 165–6.
Theydon Bois, 106.
Tilbury, 106, 114.
Tile floors, 73.
Tile hanging, 55, 108.
Tile roofs, in England, 83.
— in America, 136, 166.
Tillingham, 111.
Timber in America, 127–8.
Timber-framing in England, 19, 22, 53–71, 92–115.
— in Holland, 35–41.
— in America, 123–4, 130–1, 131–2, 136, 137–40, 141–71.
Tonbridge, 80, 104.
Tools, early carpenters', 69, 126–7.
Toppesfield (England), 43, 81, 83, 109.

Topsfield (Mass.), 43.
— 'Parson' Capen House, 154, 161, 163, 170, 175, 176, 178, 182, 190–2.
Tottenham, 97.
Trevelyan, G. M., *quoted*, 25, 44–5, 46 n., 47 n., 56.
Tring, 49.
Troedrhiwdaler, 48.

Utrecht, cathedral, 32.
Uxbridge (England), 43, 46.
— (U.S.A.), 43.

Vange, 114.
Virginia, 1, 116, 122, 194–8.
Vitruvius, 32.
Volendam, 35.
Vrederman de Vries, 33.

Wailes, Rex, *quoted*, 140–1.
Waltham (England), 43.
— (U.S.A.), 43.
Walton (Essex), 106.
Wampum, 133.
Wartling Hill, Sussex, 100.
Wash, the, 52.
Waters, J. F., *quoted*, 152, 185.
Watertown (Mass.), 140, 145.
— Abraham Browne House, 178, 181, 184.
Watford, 104.
Wattisfield, 49.
'Weald,' the, 76, 101.
Weatherboarding, in England, 13, 22, 77–80.
— in Holland, 35–41.
— in America, 134, 167–9.
Webb, John, 88.
Wenham (England), 43.
— (Mass.), 43, 145, 155.
Wesley, John, 14.
West Blatchington, windmill, 99.
West Hartford (Conn.), Webster House, 182.
Westminster Abbey, 52.
Wethersfield (England), 43, 90, 109.
— (Conn.), 43, 154.

Wethersfield (*cont.*)
— Older Williams House, 152, 155, 156, 162, 176, 182, 188.
Wickford, 81, 113.
Wickhambreux, mill, 102.
Wigge, Gilbert, 67.
Winchelsea, 101.
Windmills, in England, 13, 99, 105, 109, 111, 115.
— in America, 140–1.
Windows, in England, 16, 88–91.
— in Holland, 34.
— in America, 136, 172–5.
Windsor (England), 43.
— (Conn.), 43, 137.
— — Moore House, 181, 186.
— — Loomis Homestead, 181.
Winslow, Edward, 54, 123, 125, 130.
Winthrop, John, 50, 138, 139, 152, 167.
Witham, 46, 106.
Woburn (England), 43.
— (Mass.), 43, 145–6.

Wolsey, Cardinal, 10.
Wood, Wm., *quoted*, 126, 127–8, 129, 136, 139, 140, 175.
Woodbridge, 49.
Woodham Walter Church, 111, 196–8.
Woolwich, Bostall Farm, 101.
Worksop, 19, 29.
Wrangle Tofts, barns, 22.
Wren, Sir C., 70, 189, 195.
Wrentham, 49.

Yale College, 144.
Yarmouth (England), 43, 91.
— (U.S.A.), 43.
Yorkshire, huts in, 24.
— stone houses of, 59, 92, 189.
'Yorkshire lights,' 90.

Zaandam (Holland), 36.
— 'Czar Peter's Hut,' 36–41, 80, 136.
— Other buildings, 37.
Zuyder Zee, 35.

www.ingramcontent.com/pod-product-compliance
Lightning Source LLC
Chambersburg PA
CBHW071329190426
43193CB00041B/1021